RIPPED AND TORN

RIPPED AND TORN

LEVI'S, LATIN AMERICA AND THE BLUE JEAN DREAM

AMARANTA WRIGHT

EBURY PRESS

First published in Great Britain 2005

1 3 5 7 9 10 8 6 4 2

Ebury Press, an imprint of Ebury Publishing.
Random House, 20 Vauxhall Bridge Road, London SW1V 2SA

Random House Australia (Pty) Limited
20 Alfred Street, Milsons Point, Sydney, New South Wales 2061, Australia

Random House New Zealand Limited
18 Poland Road, Glenfield, Auckland 10, New Zealand

Random House South Africa (Pty) Limited
Endulini, 5A Jubilee Road, Parktown 2193, South Africa

The Random House Group Limited Reg. No. 954009

www.randomhouse.co.uk

A CIP catalogue record for this book is available from the British Library.

Cover design by Antigone Konstantinidou
Typeset by seagulls

ISBN 0 091 90083 2

Papers used by Ebury Press are natural, recyclable products made from wood grown in sustainable forests.

Printed and bound in GB by Mackays of Chatham Plc

To the courageous and ever hopeful young of Latin America.

To my Mum and my Nan.

contents

1

WORLDS AT MY FEET

I twirl around on my white leather stool at the bar of the Marlin Hotel, a stunning art deco masterpiece restored to its original brilliant-white glory, a block away from Ocean Drive, South Beach. The chrome clock on the wall shows seven forty-five. There is a glow from the lime-green suit of the man sitting behind me, sleeves rolled up to his elbows and a radioactive tan that looks as though it could be contagious. Must be a Venezuelan crooner, I say to myself, and almost jump off my stool when I hear the Yorkshire accent boom out at American volume: 'Eeee oop, we'll mek a man out'hat Latino pansy.' Is he signing Ricky Martin to Leeds United?

Miami is where the big deals are cut, from Ricky Martin to gas pipelines through the Amazon. On the clinking rims of sun-kissed Cosmopolitans, dreams glisten. Fantasies twinkle in the corner of D&G shades. Everywhere, you see licking lips, lustful glances and grins – naive and decadent. I have come up from the south, waiting for something to happen, just like all the rest – models, actors, entrepreneurs, hoping to meet their makers from the north. In a more distant past, I also came from the east. East enough to recognize a Yorkshire accent anyway.

I still feel spellbound by this vacuum of time and place, where reinvention is king. In this coral and baby-blue no-man's-land lies the secret to an enchanted life, I am sure of it. If you just catch that lucky wave and drift out into the sunset's toxic intensity. Or eternal ecstasy will be handed to you in a sparkling pink pill under disco lights and a reflector ball.

I pinch myself. Stupid. Think about bushy-eyebrowed actors in polo necks and corduroys sitting at rickety wooden tables in the small hours discussing Borges and Brecht. This is my trick, when things get too blurred. I try to revive memories of the dark, decaying, smoke-filled bars of Corrientes Avenue in the centre of Buenos Aires, where I lived for four years before coming to Miami. I have to remind myself that I know another reality, solid, entrenched down there, 'Forgotten in the world's arsehole,' as the Argentines say. From that dark place, clarity frowns upon me.

Like the insane love of a suffering mother, Buenos Aires pulled me to her bosom with her warmth and tenderness while pushing me away with her dramatic melancholy and neuroses. She drove me mad. But the feelings come flooding back, twisting my insides, dispelling this pastel-coloured world of

Euro-trash, Latin flash and wads of US cash. That little voice in my mind begs me again to leave this place, back to England maybe. Anywhere but here.

A minute later, Bill strides in with his triumphant air and confident grin and orders a Martini. I met Bill in Buenos Aires where his office, Levi Strauss Argentina, commissioned some vague journalistic work from me on young people's attitudes in the city. The assignment gave me a month-long break from the 'foreign' reporting I was doing for British and US newsrooms, and paid far better. A year later, Bill has tracked me down. We chat inanities. But I am absorbed in the lemon twist of my third Cosmopolitan. Then Bill's flash of childlike excitement, a vision of blue jean glory and a dollar sum snaps me out of my dizziness.

I think he just made me an offer, but his words seem to fuse with the deep triumphant vowels coming from the mouth of cool-as-ice-Don-Johnson-of-the-shires over there. Something about investigating youth, Latin America, continent-wide, top to bottom. I have to concentrate here, as I have acquired a penchant for blur over detail.

Competition has been getting intense in the jeans business, Bill says. Levi's world sales have plummeted and the Original Jean is no longer seen as cutting edge in the US. The company has had to downsize and invest in reimaging for a new era of corporate branding. Still number one in Latin America, however, they want to make sure it stays that way by investing in new countries where counterfeit Levi's have been dominating the market. The company needs to 'understand' these new markets in order to build a brand identity that will be an indispensable accessory to Latin American youth.

Levi's wants to know exactly what is going on in the minds of teenagers – their ideas, their vulnerabilities, their desires, their needs, their hopes, their fears, their ideals. Don't bother about jeans. On top of a generous salary, they will pay expenses for travel and a month's stay in each Latin American city. After my return to base, wherever I decide to make it, I have a month to write the report and get it to San Francisco before setting off to my next destination.

I am on my fourth Cosmopolitan now. Bill is whipping back the Martinis. Exactly how I infiltrate youth and get the information, he says, will be my business. But, we agree, it's best no one knows who I'm working for. Get more honest information, without Levi's notoriety clouding my subjects' judgement. Besides, there is the obvious danger in countries like Colombia, where working for a multinational makes you a prime kidnapping target for the left-wing guerrilla groups.

Is this the magic pill I have been waiting for? Surely this *is* the dream? I can have both worlds – the fantasy of Miami and the reality of my past? How rich life will be on this adventure! I can get out of this lull of distraction, this haze (I've been smoking too much). Yes, the pill of vitality has been given to me. I know this is my big break, my chance to explore the other part of me, the other knowledge, the one that I'd touched in Argentina, my awake side, not this dormant blob I've become.

■

This 'other knowledge' I talk of is still only a flirtation, rather than a love in full bloom. It began when I was about seven years old. We lived in a large Victorian house in north London, Crouch End to be precise, the four of us, Mum, Dad, son, daughter. Church of England primary school, choir on Sundays, tennis club, piano lessons, pink tutus, camping holidays in France – you could say it was a pretty average life, but for the flocks of dark, bearded men who began to appear.

I don't remember feeling invaded or jealous: these creatures swanned around our house with such confidence and panache that they seemed to really *belong* to life. They were Mother Earth's prime pickings, while I was still a foster child whose fate she had not yet decided. My eyes followed them as my soul yearned to go with them into their secret world. I was told they were political refugees from a far-off land.

Alejandro was my favourite: he let me play for hours in his room and brought me back sweets and presents every time he went out. I was so infatuated with him that I would sneak into his bathroom every day to use his toothbrush, just to have shared something with him. He soon caught on and gently told me that it was not a healthy thing to do. I felt embarrassed, but his affection for me never waned. One day, he told me that we were related '*por tierra*': I too belonged to the place he came from. This delighted me.

I was born in Buenos Aires in April 1972 to British parents. My father managed Reuters, and was dazzling the beautiful bourgeois brunettes at the Buenos Aires Lawn Tennis Club with his Robert Redford looks. My mother, with two toddlers in her arms, vacillated between watching a precocious Guillermo Vilas wallop balls on his way to a number-one world ranking and soaking up the revolutionary fervour of the day.

The first socialist president in neighbouring Chile, Salvador Allende, had just been elected, and where we lived the Perónist Youth were clamouring for former nationalist president Juan Domingo Perón, who had been exiled to Madrid in 1954, to come back and lead their left-wing movement.

In 1973, as I happily sat in my high chair smearing puréed pumpkin over myself, my mother watched Perón's return on TV. A million Argentines from both the extreme left and extreme right went to meet him at the airport to claim him for their own. Then, as the spoon approached my open mouth, the screen went black. Right-wing Perónists, installed in trees, were gunning down left-wing Perónists as they made their way to the podium where Perón was to speak. Dozens died and hundreds were taken to be tortured in the airport hotel. It was the turning point for Argentina's troubles. The ideological battle for Argentina had begun again.

I, oblivious and chubby, rolled around like a football under the shade of the ficus trees in Plaza San Martín, while my brother hung from their sprawling tentacles. We lived on top of Harrods, the pathetic replica built in the last days of British Empire, where we attempted to resurrect Christmas in the ninety-degree heat. Mum would take us to see Father Christmas suffocating in his red suit outside while his assistant poured soap powder from our apartment at the top of the building.

Dad found opportunity in a city brimming with ideas for study. He and his new friends – a mix of expats and Argy-Polish, Argy-Lebanese, Argy-always-from-somewhere-else – formed a film club and hired a professor from the university to teach them Latin American history. They energetically contemplated utopia in the new world over dinners, chewing on politics and Pampa beef, exchanging ideas with salads and guzzling them all down with rich, dense Argentine wine.

Weekends we'd spend on the farm of Enrique, my parents' sociology professor friend. In his towering cornfields, we'd play hide and seek; Mum and Dad on a horse each, I on the back of my brother's. We'd come to a clearing, and I'd spot Dad amidst the hanging cow carcasses, leaning against a eucalyptus tree, chewing on a long thread of wheat as he talked to *gauchos*. In his poncho, his hair long and moustache bushy, this mousy *gringo* looked curiously at home in the golden Pampa evening. This moment remains my definition of happiness to this day.

Enrique introduced Mum to their political struggle. Every time she heard that one of the guerrilla groups had robbed a casino she celebrated with her friends, for whom these activities seemed to hold a kind of Robin Hood romanticism. There was the more serious armed conflict carrying on outside the capital, but the people Mum knew were not bloodthirsty; they were humanists who believed they could bring the establishment down through the force of a mass social movement. The way they talked made you believe it was all possible.

It made her nervous, how lightly they took it sometimes. Once, when she was having a drink with Enrique, the local police chief came over to say hello and asked who she was. 'Oh, she's an agent they've sent us from Czechoslovakia,' Enrique joked, slapping the police chief on the back. This was the early 1970s – no one had any idea what was in store for them. A few years later Enrique would be running for his life.

It soon became clear Perón had no intention of signing his name to any left-wing revolution. His populist rhetoric hid a reactionary and authoritarian core. When the Perónist Youth came to honour him at a mass rally in the Plaza de Mayo he sent them away, and then ordered the secret police to root out the leaders. It was a bitter pill to swallow, but there was no time for bearing grudges. Perón died in 1974, his second wife Isabelita took power, and the political and economic situation spiralled out of control. A death squad known as the Triple A intensified the witch-hunt of guerrilla fighters and their sympathizers.

Slowly, light-hearted red-wine idealism became clouded with terror. One day Mum took us to Enrique's farm to find nobody at home. We waited until a friend of his came to pick us up and take all the hunting weapons from the house. Enrique had been arrested. Paranoia ravaged the city like a plague as people began to disappear. Just your name in a phone book could warrant a midnight visit. At the conservative Buenos Aires Lawn Tennis Club, Mum noticed people acting peculiarly towards her. Rumours were going around that she was involved in 'funny business'. When she asked her friends why they no longer invited her to play bridge, they replied disconcertingly: 'It's best to leave things.'

In the next few years, a military witch-hunt would make thirty thousand people 'disappear', drilling a hole through an entire generation of educated professionals and students. We left in 1976, the year the coup finally happened. My father's contract was ending, and his request for another extension, his third in a row, was rejected. To the company's disapproval, he had already 'gone native', thus clouding his capacity for 'objective analysis'. My mother was devastated. On the day of departure we missed the plane and had to spend our last night in the hotel whose rooms had been the torture chambers the night of Perón's return.

Back in England, my childhood years were full of reminders of another place that held part of me. I watched the Sunday football matches on Hampstead Heath, Argies vs Brazilians, which would invariably end in macho sparring and a punch-up. I stayed up at dinner parties, stroking the long black silky hair of mysterious Amazons as they left bespectacled Anglo intellectuals in awe of their passionate intelligence.

My brother, by contrast, wanted to forget about the place we left behind, even the language. 'Here, Spanish is no use,' he announced on arrival. My mother noticed how nervous he became at the Argy-bargy around the house, both the demonstrative affections and the mysterious whispers. At our parties we'd find our latin lodgers huddled in our nursery at the top of the house talking revolution. From the way he winced, it seemed the mere sound of Spanish aroused feelings of fear and images of violence.

Dad travelled back there a lot, more so as my parents' marriage fell apart. He had started a magazine on Latin

 America, but I liked to imagine he was a spy, enigmatic and dashing as he was, like James Bond. During the Falklands War I was teased at school with the threat of being deported to Latin America. I should be so lucky, I thought. It was the bright corner of my imagination that I kept alive, even though I always hid when Mum picked me up draped in poncho and painted leather satchel so that my schoolmates wouldn't laugh. In my mind I scolded them. Did they not know that the satchel was that funny shape so the *mate* and flask could fit in? Everyone knows that! I felt the misfit, but proud when Dad would come home from a trip, tanned and trim, knowing he'd show me the new football tricks he'd picked up on Copacabana beach. He'd dress me up in the black and red strip of Flamengo, Brazil's Man U, and we'd take the ball to the park. I'd be Zico, he'd be Socrates: the stars of the Brazilian team. Only now I understand why we shared this passion: he too was born in that warm continent, as the son of diplomats, and lived in Cuba and then Ecuador before coming to England for the first time aged six.

From my London comprehensive I went to Oxford, thrown in with a species of Englishness I'd never encountered before. They seemed so confident that they were destined for great things, and so at home in those ivory towers, as if they had been created specially for them. But they were unlike the self-believers who had swaggered through my house appearing to own the world, even while displaced in it, and I neither understood nor felt attracted to the students' self-assurance. Was it their (already assured) class or power that made it so distasteful? And the exam-obsessed procedures seemed to me more like military training, arguments thrown up like a clay pigeons all for the purpose of shooting them down. It was more about conquest than reflection. Even the suicide of a fellow student from Singapore a week before finals failed to raise questions about a system that isolated rather than stimulated. Then the day came when I could go back to find the part of me that might make sense of my awkward existence.

■

I arrived in Buenos Aires in November 1993, leaving winter behind. At the bottom of the aeroplane steps I paused, lifting my face to the warm, moist air, letting the rays of the austral sun dance on my skin and leave their tingle. I breathed in the eucalyptus breeze, right down to the bottom of my lungs, as far as breath could go, and then let it go. Aaaaaah. It was like rebirth.

But I was not to find the Buenos Aires spirit – tender, vibrant, funny and easy-going – that my parents had known, and which had filled the corners of my mind. Andres, Mum's Argy-Romanian-Jewish friend, whose intellect and wit had made him the life of all parties, reminisced about times spent with my parents, but I could see his memories were drenched in pain and sadness. Such terrible things had happened since. Unthinkable, unspeakable things. Against my will, I did not ask for details.

There was a brief period, Andrés told me, after the dictatorship fell in 1983, when they hoped the victims of state terror, which included friends, colleagues and relatives, would at least be recognized, and the country would face the truth of what had happened. Raúl Alfonsín, the first post-dictatorship president, instructed civil courts to try the generals responsible for atrocities. But the economic crisis left by the military government began to undermine his noble efforts. Enter charismatic Carlos Menem. Using the old Perónist euphoria-inducing tricks, he presented himself as the man of the poor while opening up the bankrupt inflationary economy to foreign investment – the best way, agreed international governments and financiers, to heal the past and to progress. The military generals who had ordered the torture, murder and disappearance of their own people were officially pardoned.

The children of my parents' old gang would naturally have become my friends. They were almost long-lost cousins. But they did not want to talk about the period our parents had lived through. Look what it had brought. Violence and economic crisis. They wanted the shopping malls and the Häagan Dazs, Levi's, Mango and Diesel stores that filled them. They relished the magazines full of the new rich celebrities. They even liked Menem, his huge sideburns and *Saturday Night Fever* suits and his soap-opera marriage. Once cameras showed his wife, Zulema Yoma, furiously rattling the gates of the presidential palace, and him refusing to open them because she was driving him nuts.

I began writing for British and US newspapers, and was assigned to investigate Menem's cronies – politicians, businessmen and judges who were alleged to be dividing privatization assets and profits between them in deals made outside the official bidding. One of them, Alfredo Yabrán, had managed to sweep up all the customs administration companies, the private postal services, armoured car and security firms, where he employed ex-torturers of the dictatorship – an eerily convenient infrastructure for international drugs and arms trafficking. Allegations of such implicated the president and his wife's family in a scandal, but investigations never made it to the courts.

The economy minister, Domingo Cavallo, darling of the IMF and foreign investors in Argentina, began implicating some of Menem's ministers in Yabrán's corruption ring. He was sacked. But his voice was soon replaced by that of the president's now ex-wife when their son, Carlitos Menem, was killed in a helicopter crash. She was convinced it was the work of Yabrán's mafia, in some kind of settlement of accounts with Menem. On top of it, she even claimed her ex-husband knew about it and was covering it up.

'Do you think your husband would really cover up the death of his own son?' I asked her one day, watching her sob on her white leather sofa. 'I have seen that anything is possible in politics,' she replied, looking up as the mascara ran down her face. The president dismissed her as hysterical and delirious, but she received much public sympathy: after all, a lot of people knew what it felt like to live with an unexplained death in the family. 'Sure she's mad,' one of my friends said when we were discussing the matter. 'She's so mad she's the only one willing to tell the truth around here.'

My *Sunday Telegraph* editors relished the stories about shady Yabrán, the playboy president and his hysterical wife. It was the 'funny foreign stuff' that amused their readers; a sleazy comic-thriller that only happened in third world politics. The story wasn't so amusing for Argentines, especially when a photographer, whose secret snapshots of Yabrán had featured on a news magazine cover, turned up dead, having been gagged, handcuffed, tortured and burned alive, in true dictatorship style. In the dictatorship, people had been punished for speaking out against the state; now they were punished for speaking out against businessmen.

President Menem had a remarkable ability to survive all the scandals, and was re-elected in 1995 for a second term, having got the constitution changed to allow him to run again. His penchant for famous blondes – Madonna, Claudia Schiffer, Lady Di – whom he'd get round to the palace for tea as soon as they stepped off the plane, provided the necessary distraction. The survivors of my parents' generation, who would have put up resistance, were not only psychologically destroyed but also grappling with economic marginalization because of the crisis in local industry. Their products could not compete with those of multinationals and, with the peso pegged to the dollar, export was out of the question.

My almost-cousins submerged themselves in hedonism. Whether at a football match, or a concert given by the Rolling Stones, the symbol of a rebellion that military government had denied them, everyone took any opportunity to scream, jump around and do crazy things just to release the collective built-up tension. My boyfriend's way was to speed down the motorway with a maniacal grin on his face while I sat paralysed in the front seat. The president covered up psychological scars with plastic surgery, and the fad was becoming as fashionable as psychoanalysis had been for my parents' Argentine friends.

I couldn't really relate to all this *frenesí*. Maybe belonging here was a fantasy I could only have from afar, I said to myself sadly. Yet nobody in Argentina accepted I was English. Whenever it was found out I was born in the clinic down the road, their Anglophilia would dissolve and they'd mock: 'You're just a pretend European like the rest of us!' Here, land was thicker than blood. I had to resign myself to the idea of being some kind of displaced Argentine.

I still wanted to be inspired by those things that had inspired my mother when she came, even though I wasn't quite sure what they were. What used to be a bright spot in my imagination was now a dark place. 'Everyone seems so angry, defensive, yet passive and numb at the same time,' I complained to my father when he came to visit me. 'They're kind of mad, the Argies, aren't they?'

Dad flinched, irritated, but quite calmly replied, 'Really? I think people are remarkably sane considering what has happened here.'

So I searched on. I made new friends: people my age who did not believe you could patch up the psychological scars with plastic surgery, and who refused to get into Ford Falcon taxis because, though now yellow instead of black, the stench of the secret police who took people from their homes to the concentration camps in them still lingered. I used journalism to go back into the past, tracking down ex-dictatorship officials who used the money from the property they stole from their victims – an estimated seventy million dollars' worth – to set up security firms.

I met a man called the Turk, one of the dictatorship's cruellest interrogators, in a seedy bar. He was out of work, and groaning that what he did against subversives was no longer appreciated. I could not keep my eyes off his twitching hands as he told me how he had put electric shocks through the genitals, nails and heads of men, women and teenagers – 'When it comes to the enemy one does not discriminate.' He wanted me to pay him for more information and assure him that my article would bring him some work 'where my expertise lies' from overseas. He would be happy, he said, to get rid of scum wherever they were. 'In England you have a problem with terrorists too, right?' he asked hopefully.

Then there was Elena, who had discovered that the parents she thought were her own actually worked in the concentration camp where her real mother 'disappeared'. They had nursed her mother before they killed her, so that the Elena they were to adopt wouldn't be damaged.

For years, Elena wished they had let her die with her mother. But now she felt fortunate to have discovered the truth in time; she was slowly rebuilding her identity. To free all the others from their lie had become her mission, especially since 'baby-snatching' had not been included in the amnesty given by Menem and military officials could still be prosecuted for that particular crime. But not everybody wanted to be freed. 'My mother says I am not the daughter of subversives, and I believe her,' said one girl I rang. The people who had brought her up had filled her with so much hatred for what her real parents stood for that the thought of being born to left-wing scum was more abhorrent than the idea that her adoptive parents had killed her own parents. This ideological cleansing had been the military's rationale all along.

Sometimes I thought: What am I getting so involved for? Whose banner am I carrying? What am I trying to prove? It seemed pathetic to have come back with expectations and to have ended up rummaging through the debris of others' broken hopes. For what? It was about this time, in 1996, that Levi's approached me. They wanted me to do some 'street research', a kind of general survey on youth attitudes in the city so that they could break the code of post-dictatorship youth. And I needed a break also.

■

The first thing I did was jump on a bus, in a convoy with fifty thousand maniacal rock fans to see Argentina's most famous band. Argentina was the rock reference for the rest of South America. Argentine rock groups had bizarre names – The Grandmothers of Nothing, The Paranoid Rats, The Burning Gentlemen – but the band of all bands I was travelling hundreds of miles for were The Little Balls of Ricotta. Their ten-year career defied all commercial rules. They had never made a video, never signed a record deal and never gave interviews. The big labels were desperate to sign them up, but they flatly refused. Only word of mouth advertised their concerts.

The fans, known as *Ricoteros,* were so many and so passionate that the police couldn't control them without their usual resort to brutality. The group had been banned from playing in the capital ever since a fan got killed in police custody. So instead thousands of kids would descend on some little town in the interior. There the police were waiting, and *Ricoteros* would have to get through their pounding batons and drag each other from under their boots before they could get inside the stadium.

Enemies in the football stands, united by *Ricotero* passion. The solidarity on the bus was breathtaking. People put in a dollar for meat to barbecue on arrival and everyone got food, even those who couldn't afford to put money in. And inside the stadium the emotion was intoxicating as I struggled to jive with thirteen-year-olds in waist-high mud. A rock'n'roll rave.

I couldn't believe the respect this fifty-thousand-strong rabble, all off their heads, had for Indio, the bald band-leader. He was in absolute command of them, without use of violence or media propaganda. Indio had only ever given an interview once, to explain why he never came out in public to mourn for the fan who died. 'I didn't make a statement because I would have had to recreate the emotion for TV and that is where the lying starts. But you can be sure that the only place where Walter Bulacio is remembered outside his family is at a *Ricoteros* concert.'

I understood then that this post-dictatorship generation didn't loathe ideals. They weren't apathetic. It was just that their heroes didn't appear on TV. Argentine kids knew what was going on under the Menem regime. Helpless, they flocked to the only man who had principles and, unlike Maradona, would never let himself be used by politicians. 'He is the only one we can rely on,' said my fourteen-year-old *Ricotero* companion, who looked after me all weekend, never leaving my side. Indio was about loyalty and honesty and that was all they wanted.

I left Argentina in 1997, four years after my arrival, to a small *Ricotero* feeling of victory as fans witnessed a local popular music station fight off Miami-based MTV in the ratings.

'They are like the McDonald's of music, we are like a good local restaurant,' my friend Ralph, owner of this local music channel, told me. 'You cannot tell us that a McDonald's hamburger is better than an Argentine steak.'

Brave talk. Ralph soon learnt that patriotism could not compete with might. MTV single-mindedly poured more and more money into its channel, and, stealing a few leaves out of Ralph's book on the way, the channel finally began to stick. Ralph ate his words when, realizing his channel could never survive without huge financial backing, he sold up to a Miami-based media giant. Ironically, it was this company, the Cisneros Television Group, that I began to work for in Miami.

■

I don't quite know how the Miami saga happened. It was supposed to be a stopover, to wean myself away from Argentina, after I'd agreed to take a desk job at the *Scotsman* in Edinburgh. Ralph, who was now the Cisneros TV creative director, asked me to interview his boss, Carlos Cisneros, nephew of the powerful Gustavo, an anti-Castro Cuban who fled to Venezuela to become one of Latin America's most powerful businessmen.

 Carlos was in charge of the Cisneros empire's media arm, which in itself owned Venezuela's main TV station, Venevision, as well as Univision, the main TV station for Latinos in the US. With new US partners they had just bought twelve new cable channels and the rights to the Direct TV satellite network to distribute them through Latin America. Thirty-three-year-old Carlos was like a younger, hipper Latino Rupert Murdoch; his company's influence over Latino opinion throughout the US and Latin America was virtually unrivalled.

He asked me about my history and I told him about a little internet project I had in mind, an internet site about Latin America in English. By the end of the interview I had a job, and Edinburgh became a blip on the landscape of missed fate.

To my Argentine friends, Miami represented the dumbing down of their continent. It was the pleasure emporium where Menem's cronies spent the profits of the privatizations they had secretly divided between them. Even so, I was drawn to it. After four years in Buenos Aires, with its Giselle-like figures flaunting their German, Polish Jew, Italian, Libyan, English, Irish, Basque mix, as if they were genetic experiments in European perfection, I finally met the continent I had not seen, in the indigenous faces, in the *mestizos* of Central America and the *mulatos* of the Spanish Caribbean, not to mention the Miami *Latino,* a strange evolutionary phenomenon Darwin might have studied.

My home became South Beach: America's 1940s Côte d'Azur, gangland in 1970s, now resurrected to its neon deco glory thanks to the gay community. The run-down condo where Scarface massacred his enemies is now a restaurant owned by Ricky Martin. Gloria Estefan has a Cuban restaurant called *Lario's* a few doors up.

Inside the Cisneros pastel palace, my office had a spectacular view over the turquoise Caribbean. I sat next to a young square-jawed blond called Guido, who would have made the perfect Chippendale if you tied a dicky bow round his neck. He said he was Argentine, but I was sceptical. I had never known an Argentine shave himself from neck to toe, or have the delightful combination of bleached crew cut, fried orange face and squeaky American accent. As far as I could make out, Guido was in charge of developing content for the company's porn website, Venus. He surfed nude women all day, with no apparent pleasure. His voice was so high it put David Beckham in the Barry White league. He would spend hours on the phone to his friends describing in squeaky, lithpy excitement his day's adventures in cyber-porn, while dissecting the crude details of the weekend's gay gossip. 'Oh my gaaaad, he did *that*?' He must have shrieked at least fifty times a day.

Guido thought my accent was '*sooooo* cooool'. He would twitter on about how he thought English people were all '*soooooo* intelligent, and *soooooo* funny'. He kept trying to get me to say things that he thought only a British person would say, like 'How awwwfully nice' and 'May I have a glaaahhs of waaahter, please?'

Carlos Cisneros also seemed to be glued to the small TV screen on his desk every time I walked past his office. His vice was *Infinito*, the 'esoteric' documentary channel specializing in saintly apparitions, alien-possessed humans and other pseudo-spiritual and supernatural phenomena. To Carlos it was not only the jewel in his company's crown (a huge hit all over Latin America), but his personal swami. In questions of superstition, billionaire Carlos and other top executives appeared to feel a special affinity with the impoverished masses. They even solicited the channel's producer, a bearded man with enlightening powers, for private consultation on where they should be when the end of the world came. Out of the seven spots designated as life sanctuaries amid total destruction, it was decided that Machu Picchu would be the fortunate touchpad for the Cisneros helicopter at the final hour.

■

My life in Miami was like a hazy dream of blinding brightness in which I floated feather-light and oblivious. Argentina was a weighty memory of complex reality and intense emotion. Here, I belonged, a phoney just like everyone else, with the title of 'chief new media developer' printed on a snazzy little business card, even though I had probably surfed the net once in my life, and got very bored doing it. The only indication of my cyber knowledge was my spiky peroxide hair, big clumpy shoes and a reflector vest I'd bought in a shop in Covent Garden called Cyberdog. But image is always a precedent to empire building, and my English accent and *Blade Runner* hair earned me the dual role of the company's cyber ombudsman and English muse at the Cisneros Saturday lunches on the back veranda of the Delano Hotel.

Cubans with crew cuts welcomed you through the white chiffon curtains into a long mahogany reception area with mock-Elizabethan panelling and little red lamps, adorned with a Louis XIV-style coronation chair in the middle. In the hotel's Blue Door restaurant, predictably owned by Madonna, we chewed on lobster ravioli with caviar cream and overlooked the *Alice in Wonderland* garden, with its giant chessboard, bright green lawn and symmetrically planted sky-high palm trees bursting green bouquets into the air. The swimming pool played Vivaldi underwater, overflowed at the sides, and had a white wrought-iron garden set in the shallow end so you could have tea while you cooled your feet. Around the pool, sun-scorched dinosaur men sporting tiny yellow trunks, straggly bleach-dried ponytails and frazzled chest hair conducted business by mobile phone.

Carlos Cisneros always sat at the head of the table, smirking at his audience made up of various members of Miami's gay elite: fashion designers, photographers, local politicians, playboys and me, who he thought was funny, cute and a possible traitor.

'Amaranta dear!' he said to me one Saturday. 'A little bird has told me that you have communist tendencies.'

'Communist?' I said. 'I've never read any Marx, Carlos. Mind you, in the end you have to know what side you're on, don't you?' I had no idea what I meant; it was just a reaction. After a glance of uncertainty, he burst into laughter. Then an abrupt halt, as he leaned into my ear. 'And whose side are you on?' he whispered. I remained silent. Maybe clarity would come one day, though through Marx I'm not sure.

■

 Miami was the kind of place that encouraged chameleon behaviour. Its residents – migrants, immigrants, business visitors, tourists – either lost or being found, invented their own fantasy identity and, if they stayed long enough, became caricatures of it.

The Argentine friends who came to visit me were worried about mine. My hair was growing out into a long golden mane, which, they teased, I flicked around as I sprinted along the beach in my red, white and blue Lycra outfit like a *Baywatch* girl. They accused my Argentine accent of fusing into whining Miami Spanish, the equivalent of mid-Atlantic English, replacing luscious rolled Rs with growling cowboy Rs. I had become a functionary of the aspiration industry, which produced next week's Latino *Hello!* magazine exclusives: 'Ricky Martin confesses: "I am scared of dying."'

Back in the office, the bogus internet specialist was struggling to maintain her pose. Web-builders would talk at me in indecipherable sentences, and I had to keep popping off to the toilet to write down all the web lingo on a bog roll. And yet one day a single announcement of the company merger with internet giant American On-Line (the first I'd heard of it) seemed to render my monumental inadequacies insignificant. I would be lucky if my little project survived at all.

We were visited by AOL in the form of a small thin android in a grey suit with a military haircut, little round glasses and robotic monotone voice. He oozed passion like a vegetarian eating steak, but his squinting eyes flashed when phrases like 'number one in the region' came out of his mouth. I switched off as my eyes zoned in on his thin lips. In my dream like state, I swear I could hear a muffled Dalek zumming the words: 'We will exterminate, we will exterminate.'

That day I ended up in the Marlin drinking Manhattans. Like this city, so busy reproducing itself for the Latin media, so entranced by its own reflection, it was easy to get lost in one's own self-invention. I did try to belong for a while, but once the circus stopped being so entertaining, I was left staring into the vacuum of a city with no soul, and facing my own sad and lonely existence. It was like finding yourself at a never-ending party, your friends have left you, the drugs are wearing off, all you want to do is go to bed, but you are forced to stay awake in a room with Buñuelesque creatures you wouldn't wish on your worst enemy.

After my second Manhattan, a wave of dizziness suddenly came over me. The barman's hair transformed into a big red blur and the room began to spin. I could see his face peering into mine with a look of concern but could not hear what he was saying. I fell off the bar stool and only just managed to pick myself up off the floor. With the help of the barman, I made it out of the door, where I vomited all over a red Porsche.

And now, a week later, I am sitting with Bill on the very same bar stool that witnessed my collapse. Just to be safe I have changed from Manhattan to Cosmopolitan and the world already looks a brighter place. Things aren't clear. For example, why I am here, halfway between two half homes. But I know there is more to this continent that lit up my childhood than the devastation, sadness and confusion I felt in Argentina, more to life than this place of crude inanity, or England's aloof and smug status quo.

I've been leaping from dot to dot in a big picture without the ink to join them. There must be some connection between one lost world and another. Now I can stitch together realities with golden-orange thread and clinch them with rivets of truth. I'll announce my clarity by fastening my red tag, like a true explorer. What a thought! This really must be a mad world if enlightenment can be found at the end of the blue denim road. But I have no choice. I must make this my chance.

2

DISCOVERING THE ATAHUALPA COMPLEX

'We don't want to be like the people in Hollywood films, we want to be like we are but with a bit more money.'
HÉCTOR, 17, LIMA

Had Bill really been here? Did our conversation happen? The pink-stained paper with blurred country names left on the bar after a whipped-off glass was evidence. Bill had whirled out of the chrome doors like a sorcerer and I was left staring at a barely legible doodled-on list: Costa Rica, Panamá, Perú, Venezuela, Chile. Colombia was there also, the one that Bill had said I didn't have 'to do'. Why do people in Miami always refer to 'doing' countries rather than 'going' to them, as if they were problems to be solved? Ticked off list. Done, fixed. Clutching my mission list, I drifted amid the convoy of topless cars inching along Ocean Drive, drivers' grins reflecting in neon flashes as they relished the swerving bums on skates. Grimacing table-dancers gyrated in leopardskin to the bongo sounds of the tropical disco and waved to passers-by. Thank you, Levi's. Thank you for saving me from this purgatory. My Angel Gabriel.

Now I clutch an email with the instructions for my arrival in Perú. I am on flight AA2117 going south, over the Caribbean sea, the jungles and mountains of Colombia and Ecuador. I descend at dawn over Lima's strange desert coast. Salsa music plays on the radio of the taxi from the airport – an odd theme track, I think, to the very untropical grey drizzle we drive through along the city's granite coast. The drabness unsettles me. I feel suddenly naked, as if Miami's brilliant pastel humidity had been a sugary film of protection I have now been stripped of. I can no longer hide in self-invention. What will teenage sensibilities, raw and cruel, expose in me? The sudden swerves interrupt my thoughts as we miss the boulders tumbling onto the road from the cliff above.

I arrive at my step-grandfather's house, the father of my dad's second wife, who is Peruvian Japanese, just like the current president, Alberto Fujimori. I arranged to stay here partly to pre-empt the negotiation of expenses, which I grew accustomed to when trying to get newspapers to buy a story. Although now I wonder why I am living off an old man to save Levi's money.

Later, I head down to Levi's headquarters. Levi's Perú is a brand-new venture, licensed by Levi's Chilean subsidiary. These days the Chileans are buying up companies and expanding their business all over neighbouring Argentina, Perú and Bolivia. The tigers of the Southern Cone. Levi's man in Lima is a thirty-something, business-school-trained Peruvian with a crew cut, slacks and a shirt with a polo player on his breast. Percy emerges from his office with his architect, a very attractive woman in high heels and stockings; immaculately presented, apart from her blouse, which is not quite tucked in at the back.

Percy says he has very little time, and is in an obvious rush to get our business over with. He has the items I requested by email: a map of the city and some coloured markers and highlighters, but is clearly unimpressed with my primitive work tools. When we sit down and I ask him to help me mark the parks, schools, universities, so that I can start colouring in my map, he keeps glancing at me and frowning. He probably expected me to pull out the latest in CIA technology: a talking compass or a fingernail-sized computer atlas.

He seems confused and slightly defensive as to my purpose here. He has not been briefed. Perhaps he thinks I have been sent from head office to check up on him. I reassure him that once I have my map sorted out, I'll have no reason to return during my stay. This seems to inspire an immediate interest in my map; he grabs the pens and begins marking places and even offers to show me around the city.

The tour consists of a trip to the new, open-air shopping mall called LarcoMar perched on the cliffs of Lima's coastline. Percy claims it is the city's most important feature as it is where our safest market, the Levi's loyalists that we must not lose, hangs out. We munch on a bagful of Ben and Jerry's chocolate-chip cookies and Percy reveals that Levi's are up against fierce challenges in Perú, not least the counterfeit industry, a much better-organized and successful business than those of the import brands they copy.

The retail terrorists that run it are nested within a few blocks in central Lima called Gamarra. It is a traditional marketplace where the people from the *sierra* used to come to sell their artisan goods, but they have recently realized the far greater interest in global brand names. 'My dear, *cholo* gear went out of fashion five hundred years ago,' says Percy, referring to the colourful woolly hats with earflaps and llama-breasted sweaters favoured by tourists. 'Peruvians don't want to look like Indians. Fake Tommy Hilfiger and Levi's, that's where the money's at.'

The next day I find myself nudging through a multitude of shoulders between the decaying houses of Gamarra Avenue. The main bits have been renovated. The whole cleaning up of the area is apparently the thorn in Levi's side, since now it is safe enough for middle-class people, who would never have ventured here before, to buy their fake Levi's.

Heaped in converted living rooms, thousands of jeans and T-shirts of the finest quality are piled, all in the latest Calvin Klein and Guess designs at practically no cost at all. Feeling the quality makes me realize why Percy was complaining so much about the flimsy test garments that he was being sent from Chile. My stepmother had once told me that Perú's textiles tradition goes back thousands of years, while Chile has no such history. I feel an almost patriotic duty to tell Levi's about this cultural detail, but have to remind myself that I am not here to lobby for the Peruvian textiles industry.

'How am I supposed to sell this stuff?' Percy had screamed. 'Those *cholos* will be raking in more money than Levi's. And the last thing we need in this town is more *cholos con plata*.'

I spend my first days with Percy's 'safe' market in LarcoMar, because I reckon it will provide the gentlest testing-ground for my new job. It is also a 'safe' environment for a *gringa*. Instead of Gamarra hagglers, bored store assistants (not *cholas*) lean on piles of Diesel, Levi's, Guess, faces cupped in hands, dreaming of Prince Charming out of the windows of chain stores. Plastic, cheap and clean, it could be any mall in Florida, but here it's a piece of exclusive paradise. The McDonald's greasy stench is the perfume of the rich. A giant Donald Duck and Mickey Mouse sing happy songs to groups of children. In the background security guards escort the riffraff out by the arm.

It is three thirty in the afternoon and the kids are out from school. I spot two boys, hair short and parted at the side, wearing freshly ironed shirts with crispy creases – I assume these are specimens of the 'safe' market, which we must nurture. They are sitting at the plastic table with a girl, talking over the remnants of their Burger King tea. I hover, feeling like one of those paedophiles who hang around play-grounds. What am I supposed to say to them? Offer them my bag of sweets and ask if they have had any problems recently that they'd like to talk about?

'Hi! Can I have a chip? I'm...' is one introduction I consider, or, on seeing an eighth of a cheeseburger left in its foam carton: 'Finished with that? Don't mind if I help myself, do you? By the way...' Embarrassingly, I catch the girl looking at me. She smiles, and pats the empty seat beside her signalling for me to sit down. The boys are fifteen: Lucas and Yuri. Violeta, still in the little blue uniform of her English-style girls' school, is sixteen, but fast developing into a woman. They are full of curiosity and bubbling with life.

They tell me that Lima is going to the dogs and that they come to LarcoMar because it is the only place they can get away from the *cholos*. They refer not to the trading *cholos* that Percy despises, but a comical variation who make a living by dressing up in fishnet stockings and plastic boobs, stuffing cushions down their bums, and then stomp around the streets in stilettos spanking men to get laughs and a few bob from drivers at the traffic lights. Ambulant Comics they are called. They were amusing at first, Yuri says, but since someone began making TV programmes around them, the whole of Perú has gone insane over *cholo* slapstick – a far cry from the usual depiction of tearful *cholos* in the ghetto, surrounded by hungry children and begging for charity.

'Now any *cholo* thinks he is famous just by dressing up as Cinderella's ugly sister and expects you to give him money. If you don't, they get nasty,' Lucas complains.

'So what is a *cholo* supposed to be like?' I ask, feeling strange just saying the word, as if it were like saying 'nigger' or 'paki'.

'My maid,' blurts out Violeta instinctively. They look at each other and giggle.

I wonder whether they'd rather the *cholos* be how they were when the Francisco Pizarro, the Spanish explorer, arrived in Perú in 1532. The Inca kingdom was a strict and tightly controlled hierarchical society. Decision-making was almost exclusively reserved for King Atahualpa himself. When Pizarro killed Atahualpa he inherited an ideal indigenous civilization of law-abiding citizens, reverential in their attitude to the ruling class, reluctant to impose their individual will. The new European rulers, however, deprived the Inca subjects of their basic rights and the high living standards that had kept them so loyal to the king. They broke the deal.

'I don't want more equality,' says Violeta. 'If we had more equality, we would have to share more and work harder to stay where we are. In Perú there is not enough wealth for everyone. You have to keep what you've got.'

She complains that the newly rich *cholos* even turn up at *their* discothèques. 'We go to a place and make it really happening. Then the *cholos* turn up and you think uuugh, and you have to start going somewhere else and then they turn up there! It's impossible.'

It seems that Violeta and her gang spend the whole time escaping from the *cholos* as if they carried the plague, a quest that strikes me as slightly futile, since the large majority of the Peruvian population is of Indian descent. They would have to run very, very far before they were rid of the *cholo* face, and even when they reached the USA they'd find them there, in baseball caps and Levi's jeans. The most ironic thing about it is that both Lucas and Yuri, who see themselves as refugees of sophistication against *cholo* persecution, don't, to my foreign eyes, look much different from the people they claim to be escaping from.

'You don't understand,' says Yuri. 'Being a *cholo* is an attitude.' He explains that you can have Indian blood but not be a *cholo* if you didn't act like one. For example, he has Indian blood, mixed with European, but his dad works for an international bank, they live in Miraflores, so he could not possibly be a *cholo*. 'Some *cholas* are quite pretty. But I couldn't go out with a *chola*, even a pretty one. It would be like going out with my maid.'

All maids are *cholas* and having a maid to order about is key in the ability to *cholear*, a verb created specially for the task of putting others down. *Yo choleo*, I cuss. *Tu choleas*, you cuss. *El/ella cholea*, he/she cusses. If you have a *cholo* maid it automatically excludes you from being a *cholo* yourself for it puts you in the class of ordering and not of obeying.

'My mum goes to church and she criticizes all the women for looking down on her and then she comes home and shouts at her maid and feels better,' admits Lucas.

But, Violeta tells me, many middle-class Peruvians are now struggling to keep staff on in the current recession, and this is causing catastrophe. 'My friend's dad lost his job and they had to sack their maid. My mum runs away if we see her mum in the supermarket so as not to embarrass her.'

I wonder if this is why they are here eating American burgers, because it makes them feel whiter. Like the sacrament, each mouthful bringing them closer to salvation, as seen on

Friends, and a little further from *cholo* damnation. I wonder if a pair of Levi's is also a sacrament.

Next time I go back to the office Percy wants to get my opinion on Perú's first Levi's publicity campaign which he shot at LarcoMar last week. In the ad, a blonde Germanic girl, a very handsome Italian man and a black man smile gaily across the neat wooden balcony over the sea. But no *cholo*. 'We could never put a *cholo* in an advert,' says Percy, 'because nobody wants to look like a *cholo*.'

■

Four days after my arrival in Lima some men appear on my doorstep. The doorbell rings just as I am about to sit down to dinner with my grandad, and Vanessa, the maid, shouts that it's for me. I wait for grandad to shuffle over to the window of our second-floor apartment and peek through the curtains, as he always likes to do at any unexpected call. He tells me he sees three shady men on the pavement. 'Thugs,' he grunts in his usual way. I go over and look down. Indeed, three ominous figures with coat collars turned up and hands stuffed into jacket pockets shiver in the cold, shuffling their feet.

I make my way down. The three men say that they have been informed of my arrival and that I am to go with them. So I do, leaving my dinner on the table and waving to grandpa as he looks disapprovingly from the window. I sit in silence looking out of the taxi window, carefully noting every detail of the journey (just in case) as we bomb down the death-wish road heading south along the coast, rocks tumbling down from the cliff on my left, waves crashing on my right. On the pebble beach (alas, a bit like Brighton's), steamy makeshift halls filled with dancing silhouettes are pumping out techno. Straying figures stumble over rocks and lovers huddle under the sea spray. We climb up again onto the edge of a cliff on the south of the city, a more tranquil setting of old churches, nineteenth-century houses and giant winding trees. Yellow light pokes out from the tiny windows of old wood-panelled bars – a little bohemian oasis in the desert.

We reach a square where silhouettes sit dead still hunched on the benches in the moonlight, their shadows stretching over the cracked paving stones of the intricately designed park, like monuments to its faded glory. Our taxi stops a few blocks past the square. One of the men is already unlocking a big red iron gate as I get out. With a huge grunt and the rattle of metal his push reveals their hideaway: a studio filled with half-finished paintings and paint materials, lots of old printing machinery, rusty fridges, prams, go-carts and other strange rubbish-heap items. They bring out some small glasses, a bottle of *pisco* and several boxes of cigarettes. They put on some music, Joy Division if I'm not mistaken. They fill a glass and bang it on the table in front of me in a manner that suggests my refusal would offend.

They gulp, I sip, and they ask me what I am doing in Lima. I get the feeling they already know. They tell me they will help me. They will tell me everything I need to know, guide me and watch over me. I have no choice, it seems, so I nod my head.

I like not knowing who they are. It excites me. I like wanting to trust them and I imagine that someone has sent them to protect me.

Perhaps they are kidnappers, I suddenly think. Perhaps it is a special do-gooding branch of the famous Shining Path, the left-wing guerrilla group that held the country under its terror grip for a decade until President Fujimori crushed them, or perhaps it's the other group that took the Japanese Embassy. Perhaps when they say 'help' it has some other meaning. Maybe I will have to cut a deal.

I remember the American girl who got caught a few years ago stealing documents from the Peruvian Congress for the Shining Path. Lori Berenson was her name, a twenty-six-year-old student from a wealthy New York family, and now she's serving a life sentence four thousand feet up in the Andes. Even her parents' status and influence couldn't get her off the hook; ideological turncoats, it seems, get little sympathy from the US government.

I cannot, however, identify the ideology of these kidnappers. Their common trademark is curly hair. There is César, with little round Lennon glasses and short curly hair (the intellectual), Marcel the podgy one with big medusa hair, a beard and dark rings around his eyes (a touch Arab, I think), and Alfredo who has his long Afro tied into a neat ponytail. His expression is so severe, his lips pressed so tightly, I fear a terrible explosion might occur if they were ever to part.

It doesn't take long, however, under the effect of *pisco,* before my supposed kidnappers begin slapping each other on the chest and kissing in tender nostalgia, all to the songs of Joy Division. 'Ah, this is my *pata*, I love this guy... Ah, the things we have been through together. I love him so, I love him so,' they say. Have I been brought specially to witness these teary declarations? I melt into the contagious emotion, giggling at their bad pronunciation of Joy Division lyrics. Then again, perhaps all this is a ploy to soften me up. Perhaps this is how they seduced Lori Berenson into spying for them.

By midnight everything has become a blur. All I know is that I am very drunk and I am laughing a lot. If my new friends have any bad intentions, I am in no state to resist. The next thing I know we are in another taxi heading towards the outskirts of Lima, where millions of little sparkles glisten on the horizon. For a minute I think they are stars, until I realize they stop where the *sierra* meets the sky rather than the other way round and are in fact the lights of the shanty town that goes on and on and on. I am grateful they have brought me here after dark. A magical star-studded vision by night; a blanket of dust and debris by day. This is where the *cholos* live. Over a million have come over the last ten years, first fleeing civil war between the government and left-wing guerrillas, and now fleeing poverty. 'Lima is a time bomb,' says Marcel, 'ready to explode any minute.'

A salsa tune is playing on the car radio. It's one of those anguished Puerto Rican crooners singing about his ghetto, 'where the true patriots lie... and suffer the bitterness of a defeat they never deserved'. I wonder why Peruvian taxi drivers love salsa so much, when nothing in the country's dense jungles, dry Andes or hostile Pacific coast could be further removed from the sunny sands and palm trees of its Afro-Caribbean birthplace. Yet they talk admiringly of salsa's dead heroes, and in the Lima market stalls you find 1970s salsa martyrs, Héctor Lavoe, Ismael Rivera, on T-shirts alongside Bob Marley and John Lennon.

Finally we reach Comas, and the faint salsa melody echoes again out of closed-up houses. Inside families are dancing away their sorrows to its happy beat, while crying to the reality in the lyrics. I suppose that's why they like it. Salsa is the music of the poor, whose condition and sentiment is the same in Puerto Rico or Lima.

The grime of Comas begins to reveal itself. Under the occasional yellow street light late workers shuffle home, hunching in their jackets against the cold wet Pacific fog. Apart from these sporadic figures, the streets are deserted.

It is a Monday. César is trying to tell me that this is the time and place where Lima's secret dreams of glamour and liberation come alive. By no stretch of the imagination can I envisage the celebrities, hedonist vamps and secret liberationists they talk of springing out from the cracks of this grimy labyrinth. I don't know if I want to see these creatures anyway, but I have been told to shut up and cooperate. We circle the deserted blocks, and I begin to wonder if I am about to be dumped in an alley to be sacrificed in some voodoo ceremony.

Then we turn a corner and suddenly the whole world lights up in sparkling greens, reds and golds. There are things flashing everywhere: giant champagne bottles with gold bubbles bursting out, fluorescent female silhouettes, pianos, penises and cocktail glasses in interchanging pink, red and yellow. We nudge along in the traffic jam that has appeared from nowhere. I swear this is not Lima; I have been transposed somewhere between Ocean Drive and Las Vegas. There are roller-skating *cholos* in tiny miniskirts who ride between the cars and offer us trays of drinks. There are *cholos* on stilts dressed up as women, weighed down with make-up, false eyelashes and silver Beethoven wigs. And little fräulein *cholos* with bleached pigtails, painted red circles on their cheeks, carrying baskets of red apples. César points out a creature in a bikini with huge breasts and says that he is a famous cabaret star.

They take me into one of the pleasure domes. Techno is blaring, mixed with sounds of salsa and Latin house. Inside everything is sparkly, magical, like Cinderella's ball. A transvestite fairy godmother all in white and silver with a huge glittery bouffant, his *cholo* skin powdered in white and a beauty spot painted on his cheek, is grinning and waving his wand from the balcony and throwing angel dust onto the crowd.

The place is packed and the atmosphere euphoric, like a weekend release in London, when the slaves of the system throw off their suit-and-tie stress and free their repressed sexuality. Except this is Monday and I am in Lima and I get the feeling they are throwing off something more intense than stress.

This is the only place in Lima, Marcel tells me, where you can be anybody from anywhere and nobody cares. Nobody cares if you are gay, and nobody cares if you are *cholo.* If you are from the traditional elite, you can come here and escape from the social pressures. If you are poor no one will turn you away. If you are a girl in a short skirt you will not be called a whore; if you are young you are safe from the police. The celebrities of the new *cholo* TV shows come here because, even though they have moved up in the world, this is their home.

Inside everyone is united by a common goal to liberate themselves from the taboos of closed and conservative Limeña society, where discretion and submission to tradition are of essence. I dance with the ecstatic crowd, jumping around, throwing my arms up just like them, as if I too am throwing off my shackles of guilt. I soon find myself under the gaze of an entire table of men, observing and whispering to each other like schoolchildren. I feel a bit self-conscious. 'Don't worry, they are gay, they just want to look and learn from the way you move. They've probably never seen a *gringa* dance,' says Alfredo. They soon begin to dance around me, but none of them reach my shoulders and all of them combined have even less rhythm than this *gringa.*

I am saved when the DJ stops the music to the sound of rolling drums. A booming voice announces the night's special performance as a trapeze lowers a man dressed in the bottle-green uniform of a Lima traffic warden. On touching the stage the young man whips off his jacket and shirt. The crowd roars. Then go the belt, the trousers and the socks, leaving nothing but a hard white hat in the shape of a tea cosy, white gloves and a leather thong. He climbs the balcony and pumps his gyrating pelvis against the rails. He lets himself down and crawls on the floor, stroking himself with a rose that he seems to have produced from nowhere, and then, to the audience's gasp, he pushes the thorny stem down through his underwear. Off goes the thong, and with his back to the audience a most strange show-piece follows in which, by clenching and releasing his muscles, the performer makes the rose dance between his buttock cheeks. Marcel, César, Alfredo and I fall over each other laughing.

We leave in the early hours. The carnival has petered out and the seedy reality of our setting slowly encroaches with the grey dawn. We stop at a stand that sells juicy cow-heart kebabs, where a small crowd is gathered – famished post-partyers scoffing down their food like daytime scavengers, huddling around the kebab grill to keep warm. Their *cholo* faces now look like the everyday victims of downtown's cruel rat race. Their skin is leathery, their faces full of scars, their Nike tracksuits dirty and their eyes darting electrically with the paranoia of *pastabase*, the lethal cocaine residue, Latin America's crack.

One of them has an eye that looks like it has been scraped out. His nose is flat and his face is full of cuts. He tries to talk to me, but I can't work out what he is saying. When I turn away he begins tugging my arm. 'Did you see, did you see the fight?' I think that's what he's saying. And then the words drop off and he just looks at me with a bewildered gaze. He seems to want to tell me something. He looks so pitiful, so vulnerable. Other people butt in, pushing and shoving, and everything is getting out of hand. Alfredo drags me away, but I turn back to look at the man with one eye. Only a few years back, Alfredo tells me, he was the national featherweight champion.

■

My research continues. By day I frequent the universities and schools, recording their moments of pain and anger, joy and laughter. I have started to notice how brands associate themselves with intense feeling at TV football matches here. Just when someone scores a goal, an important and victorious voice booms over the cheer of the crowd: 'Banco Santander, the bank of the people.' Almost undetectable in the euphoria of the moment. Funny how I never noticed that before.

At night my kidnappers appear. They have now revealed that they were instructed to look after me by some Argentine friends of mine. Alfredo is the stern, ethical one, sometimes annoyingly so. César is Mr Melancholy, always crying into his whisky into the early hours, and Marcel is the Joy Division fan.

I've discovered that they are artists or '*cholo*-bohemians', as they joke, because of their humble means and lack of connections. Only aristocrats can make it as artists here, they say. Gallery owners find their work 'interesting' but can afford to treat them with contempt. Luckily, foreign institutions in Lima – the Alliance Française, the British Council and Spanish institutes – exhibit their work and award them prizes that help them with their payments on their studio.

'After years of our continent being raped, we get the dribbles of your guilt,' Alfredo laughs.

We are back in their studio. Since we met they have barely let me out of sight. Every night at seven thirty they appear outside my door; if I'm not there they wait outside in the cold until I come home. Grandpa will not let them in. Riff-raff, he says.

Everyone is heading for Cusco, César says. 'Cusco is about the only place in Perú where it is cool to be *cholo*.'

In fact, it is a virtual prerequisite to be *cholo* if you want to seduce a *gringa*. Buxom blondes will treat a white Peruvian suitor with dismissive indignation, as if she is being sold a souvenir that's not authentic, whereas the *cholo* will blind her with his exoticism.

'A friend of ours now lives in London on the back of a night spent with a smelly-knickered backpacker,' says Marcel, who laments he could never be a *cholo* because he looks too much like an Arab terrorist. 'Seriously, all he did was talk about "*my* people" and "*my* culture" and took the girl to all the corners of Cusco saying things like, "This was where my ancestors ambushed the Spanish and died a terrible but heroic death"... and bam, she went wobbly with historical sympathy.'

It is midnight again, time for another journey into the Limeña night. I watch Alfredo clear the table, rinse the glasses, put everything back in its place and wipe down the surfaces. I am fascinated by his meticulous manner. He learnt these habits in prison, he says.

We take a taxi to the centre of Lima and get out just behind the old Plaza de Armas and the Presidential Palace where the original colonial residences and churches lie crumbling around us. When Perú was the jewel in the Spanish crown, this was where imperial wives lived a life of opulence and idleness while their husbands were out looting the country. Mahogany box balconies hang above us, clinging tentatively to the walls where young Spanish virgins would sit doing their embroidery, surveying the men of colonial society through the holes in the elaborate wood carvings. Now all is quiet. During the day the narrow streets are heaving with the nimble traders weaving through each other trying to earn one more day's survival for their family. Each face in the scavenging crowd has defeat written on it; an ambush on the conscience of the onlooker. But even as you tussle with this, you can feel an energy rumbling under your feet: the layers of a rich history, a memory store of pain and suffering, lost struggles and noble civilizations.

Earlier today, when I strolled into the centre, I came across a little square, almost buried beneath the traffic's black fumes and blaring horns. A hundred *cholos* were sitting on the steps around an auditorium, looking down at a *cómico ambulante* standing on the podium with a microphone. His jokes sent them into roars of laughter, but his sketch was imbued with a message, which he summarized in an endnote.

'Don't spend all your hard-earned money on horses and getting drunk! There is no excuse any more!' shouted the small brown man, with shiny straight black hair, hooked nose and sad intelligent eyes. 'The situation is the situation and whatever the obstacles against us are, we are only shooting ourselves in the foot by drowning our sorrows and evading our responsibility to our families... Living like this, we are the scum they want us to be: easier for them to trample on, easier for them to sell us their cigarettes and their liquor. We must be productive; we must help each other. We must help ourselves.'

The audience nodded in agreement and whispered words of approval into each other's ears. I realized the *cómicos* had nobler roots of community commitment and social criticism than the mere escapism that TV entrepreneurs reduced them to.

The place is apocalyptic in its chaos of cars and *cholo* street traders by day, and depraved and dangerous by night, but Marcel, Alfredo and César love their forgotten city. Though diseased with failure, it vibrates with their history and culture. Within it lies the key to their identity. We wade through the day's residue of rubbish, its stench. The only sounds are the occasional salsa rhythms floating up from a basement, the mumbles of zigzagging drunkards, and ourselves, linked arm in arm and staggering along in a heap of slurring rowdiness.

I watch the boys rescue the redundant objects from piles of rubbish, nursing them as if they were the most precious things in the world. Between these objects and their imagination they revive and reinvent their discarded identity. In oil, acrylic and installations they fuse representations of Inca giants, gods and symbols with images of contemporary brand culture, technology, poverty and power, always challenging the Peruvian self-perception and historical confusion.

In one of the streets Marcel knocks on an old wooden door. We wait for what seems an eternity. Finally an old man opens the door and beckons us into a Spanish-style bar with dirty walls. It's like an old pharmacy: all the walls are lined with wooden cabinets stocked with *pisco* and whisky bottles. The laboratory lighting magnifies the glowing pimples and breathing pores of the clientele, unforgiving of their sunken eyes and facial crevasses. We sit down, accompanied by the thud of a *pisco* bottle on the table, and César makes a toast.

'To the lovely losers of the world!'

Losers? Why losers? Maybe because they spectacularly fail the Miami-aspiring criteria of neo-liberal Perú; they are neither believers in social status nor consumers of its symbols. Yet they are proud to be losers and are open to everything, never anti anything. Marcel dreams of seeing the paintings of Andy Warhol, which he has admired for so many years in books, hanging in the galleries of Europe and New York. But he has been denied a visa three times because he does not have the ten thousand dollars in the bank required by most rich nations as a guarantee. He is not *cholo* enough to sell himself to the *gringas*, but too *cholo* to get a visa.

'I don't want to live anywhere else. I want to live here. I just want to see some paintings, that's all,' he says. 'They interview you through a sheet of glass like they are scared you will attack them. Do they think we are animals?'

I couldn't say; no nation has ever questioned my motives to enter its borders. There is no such thing as a European or American parasite. Grungy backpacker haggling with a hostel owner over a three-pound bill? Never! We are explorers, adventurers, our free spirit a product of some inherently brave national character.

In the early hours of the morning, while César is crying into his *pisco* about some girl, I learn that Alfredo has just been released after serving four years of a life sentence, accused of terrorist crimes. Twelve months ago Fujimori gave the official pardon to twelve innocent prisoners – Alfredo was one of them.

'I'm the lucky one,' is all he says, his eyes smiling. 'There are about three thousand innocent prisoners whose name was found in a telephone book or who received left-wing people in their house. They will have to stay there for twenty years at least. So you see, I am the lucky one.'

'But how did they convict you if they didn't have any evidence?' I ask. Alfredo's serious face breaks with a mild chuckle. My naivety clearly amuses him. He tells me about his trial – a closet, a sheet of black glass and a speaker through which a barely audible voice recited the crimes he had supposedly committed. He had been tortured and kept awake for a week, and the questions confused him.

'Many of the men accused just bowed their heads and said, "Yes, señor, yes, señor, I did all that," because they were told that it would lessen their sentence and no harm would come to their families. But I was defiant and sarcastic. I was stupid. I assumed that because I had done nothing wrong it was simply impossible they could ever convict me. I treated my accusers like ignorant, narrow-minded brutes, not as people who had the power to put me away on a whim. I have been humbled by this experience. You are treated like an animal and it is easy to start behaving like one. You have to find a way to maintain your moral composure. The food is the filthiest thing you've ever seen: fat, water and rotten left-overs from the street markets. I would always keep a tomato or an onion that a visitor would bring me to add it to the stew and make it something close to edible. It was my way of feeling human.'

'How is it you are not bitter?' I ask.

'In jail I saw things so horrible even the imagination could not invent them. But among us political prisoners I experienced a solidarity, compassion and generosity I have never seen or felt in freedom. When my prisonmates heard the news of my liberation, they cried. I thought they were crying because they had not been chosen. But now I know they were crying out of joy for me. I will never forget their faces as long as I live.'

■

Our nights end in the early hours, but around mid-morning I manage to wake up, grab my notebook and go on the hunt for kids. I have a system now. I choose an area on my map where I can see there is a school near by, a park or square. I take a bus to it and then walk, walk, walk. I look for kids on street corners, on benches, lying on the grass or on the grey beach. Sometimes I feel eyes upon me, and that is the moment I make my move.

As I introduce myself, a *gringo* writer, they stare at me, jaws hanging in disbelief. *Me*, interview *them*? What for? But then I ask them who *they* would interview if they had the choice. They smile and I can almost hear their imaginations begin to tick – tick tock, tick tock. Maradona, Che Guevara, the Pope, Alan Garciá. Oh not *him*, or not *her*, I respond, or wow that's a good choice, what would you talk about? I ask them when was the last time they were angry, the last thing that gave them joy, what they hate about their country, what they love, what they think about most often. And how they talk! It would seem nobody had ever asked them anything about their lives.

We talk about everything: life, love, loathing. We laugh. Sometimes they make me laugh so much I forget to write it all down (later I recap). Sometimes their stories are sad. But I love the roaming, the talking, the sensations and moments we share. The more kids I interview, the more I am fascinated by the details that make each one of them different.

So far I have interviewed six hundred kids (in groups, of course) and I swear I can put a face to each one. I think a thousand will be enough, a whole pool of emotions. The real problem is that in the 'safe' areas the security is so high that sneaking behind the high walls that protect them from the *cholos* is impossible. I've been caught and thrown out of two schools. Even a normal middle-class house looks like a mini high-security prison.

In search of a broader Levi's market, I leave the nice areas of San Isidro, Monte Rico, Santa Anita and Miraflores for the poorer ones of Callao, La Victoria, Independencia and Chorillos. Here they don't *cholear* each other: blessed, perhaps, by the absence of choice, or because they don't want to be white as much as the whites think they do. They call the rich *gringos,* because they watch *Friends* and dress like Jennifer Aniston and Brad Pitt and hang out in LarcoMar. But they still want their Levi's.

When I go outside the 'safe' areas, however, I also run into trouble. It is not just that I feel terribly conspicuous: the intense contrast between my colour and theirs, the brilliant newness of my clothes and the worn opaqueness of theirs, the fact that I'm alone and they are in groups. Nor is it the initial fear I had of getting my head kicked in. No, these aren't the problems. In fact, the kids, though sometimes shy, are far more trusting than they should be and slowly begin to pour out their hearts. It makes me feel uneasy. I can't put my finger on it.

It's that sometimes I spot a group of boys who look like regular teenagers, but as I approach I realize there is something terrible in their faces: they have the lines of men weathered by life, as if the map of the city's sewage pipelines in which they live were carved into their faces. Their eyes are glazed, yet wide open and darting around, almost popping out of their heads. The chemical smell of *pastabase* is so overpowering I have to hold my stomach tight to stop myself vomiting. I try to ask questions, but they just stare at me, start a sentence and stop midway, incapable of finishing.

After two or three incidents like these I try to be more cautious. Well into my third week I go to Callao, the home of Lima's Afro-Peruvian community. The taxi driver says he doesn't feel right leaving me there alone, but I tell him that I am meeting friends, which is a lie. I walk up and down the streets passing groups of boys, too scared to approach any of them.

I can see a gang of ten hanging out on a corner across the street. One of them spots me, nudges the rest and they all stop talking and follow me with their eyes. They shout something at me and I ignore them. But after a few more paces, in a split second of madness, I turn round, cross the road and walk towards them. I am petrified, but as I approach the boys begin to disperse in a panic as if I were carrying a machine gun. They trot backwards, pointing to each other and crying, 'It was him, it was him!' I have to laugh at the reciprocal fear, and they begin closing in on me, smiling too. Soon they have me encircled, inspecting me like an animal in a zoo.

They all begin to talk at once, hyperstimulated, drugged. They are dressed in basketball shirts and baseball jackets, but their gear is dirty and worn out and their hair matted and unkempt. They thought I was American, and they love America. With no prompting they shout their heroes: Michael Jordan, Michael Jackson, Tupac, Jennifer Lopez, and their brand-name idols: Nike, Tommy Hilfiger and Levi's.

When their hysteria reaches its peak I threaten to leave. 'No, no, we promise to be serious,' they say. 'Ask us a question, come on, ask us.' They try to hush each other down, like children in a classroom threatened with detention, but in doing so they get more excited and every second there are more of them until I am surrounded by twenty or so screaming over each other. I can't cope.

'Look, I have to leave,' I repeat, trying to barge my way out of the crowd that has me trapped against the wall. But they won't let me leave alone. They insist on escorting me to the main road and soon we are striding down the middle of the street, like a gang on its way to a confrontation with its rival. Mothers and children peer out of the window to see what the fuss is about as we walk down, and small children follow us. I feel absurd, and protected.

When we reach the main road the boys try to hail a taxi. I know that no car will stop for them, but they desperately want to show me they are gentlemen and I don't want to undermine their gesture. Only when the situation is getting embarrassing do I stand behind the two boys on the pavement to wave to a taxi so they think they have flagged it down themselves. They open the door for me and gently help me in. Speeding off, I look out of the back window. They are all standing on the pavement waving goodbye like the Waltons. But are they appropriate for the Levi's survey? Would they be trend influencers or consumers? Are they in the loop?

■

When the sun's glare catches the spray of the Pacific, a magical silver haze hangs over Lima's grey coast. Through the mist you can see little opaque figures gliding across the horizon. A surfers' beach lies at the bottom of the cliffs, beneath the LarcoMar shopping mall complex, the rubbish heap of the new consumer fortress. This is no Ocean Drive but, like Boulevard de Comas, it is somewhere to escape to. The surfers ride the rough, dark sea on the edge of the debris-ridden desert and jump off before they are sucked into the city. A lone rusty Inca Cola billboard welcomes you to the beach, advertising the national lemongrass cola with the logo 'IT'S OURS!' – an obvious parody on Coca-Cola's 'IT'S REAL!' and the perfect slogan for the refugee beach. Even though it possesses nothing of new Perú's plastic glamour, it *is* their own.

In the LarcoMar castle of brand names above, the castes of first-world wannabes compete to prove who is higher in shopping mall status, closer to the master breed of mallers up north. On the dirty beach below, *cholo*-surfers and the posh *pitu*-surfers sit together without hatred or resentment. Each person tramples across the giant pebbles carrying his own stories, but they are all united by a common hatred of what their city has turned into: a rats' den of urban scavengers, suffocating fumes and roaming drug-crazed youth. I too stumble over the rocks, but I am not escaping, at least not consciously. I am hunting, or at least I am supposed to be, but I am too shy to approach the surfers.

Perhaps I am the infiltrator from the world they despise, invading the utopia they are trying to create. I sit on the pebbles feeling self-conscious, and hide in the history book that Marcel and César gave me. It tells me that in 1968 a left-wing general called Velasco Alvarado took power and introduced land reform for the first time. He nationalized US-owned companies in oil, mining, sugar, banking and telecommunications, and began export-led industrialization in the effort to reduce Perú's dependence on foreign capital. He even created the Andean Pact to form a united front with Perú's neighbours, who also wanted to strengthen their respective industries. By 1974 land reform was making headway and, for the first time in history, peasants were listened to. The government toured the provinces to educate formerly marginalized groups, preparing peasant and worker communities to work alongside their newly created ministries and to participate in future democracy.

But the new spirit of radicalism, which the government had encouraged, began to work against it when world prices dropped after the Vietnam War and export revenue slumped.

People started striking when they didn't like Velasco's reforms, and he began to lose control of the military command, who were being heavily lobbied by the US State Department. In 1975, he was replaced and the new military government used heavy repression to impose the IMF-recommended austerity programme. The era of hope ended.

Three friendly faces approach and ask me if I'd like to sit with them.

Mimo, the tallest, has lovely dark curly locks and a noble, indigenous face tailor-made for a Cusco *gringa*'s fantasy. Jeison has the Zen look: his head shaved, a little goatee beard and various strings of beads hanging round his neck. And El Flaco, 'skinny', is the affectionate fatty, lavishing strokes on the surfboard lying beside him in apparent consolation for the weight it must bear.

'Here on the beach we run things differently,' says Jeison. 'The only rule is that on the wave, you respect my space and I respect yours. You don't cut across. As long as you obey the rules it doesn't matter where you come from. Up there, it's the opposite; the only thing that matters is how much money you have, how *vivo* you are.'

The most *vivo* (cunning) of them all, the man they most hate, is President Fujimori himself, who at this time is finishing his second term in government. Internationally the president is held in high esteem for having crushed the left-wing guerrilla movements. His authoritarian style is seen as no bad thing. With it he has ended hyperinflation, stabilized the economy, slashed tariffs and deregulated prices to encourage foreign investment. He has been rewarded with the rich world's loans and approval. It is thanks to the end of terrorism and Fuji's dramatic neo-liberal reforms that Levi's felt secure enough to come into the country; hence my job.

But these beach boys say that the 'Fujishock', which was supposed to put Peruvian industry through a cold shower after which it would come out renewed, efficient and ready to tackle the export market, has turned out to be more like a terminal illness. The fallout of mass unemployment and increased prices is eating away at their middle-class existence. Mimo's dad's chicken factory was forced out of business because his US chicken-feed supplier would no longer sell to him. Encouraged by the Fuji-measures, the feed supplier had decided to install itself as his competitor in chicken breeding instead. Stunned by the 'shock', local industries have not had time to readjust, reboot and reach the level of their foreign competitors. However high the quality of Peruvian textiles, for instance, manufacturers cannot compete with the marketing resources of global brand names. Their only option is to provide sweatshops for them or falsify them.

'Our government only helps foreign interests, not our own,' says El Flaco. 'And if the IMF really wanted to help us become competitive, they would make our government encourage business initiative here, give subsidies, give incentives and training, help build our industries, not just give them loans which they spend on political campaigns.'

While Perú's macro-economic recovery looks good on paper, the seven billion made from privatizations has disappeared, and a Peruvian's wages are worth a third of what they were in the late 1980s. Poverty is more desperate than ever. But the twisting dagger in Lima's wound, the surfers say, is the new drugs phenomenon, which has escalated out of control over the last few years.

'There was always cocaine here, but it was for older people who could afford it,' says Jeison. 'You didn't see so many kids walking around the city strung out on *pastabase.* Now they are everywhere. It's horrible. Fujimori has done nothing to make more opportunities here, but makes sure there is enough cheap *pastabase* to feed the illusion.'

'What do you mean, "makes sure"?' I ask. 'Why is it his fault? I thought that one thing Fujimori's governement had done was to destroy Perú's *coca* fields.'

I had heard that in the 1980s and early 1990s Perú supplied most of the *coca* the Colombian cartels processed into cocaine and crack and sold on to the US. Then the US-funded National Intelligence Service (SIN), under the control of Vladimiro Montesinos, captured all of Perú's major *coca* producers.

'You think that's what they really did?' Mimo chuckles and shakes his head. 'Montesinos just put the exporters in jail, took over their business and negotiated with the Colombians himself. There are photographs of him meeting Escobar. *Coca* growers have even admitted to paying protection money to Montesinos. Now Montesinos controls the coca export business and prevents other growers from exporting, so they have no choice but to flood Lima with their cheap *pastabase.* And that is why you have so many kids on the streets here killing themselves. So, in effect, Montesinos is helping to kill them.'

I've heard a lot about this Montesinos, Perú's *éminence grise.* His military links, people say, provide the backbone of Fujimori's authoritarian government. But I just can't believe a respected democratically elected regime could really be involved in such a lethal scam against its people. This is the era of bona fide democracy in Latin America.

'It's impossible for Fujimori not to know this is going on,' says Jeison, fiddling with the pebbles. 'Montesinos is Fujimori's closest adviser. How do you think Fujimori's governement have been financing his propaganda campaigns? They have bought every judge, businessman and political opponent in the country. With what money? Even the IMF loans are not enough to pay for the number of people they have bought off.'

I, who wanted answers, find this all too difficult to take in. It's horrible. Why would the British government support such a man?

'We are living in a dictatorship,' says El Flaco. 'Only they don't call it a dictatorship because there was no coup. But the president dissolves Congress and nobody says anything because he is backed by the army. The government has the country in its pocket, so all the allegations against them never come to anything. If there are protests against him, nothing is covered by the media. Now the terrorists are crushed, they use the SIN to destroy political opponents and suppress organized opposition in the *poblaciones.* There have been massacres, but nobody will bring Montesinos to trial. At university, people disappear from class – students and teachers who hold anti-government opinions.'

I wonder why the poor keep on voting for Fujimori. Probably because the *cholos* would rather a despised Japanese president than a white man. No white man has ever helped them. The boys, I can see, are sinking into depression.

Is it this depression, this anger and impotence, that Levi's are interested in? Perhaps it can empathize with troubled youth in its advertising. Be angry, buy Levi's. I think of that Levi's ad where the truck dragged the cowboy through the dirt to show how resilient the fabric was, how much better looking for being ripped and torn. Maybe a protestor clad in Levi's being dragged into a van by the secret police. No, I don't think that would go down well with its host government. Levi's might find import tariffs shooting up overnight.

'I'm just sick of it. Our whole history is defined by defeat,' says Jeison. 'I can't stand the way people here are so reverential... all the time they are being taken advantage of and trampled on, and they don't realize.'

'You know why?' said Mimo. 'We are a naive people; we act in good faith and embrace people and we are always betrayed, just like when Atahualpa gave Pizarro three rooms with silver and gold as a gift only to be strangled to death, his kingdon stolen from him. We have that Atahualpa complex.'

And it suddenly occurs to me: am I not about to rob them of the thoughts and feelings they are offering me? The emotions of youth are the gold sought by today's imperialists. A strange image appears in my mind of myself dressed as

 Pizarro, on my horse, brandishing my sword: the twenty-first-century mercenary with a cute blonde crop.

'We have always been defeated, first by the Spanish and now by the Americans,' El Flaco continues. 'But the problem is not that we trust foreigners too much. It's that we don't trust being Peruvian, because we don't know what it is any more to be Peruvian. That is why we are prostrate, because everyone is busy trying to be whiter than the person next to him.'

They have been taught that native Indian culture is crap. They have discovered Spanish leadership to be rotten; now Fujimori's government. Who else can they trust? No wonder my boys in Callao latch on to the US consumer dream, even while they cherish their salsa. Its marketing imagery projects the glory and victory that Peruvians crave, the irreverence that they lack. Yet their very desire for it makes them weak.

'Yes!' cries Jeison, suddenly throwing off his Zen Buddhist pose as he leaps up in triumphant righteousness. Like a sixteenth-century Protestant preacher, he announces: 'Be indifferent to them. That is our strength: indifference!'

El Flaco's entire flabbiness wobbles like jelly as he laughs and rolls over on the pebbles. When he calms down he says, 'Look, the only way we can be strong and united is by accepting all the elements we have. We have to accept that we were conquered by the Spanish – that is part of us too! At least the Spaniards lived in the land they conquered. The Americans just manage us from abroad. They can't even show us their faces. Instead they use pawns here to do their dirty work. We should know and love our culture, with all its faults, to be able to defend it, but we don't.'

Mimo broods, his locks hanging gorgeously in his face. 'For me, the Spanish are bastards; they have repressed us with their bastard Catholicism. We must look back further, when religion meant praising the sun, energy and the natural elements we depend on, and not false icons and prophets.' As he says this he stares out at the ocean. 'If I could live again, I would be born into the Inca kingdom. I would go out surfing every morning with Atahualpa.' He pauses and smiles. 'They did have surfboards in Inca times, didn't they?'

■

Our last supper must be glorious, we agree. Marcel, Alfredo, César and I book a table in Astrid y Gaston, one of Lima's most exquisite restaurants, frequented by foreign visitors and the two hundred or so members of Lima's elite who can afford it.

We stroll into the restaurant to the hostile stares of thickset women with bouffants and men in impeccable dark suits fondling the gold on their podgy fingers.

Perhaps it is the couture thriftiness of my escorts that our opulent audience finds repellent, or the forests of hair. Marcel's limp doesn't help. But I think the ultimate insult is the obvious lack of effort to appear rich with, say, a splash of cheap cologne and an imitation Italian suit.

The menu that appears in my hand, however, possesses remarkable powers to dispel all social unease. There is octopus in olive mayonnaise, mini potato trifles with seafood and avocado filling, wonderful spiced, lime-marinated sashimi called *ceviche*, hundreds of varieties of potato, new succulent meats and poultry: guinea pig, hare, duck, alpaca and huge freshwater prawns; thick bouillabaisses, miso soups, juicy roasts with crispy skins, zesty marinades and intense sauces involving new fusions of spices, creams, chillies and citrus juices.

My Limeña dinners have become the best history lessons. Marcel tells me which part of my plate comes from the Inca culinary tradition, which is the Spanish infusion (with its Moorish subtext), what the Africans contributed, what touch the French and other Europeans brought with their arrival after independence, and what the Chinese and Japanese added when they came in the nineteenth and twentieth centuries. Here on my plate, in every mouthful, the same layers that simmer below Lima's oppressive superstructure fuse in the most harmonious way. If only humanity could do the same.

We are soon lost in the happy haze of the *pisco* sour, absorbing the supreme sensations and performing our dramatic protestations of friendship and love. On the table next to us a Peruvian nods deferentially as his American business partner hollers opinions about a mining company he is interested in buying. 'Fucking' this and 'fucking' that come out of his mouth every few seconds to the obvious embarrassment of his colleague, who darts his head round anxiously every time the word spits out of the man's mouth. The volume and projection is astounding, as if the man believes the whole restaurant has come especially to hear him speak, and must indeed be grateful for his very presence in the country. The boys flinch but say nothing.

We stay late. Once the guests have gone the waiters relax and drink with us. We urge them to join us for a toast.

'To the lovely losers of the world!' declares César.

The next day they insist on taking me to the airport, to the very door of the plane if they can. There is a delay. To every half-hour they add another half-hour, and we end up waiting for four hours in the airport café. I keep telling the boys to go. Soon they will be just a memory and I feel uncomfortable with that thought in their presence, but as usual they won't hear of it.

There is a queue at passport control when I finally get there, and I stand in it while they watch me. Every time I look back they wave frenetically and shout things. Their faces get smaller and smaller until they disappear behind the crowd as I walk through the security checks.

I walk down the corridor to the departure gate where I hear a tapping. There they are again, on the other side of the glass, and I am reminded of the visa interviews they have to take in glass-partitioned rooms, like criminals. I press my face against it.

3

TRIBES AND TRIBULATIONS

'Why *did* you get so involved in Argentina?' I asked my mother yesterday when we spoke by phone. Perhaps if the experience hadn't touched my parents so, if they hadn't brought it back with them through the exiled guests, I might never have looked back. I would not be here, sitting on a plane, flying from Lima to Miami. Buenos Aires would have been just a place where I had once lived.

'The place, the people we met, the times we were living in bowled me over,' she told me. 'Their belief in society, commitment to social justice, to the ideal that a country of such abundance should be shared by all, their passion for life, their energy... was all so different from what I knew back home – you know, that insular complacency you get here.' New friends, like Enrique, brought politics alive for her in a way she had never known. 'They were not only intellectually restless, they were affectionate, sociable and vibrant. They weren't stuffy and pompous; they were funny. They could fix cars and work on farms as well as deconstruct Marxist theories. Perhaps I had not been prepared for it, having never been among people where things like these were discussed, or maybe these values triggered sensibilities in me that were latent.'

Had we been living in the posh Zona Norte suburbs along the northern banks of the river Plate, as most ex-pats did, we might have been able to ignore the struggle between ideals and might that shook Argentina. The impenetrable fortresses of private golf and sailing clubs, polo fields and mansions protected its business, political and military elite residents against the very war they were waging. In the French-style avenues of the town centre, though, lined with theatres, twenty-four-hour bookshops and cafés, a different, more politicized middle class lived.

'In the apartment blocks next to ours you'd hear desperate voices screaming out of the windows: "My name is Juan Dominguez, I am being taken! Tell people what you have seen!"' Mum said. 'You'd be sitting in a cinema and police would come in and drag people out. Once on our way to the swings in Plaza San Martín we turned a corner and a dead body lay in the street. You couldn't ignore what was going on.'

My mother found it difficult to settle back into comfortable north London life. She became involved in the solidarity campaigns that helped give asylum to the persecuted. I remember those Amazons that so dazzled the dinner parties and how we hugged on lonely nights of babysitting as they'd hunched over in pain at the fate of loved ones they had left behind.

■

The blinding white light of Miami's dawn greets me as I land. I run under the arch of two inward-leaning palm trees wrapped in little white lights and through the bright blue corridor of my new abode. Wedged between the bondage boutiques and cosmetic supermarkets of Collins Avenue, the Mermaid Guesthouse is South Beach's rustic token; a little oasis. I've made a deal with the owners to rent a room on a monthly basis and to be able to leave my stuff with them while I'm travelling.

I drop my bags at the foot of the clay mermaid spurting water into the flowers of the back patio, and head for the sea to wash off the grime of Lima's chaos. For a second, Miami's clean, sea-salt breeze and fresh blue sky almost deserve the worship of the *arribistas.* I go back to my room and crawl inside the crisp linen under the mosquito net. Nobody will find me here. Nobody wants to know your true identity in Miami. It is the palace of reinvention. It is the perfect hideout.

Julia, a butch woman who wades round the hostel like a goth-punk wrestler – a cross between Prince and Alice Cooper – runs the place. Even in midsummer when one can barely suffer the weight of a bikini, she dresses in black from head to toe. You can spot her a mile away because of the black shirt she wraps around her waist, which flaps around her big hips as she tears down the avenue, her Medusa hair flying, as if she were about to take off on a broomstick.

Her husband, Pedro, is the sensitive, soul-tormented

 trovador with a velvet voice. They met twenty years back. One look at Pedro, the Uruguayan Jim Morrison, made Julia, the daughter of a well-to-do Uruguayan family, give up a bright future in the diplomatic service. She has been his manager ever since, or rather, fierce protector from the eternal female fan club. Pedro is so beautiful that even the black leather pants and silk shirt open to the waist can't make him look sleazy. But only a woman of Julia's character could put up with his boyish egocentricity and artist's fragility, which seem to excuse him from all mundane chores.

Julia is a businesswoman with a highly mercurial streak. If she is in a generous mood you can bargain her into anything, but otherwise she is all fire and fury. Pedro puts up a sign, 'Stay out of reception, Julia's gone atomic,' so you know not to venture past the patio. She has this weird pricing system that arbitrarily favours those she considers 'proper' people – gentle, thoughtful and open-minded types – for whom rooms cost a hundred dollars; others pay a hundred and fifty.

Every room has a different colour combination: pale blue and fuchsia, violet and lime green, burgundy and lemon; with matching bedlinen and skirting boards. Net curtains hang from the ceiling over the bed to make you feel like a nineteenth-century colonial lady in some mosquito-ridden colony. There are little mermaids all over the place: brass ones, brightly coloured wooden ones, cloth ones sewn onto cushions, Haitian-style painted ones.

Behind the patio with the mermaid fountain and lush tropical plants, is the Mermaid bar, decorated with stars and moons on the ceiling, and furnished with thick red curtains and velvet loungers. Some evenings Pedro will sit on a stool by candlelight singing soft Brazilian ballads. Lured off the street by the honey voice, leggy Texan blondes will plant a chair in front of the lonesome long-haired Latino, smiling hopefully and searching for a meaningful glance. Then they notice fiercely pouting Julia in the corner, and their smiles disappear.

All these features, even mad red-lipsticked Julia, make the Mermaid a favourite stopover for European travellers. On the run from cheap, sterile office life, its shoddy wooden grot is enough to make them cough up for an rustic illusion.

I too was overpowered by the Mermaid spell, but as the days go by, the weirdness begins to creep out of the woodwork. There is Bobby, a fifty-something self-proclaimed sugar daddy to countless young babes chasing modelling careers. He appears every day in a leather outfit copied from Pedro (but with none of the elegance) and spends it chain-smoking in one of the deckchairs in the courtyard. He always comes armed with a very glamorous reason for being there, needing a rest from location-hunting with that 'slave-driver' Oliver Stone, or complaining: 'Does he think I have no other life?' after a wild night spent entertaining Al Pacino and Cameron Diaz until the early hours at the Shadow Lounge disco. 'Does a man live on champagne alone?' demands Bobby. Cameron is a 'nice gal', 'a real good partier', but he is really getting too old for all this. He needs a bit of peace.

For someone looking for peace Bobby does a lot of talking, which means none of us get any. He yaps and yaps about his career as a Hollywood film producer. All the great films? He's done them. Clint Eastwood, James Caan, Burt Reynolds, Steve McQueen? He's worked with them. He had the mansion, the Ferraris, the famous friends. And the women, oh the countless women. Oh, the crazy things he's done. 'Aaaahh,' he sighs, staring into space with a look of cheeky nostalgia as he takes another cigarette. At this point I try to sneak off to my room, hoping he might have left by the time I come out again. But no, he's always there, three hours later, rounding off his adventures to a different audience.

'Naaah… hadda get outta LA, man. That lifestyle, it was drivin' me nuts. Miami's the place. Y'know, more low-key. People don't get on toppa'ya.'

Finally, when it is getting dark, he jumps up exclaiming: 'Jesus, is that the time? Gotta run and see what Oliver is up to… gotta long night ahead of us.' Bobby always gives us the impression that he is doing us a favour with his visits, on the basis that he wouldn't usually grace such a downmarket place, so undernourished in the celebrity department.

'It's so downna'earth here. You can relax. No one to hassle ya. Aaagh, I'm finished with all those upmarket places, all those false people. Julia and Pedro are solid people. Good folk, even if they are not up there,' he says, throwing his eyes to VIP heaven.

Sometimes he drops in at night, freshly shaven and perfumed, just to show he's thinking of us as he trots off to some celebrity function at the Delano. Julia doesn't seem to mind. Sometimes he even helps behind the desk, she says, when she has something else to do. But it's me who has to spend the whole time avoiding him.

Then one morning Bobby is found dead in a prostitute's apartment.

It was a heart attack, the coroner says, induced by an overdose of cocaine and ecstasy. I should have known he'd been off his face all the time, the way he rambled like there was no tomorrow. Julia and Pedro try to find his family and friends for the funeral, but no one owns up. Even the bouncers of the nightclubs he said he frequented cannot put a name to the face in the photograph they are shown.

All his stories were lies. He was just another pill-popping pretender who spun his fantasy web around Miami.

■

I must get on with my report. What on earth will I put in it? Obviously I must segment this mass of youth. That is what they've hired me for, isn't it? To make the crowd manageable. I start to think about which kids in Perú were most similar and group them together. Obviously most of it is class defined, so that bit is not difficult. But Levi's want 'tribes', identifiable by style and attitude, by common sadness and happiness, dreams and fears.

I try to think of the pressing concerns associated with each tribe. I remember the ones who wanted to throw off society's taboos in hidden pleasure domes. The *Surfers* who wanted to wash off reality on the waves. The *Cholo-bohemios* who needed to explore their own defeats and make them beautiful so that others might face the collective truth. *Salseros* embraced the warmth and consolation offered by their Caribbean brothers, while *Patas* found no comfort sweeter than the TV cosiness of Jennifer Aniston and her *Friends.*

Young *Limeños* flash by inside my head, mouthing statements like 'Down with Arribismo!' I hear their voices: 'I want a boyfriend who doesn't beat me like my dad beats my mum, who...' or 'When I say we should value our own traditions I don't mean...' They wanted me to understand them; Levi's say they'd rather have bullet points than proper sentences to inspire advertising imagery, so I must condense them into sound-bites. Little emotional capsules that might work as campaign slogans.

To maximise the usefulness of the images and thoughts, they want me to plant the tribes on graphs and diagrams – a clearer way to decipher their consumer potential.

I was never any good at graphs and tables, or anything to do with statistics, but this is easy peasy. Under the patio's palm tree, I draw big circles on my computer screen to represent each tribe and give them different colours and sizes, according to how strongly they are represented in society. I separate and sort, just like they taught me in nursery school. Perhaps it is this my British education trains me for.

I throw down my tribes somewhere between vertical and horizontal axes. There you go, that's where you belong. Mermaid visitors look on and smile charitably, clearly bemused and wondering whether I've just been released from the local madhouse. How little they know of the sense it makes!

Sometimes I spend a long time deliberating over the category on one individual, before I slap her on the grid. Their words have made them specimens. I wouldn't want anyone to be a labelled a *Salsera* when she is in fact a *Pata.* A travesty of identity! Then I remember: It doesn't matter, because the kids are never going to see this. I will not be held accountable to them. Nevertheless, when their scrunched faces peer out of their bubbles again, mouthing their soundbites, they seem indignant, angry at me. Maybe I *am* going mad.

By the time I have finished, I am in graph overdrive, and I even create a whole new Venn diagram entitled 'Tribe Compatibility' to show which tribes flow into each other and which conflict, so Levi's can kill several tribes with one stone.

I have to laugh. I am tempted to send the end result to Marcel and crew. It would amuse them. In the last graph I have to show which tribes influence the others, which means placing my kids in the consumer hierarchy, the *arribismo* they told me they hate. Anyway, Levi's will probably send the report back to me politely thanking me for my services and informing me that they won't be needing any further reports. What the hell.

■

Outside my room the strange Mermaid regulars continue to appear. After Bobby dies, Carlos turns up, a Puerto Rican bongo player, whose claim to fame is having played percussion on Santana's famous hit 'Oye Como Va'. He barks on, too, about his glory days as the hottest bongo player of the 1980s, sharing the stage with musical greats.

Pedro and Carlos spend hours in the den together, guitar strumming and bongo banging. They stumble out late at night and knock on my door as they pass by to lure me out to a disco tour, which invariably ends with me leaving them slumped in a red velvet corner sofa somewhere at dawn, Pedro being torn apart by a yellow-maned vulture in a red PVC cat suit.

Julia and Pedro are constantly embroiled in problems with the municipality, banks and landlords. Despite the guesthouse being permanently booked up, it's clear they are in financial trouble. Rosalie, the Haitian cleaner, has to borrow money off me for cleaning materials.

Things are starting to fall apart. Even the Germans and Swedes are beginning to complain. They walk into their rooms to find gaping holes in the floors, leaks in the ceilings, water patches on the walls. A smell of damp is beginning to linger throughout the place and rat-sized cockroaches scurry across the floors and onto the beds. I walk into reception to find a Swiss man demanding his deposit back because his guidebook's so-called enchanted hostel is in fact a filthy, stinking shambles. 'Vat a disgrace, vat a disgrace!' he shouts and storms off to his musky room.

I miss Perú terribly, and the kidnappers of my heart. I hole myself up in my room to escape the senseless self-destruction around me. With its rustic façade, the Mermaid embodies even more intensely the void that exists below South Beach's seductive surface. Here, at the core of the American dream, the maggot of greed, vanity and loneliness is having a feast – trapping wannabes, has-beens, or in Bobby's case a wannabe has-been, and chewing its way through their souls.

I transport myself back to the dreary Lima landscape. Faces float before my eyes, sullen and intelligent. I long for their innocence. By innocent, I don't mean naive. Naive is Miami, pursuing a fantasy that exists through hearsay, in that bar where Cameron Diaz once played pool, or on Ocean Drive where so and so was *this* close to Puff Daddy. Success is at your fingertips but you are never quite there. Innocence only believes what she sees. Innocence can stare reality in the face, choose not to escape it and yet remain open. Like Marcel, Alfredo, César, patient-spirited yet vibrant in their apocalyptic surroundings. Never eager to impress, they watched and waited, preserving wisdom, humanity and hope, History's gift.

■

I am sitting behind the Mermaid reception desk one day, having been emotionally blackmailed by Pedro into helping out, when a tall handsome Cuban boy arrives to mend the switchboard system. Never has the Mermaid seen such politeness! Most people throw their weight around hysterically as if insolence were justified by the mere fact of being on holiday. Then this embodiment of conspicuous serenity floats in, like a goodwill ghost.

His unwillingness to intrude or draw attention to himself brings memories of Limeña natural manners. He must be new to Miami, I think. I clasp this flicker of innocence, not yet rotting in the fantasy factory. I want to know his secret. What does he seek here that Fidel has not given him?

The sum of my Miami Cuban encounters amounts to the fat tow-car lorry drivers shoving down greasy breakfasts at a Cuban café where I buy my coffee in the morning. I have heard much about the lunatic behaviour of combat-dressed *anti-Castristas* who start foaming at the mouth if you mention Fidel. It is said that Latin hot-bloodedness does not exist in a Miami Cuban, only fanaticism. They are also usually armed. But I can't resist asking the telephone technician how the Comandante is doing.

'Fidel ha done many good things in ouwer country. Wee ha better education and health than heere in the US,' says Yoel. 'The only problem ees that the man ha been in power for too long, and that makes heem a bit psychopathic.'

For many Cubans in Miami, Fidel is the unforgivable source of their riches-to-rags story, and the terrible nights they spent looking up at the stars from a tyre raft, tied together with rope, listening to the glup, glup of hungry sharks. It was petrifying and beautiful, Yoel says about his night on the shark-infested waters – just like living in Cuba.

Yoel was eighteen when he landed here a year ago. He was an engineering student in Havana, but the economy had got so bad he had to look for a place where he could practise what he studied. Frankly, he adds, he wouldn't be here if the financial situation hadn't forced it, and, anyway, the Promised Land isn't all it has been cracked up to be.

'Why heere you go to de supermarket and you have to peek from tousan' of toot'brush. Eeees stupid, man. Dey all doo the same tin'. But dair ees notin' in Cuba, no work, no money. We say Batista killed de people, but Fidel don' let you live.'

Fidel isn't all to blame, Yoel insists. It's Karl Marx's fault. 'We leev under a system invented by a man… oo never in ees life been in ower contree. So ow can ee know whas good for us?'

I try to picture Grandad Marx sitting on the beach in a *guayabera*, his white hairy knees turning red as he scribbles on his lap. Each country must find its way forward based on its own geography, history and climate, Yoel insists, rather than superimpose a system not suited to its nature.

He fiddles with his screwdriver and my mind wanders. I imagine him carrying me off into the Miami sunset, freeing me from South Beach. No more spring-breakers swirling their pierced tongues in your face as if this were the most erotic act ever invented. Oh please, I think, I know you are the world's most sexually unrepressed person but can you please just put your tongue back in your mouth? No more busty college girls who feel the need to set themselves – and their tits – free on tabletops. I practically force the poor Cuban boy to take me out. Looking slightly alarmed, he agrees and invites me to a salsa club.

Apparently the in-house disco at the Miami Airport Hilton, with its mirrored walls and rank red velvet sofas, is *the* coolest salsa club in town. Thursday and Sunday nights are free at Club Mystique, and the punters dress up like they're off to the Oscars. Even the poorest immigrant is a Cuban American Princess (CAP) for the night. In her cheap glamour, the natural swinging of her hourglass curves would make Liz Hurley break into a sweat of envy.

As they slink inside the sliding gold-rimmed doors in sparkling backless dresses, a thick fog of artificial fragrance blasts out. Long velvet-black hair swings to the rhythm of their hips as they throw killer looks to the female competition and male admirers. Behind them the boys glide in loose and lean, baggy silk shirts rippling around their wiry bodies, a gold loop hanging from the ear. They wear their hair short and gelled, slightly spiky at the front, the mark of individuality left to various designs in facial hair, immaculately sculpted.

The newly arrived Latinos tend towards the head-to-toe cream effect: cream shoes, cream trousers, cream shirt buttoned to the top and the gold chain hanging over the shirt. This is the ultimate symbol of wealth. Yoel is eager to show me how he wears his gold chain *under* his shirt, to prove that he is less hung up about money.

The greatest compliment you can give a Latino groover is that he or she is *detallista*, a champion of aesthetic detail. Unsurprisingly, there is no direct English translation. To make it all seem effortless, they look as indifferent as possible, unmoved by the slurring professors of love singing tales of suffering, desire's longing and journeys to hell and back. Emotion must be all compressed in their clinch of synchronized sexuality, microscopic movements hingeing on hip joints. He looks serious and she untouchable.

Then I see something extraordinary. I see a blonde girl like myself jumping around like Britney Spears as she drags a reluctant Cuban boy onto the dance floor. Her enthusiasm is so out of keeping with the environment that a sense of foreboding grips me. She, so enamoured with her new cha-cha-cha mood, does not notice her partner's awkward shuffle and that people are moving away in disassociation. Her partner's friends cajole from the sidelines and he laughs with them, shrugging his shoulders in a 'What can I do?' kind of way. He waits politely until the song and her dance routine are over before handing her a card offering salsa lessons. He disappears, leaving her beaming smile to slowly disappear as confusion sets in.

I take note; her humiliation is my lesson. Despite the Scarface pastiche, Miami's Latino scene is to be taken very seriously indeed. Rules are king, when retrieving roots are involved.

The spotlight falls on a man with goofy teeth and thick black-rimmed glasses: Austin Powers meets John Travolta. He begins to dance with this beautiful woman and he just dusts up that floor with the most amazing moves, stunning the crowd into 'ooohs' and 'aaahs'. It's definitely not looks that make you cool on the Miami salsa scene. Dudes queue to dance with the plain-looking fat ones who know how to wiggle their flesh. The more of it the better.

Next a little fat man with a bushy moustache gets up on stage and asks everyone to grab their partners. Each couple takes their place in a huge circle, and there are so many people they have to make two inner circles. As soon as the music starts, the couples begin the basic steps. Then the compère calls out '*Dame!*', which means 'pass her over', and the guys leave their girls to the next man, grab the next girl up and go into the next move. This goes on and on with different kinds of moves with names like 'Tell her', 'On no account', 'Goodbye and over to the sister', and 'Zorro', where in the middle of the move the man pretends he is sword-fighting. You can tell which moves have been invented in Miami from their names: 'Pizza Hut', 'Kentucky (Fried Chicken)' and 'Coca-Cola'.

The ritual is called *la rueda,* the wheel, because you just go round and round swapping partners until you come back to your own. Watching it from the balcony above is like looking through a kaleidoscope. Though *la rueda* is a Cuban invention,

Yoel tells me it has become an obsession in Miami; it looks like group therapy. Miami Cubans have also turned the communal dance expression of Castro's Cuba into a meritocracy: the best dancers are always in the inner circle, which goes faster than the rest. It's not like that in Cuba, Yoel says.

Right now, I don't care. I feel hypnotized, like I have been trapped by a religious sect. I want to be part of that community, I want to belong to it. I want to get into that inner circle. Miami makes me needy. This young generation of Cuban Americans is needy too. I suppose being fanatical about roots is an improvement on being hung up on Fidel.

We both search. And yet, they believe that salvation lies in this land of billboard dreams, the beacon of light for the purgatory below (which they've escaped from), while I'm not sure I believe in this religion. But if I deliver sacraments, and hear confessions for a faith I do not believe in, what *do* I believe in? Maybe one day the connection between this fortress of power I represent and the powerless hope I listen to down below will reveal itself. Now, I only know that I feel the south calling, like a faint flicker inside me asking to be lit up. My Perú report has reached Levi's head office in San Francisco, and been accepted. 'Good job!' is my password to continue. I am due to arrive in Panamá in a few days.

4

ENDURANCE

'He who can forget injustice and do so because he has a very good memory.'

Roberto, 15, Panamá City

From the air, she twists from Costa Rica into a horizontal position like a Freudian patient, her legs falling off the couch into Colombia. On the ground, her warm night envelopes me. Loose and confident, lean *café con leche* boys swagger past, their white welcome teeth gleaming. Their cool slither is not a pretend one, but a cultural call for confidence. My eyes follow. My muscles relax. And my Miami loneliness dissolves somewhere between the microscopic drops of humidity and the hustle and bustle of laughing taxi men.

No one has come to meet me. I am promised a contact soon.

 To compensate, I make a self-authorized reservation at Panamá City's most expensive hotel. Since leaving Perú, my Atahualpa complex has been wearing thin. I no longer feel the need to save Levi's money. The pennies it saves on me prying priceless gems of teenage wisdom is enough. Besides, I want to see what it's like *inside* the world I represent. With his sweeping certainty Bill had told me that I, being so quirky and hip, having my pulse on the street and all, wouldn't be interested in the corporate hotels on the Levi's list (I think this was meant as a compliment). But I want to know all! Is his world of business breakfasts and client-seducing dinners not part of the picture I must fill?

Jeisel, the bellboy who shows me to my room, is also fascinated by the secrets within the corridors of polished marble and gold that he guides others through. We stare into the void of the eternally reversing lights in the elevator's mirrored roof. At first he is shy to enter my room when, the following morning, I ask him to help me with my map, but soon he is pressing the buttons on every plastic gadget in the suite, bouncing on the bed and doing impersonations of his sycophantic bosses, sucking up to the Yanks.

'They tell me I have too much attitude for a nigger,' Jeisel boasts. 'I stand up for myself. But I'm not stupid. I know the limits. I know you have to play the game.'

We sit on the balcony smoking cigarettes, blinded by the burning glass of Punta Paitilla's high-rise luxury around us. Homes of Panamá's Miami-hopping elite, Jeisel says, known here as *rabiblancos.* White-arses. The Pacific stretches out before us as liberation itself, and on our right, at the other point of the long curving bay, the old Panamá city is perched. Beyond is the Panamá Canal and the Bridge of the Americas, the gateway to South America.

After my map is coloured in I take a taxi to the other side of the bay. The neglected colonial buildings-turned-whore-houses don't look as folkloric as they did from my balcony. The main road, Avenida Central, is cramped with brightly painted buses and honking cars. Traders holler in the city heat, wiping the dirt and stress from their brows, and groups of schoolgirls in clean white shirts and grey skirts skip and tease the ladies who file their nails in doorways in pink hot pants and flip-flops with rollers in their hair. Almost unnoticeable in the crowd are the portly, pink-faced foreign men walking hand in hand with teenage *mulatas.* I imagine this street fifty years ago: Richard Gere sailors dazzling local girls in glistening white. Or was that just a Hollywood movie?

As we head north-west towards the famous canal, an area of crammed narrow streets with crumbling houses and newer prison-like blocks appears on my left. By a big arrow on my map is written 'barrio de Jeisel'. Jeisel's hood, El Chorrillo, home of the canal-construction workers who were brought from the West Indies early in the last century. Jeisel told me that around thirty thousand descendants are now squeezed into a slum stretching only a few blocks.

Minutes later, on the other side of the wire fence, we are inside the pristine land of Canal Zone suburbia, where water sprayers are still hissing over the lawns of the former administrators' apple-pie homes. I've been transported to 1950s small-town Ohio, with its post office, white spire church and candy store. I imagine crew-cut boys in stripy shirts sitting on stools and sipping milkshakes while diplomats and military officials slump about with the officious glumness of the white man's burden. Now it's a ghost town and the nearby army barrack buildings are derelict. After almost a hundred years, the Canal will be returned to Panamá in a month's time.

Jeisel told me that Panamá was created when it seceded from Colombia in 1903. A treaty was signed agreeing that, in return for the military support that would make secession possible, the US would have the rights to build a canal, own it and a vast area around it. The treaty, US Secretary of State John Hay admitted privately to staff, 'was vastly advantageous to the US and, we must confess, not so advantageous to Panamá'.

Now, most of the forty thousand Americans who used to be based here have already packed up and gone.

'They'll be back soon. This is going to become a tourist resort. All the big hotel names will be coming,' Hernan, my driver, announces proudly, as if to reassure me it will not be abandoned to reckless locals. I envisage giant Miami-style wedding cakes on the Pacific horizon plastered with Hilton or Radisson, and spring-breakers speeding across the tranquil lawns in their jeeps into the sunset... Weheee! Yeeehaa! The children of Chorrillo's bare-backed ancestors will be invited to wear white as they serve cosmetic mutants and their sugar daddies by the swimming pool. The government will probably claim this a sign of great progress.

'I thought the point of getting the Canal back was to get the Americans out,' I say.

Hernan shrugs. 'They put the bread on our tables, don't they?'

I suppose that is the best relationship they can expect. If, since the very beginning, foreign occupation has set their course, why should anyone now think they could control their own destiny? Maybe he feels grateful for the crumbs off another's plate. But who am I to talk of these things? Am I not also a servant to this power?

By the time we cover the Canal Zone, up to the mansions of Balboa and Cerro Ancón, most of the afternoon has gone and I decide not to go to the great canal itself. Instead we head north of the city where migrant squatters have cut back the long grass and banana trees to erect humble wooden shacks. In the last of the orange sunlight children play barefoot in the streets, fat ladies swing in hammocks on verandas and plump couples in flip-flops are pressed together in chubby harmony as they shuffle in rotation to the salsa. I ask the taxi driver to drop me off. On one porch an old man sits alone in his grubby T-shirt, shorts and sandals, beer in one hand and barbecue stoke in the other. His bloodshot eyes lazily follow this conspicuous white-faced and yellow-haired woman stealing around in a night that doesn't belong to her.

I come across a group of teenagers, still in their school uniforms of short-sleeved white cotton shirt and grey slacks, or skirts for girls. The two *mulatos* are tall, slim and handsome, and the girl stands chest out and proud. Her Afro is braided and tied with colourful bows and her lilac eyeshadow makes her hazel eyes even more striking. Leidy, Rory and Oosnavi are their names. Oosnavi – that's a strange name, I say. The boy replies that it is taken from the famous plane that flies daily over their skies.

The kids are warm and friendly. They ask me where I am from, and bombard me with questions.

'Someone told me that in England they all eat out of tins because there's no proper food. That you don't have fresh fish and vegetables, like we have here. Is that true?' says Oosnavi.

'England?' Leidy continues, with a cheeky smile. 'Isn't that the place where people commit suicide because it's so dark?'

'No, that's Sweden,' I reply, almost offended. After all, it is the home of the English princess she is named after. She thinks Lady Di is Britney Spears's mother. I suppose she is perfectly entitled to; why should it be only Brits and Americans who are careless with foreign facts?

It occurs to me that none of the kids I have questioned has questioned me or exposed me as I feared at the beginning. I find it moving, and unsettling.

■

At breakfast under fake chandeliers, international loneliness often sits down uninvited at my table: a British engineer, a Tommy Hilfiger salesman, a New Yorker who tells me about a photography book he is working on to celebrate the handing over of the Canal. If there is one thing I must do in Panamá, he insists, it is to see this eighth wonder of the world, this historic feat of engineering, this monument to human enterprise, this gift of bolted steel to the world, and now to Panamá.

The pride and patriotism he exudes reminds me of my grandmother when she would tell me of the great railways we built and kindly left for 'those wretched Indians'.

I have finally established a relationship with Levi's Central American office, stationed in Costa Rica. Costa Rica is Panamá's richer, more reliable neighbour and, I've been told, to Central America what Chile is in the Southern Cone, safe and stable for multinationals to run their operations from. Panamá and Costa Rica are both on my list of 'non-risk' Central American countries. Bill is also considering Honduras. Sipping my breakfast broth I stare north across the Pacific towards Panamá's other neighbours – Nicaragua, Guatemala and El Salvador – and wonder why they have not made the Levi's selection.

An image comes to me. I am seven, clad in my favourite red clogs, tracksuit bottoms, a yellow tie and an Argentine sheepskin coat that was already short on the arm but I was refusing to grow out of. You could tell fashion was my destiny. Hyde Park's Speaker's Corner is behind me. My mother, in purple boiler suit and perm, is chatting animatedly in Spanish to another sheepskinned bloke. After long being depressed about having left Argentina in its worst moment, her mood is jubilant. My own little banner reflects it: 'The tide has turned... It is unstoppable.'

We were rooting for El Salvador against American intervention, and Nicaragua too. It comes back to me now. In Nicaragua, the Sandinista National Liberation Front (FSLN) had wrested power from the hated Somoza dictatorship, a family who for forty years had kept its people in poverty while it appropriated vast areas of land. Anastasio Somoza, the first in the US-supported dynasty, had his terse liberal opponent, Augusto Sandino, murdered in 1934. Somoza's sons continued to murder peasant activists who, inspired by Sandino, tried to better the situation of the poor. In 1972, the year I was born, the 'tide' began to turn as Somoza was discovered to have stolen international aid sent after a devastating earthquake had killed six thousand people and made 300,000 homeless. Even the conservatives turned against him and, in 1979, the Sandinistas marched victorious into Managua. I remember celebrating, with flags and fluorescent dyed wools draped around our house. We danced to the guitars, drums and resistance anthems that had accompanied Nicaragua's victory, but I knew nothing of what it meant.

Our joy was short-lived. Just as the new Sandinista government began dividing up Somoza's land, US congressmen awarded ten million dollars to fund counter-revolutionary groups. When that didn't prevent the Sandinista government from winning a landslide election victory, Congress authorized a trade embargo and pressured financial institutions to stop lending it money.

El Salvador suffered the same treatment. There, in the early 1970s, it was church leaders who began to challenge the corrupt US-supported government. After witnessing the murder of fellow churchmen who sided with the poor, Oscar Romero, a formerly conservative member of the Catholic hierarchy who became Archbishop of El Salvador in 1977, also began to preach that it was not God's will that poor people should suffer, as their schools and churches told them. It was the will of the rich, including the church hierarchy and foreign companies, who sought to preserve their own wealth at the expense of others. Archbishop Romero's assassination while saying Mass in 1980 reinforced an armed insurrection. As I held my banner to support the 'unstoppable tide', the US was pumping in what would amount to over six billion dollars over twelve years to train the Salvadorean army. The civil war killed 750,000 people.

In Guatemala, when peasants began demanding reform of their land, CIA-trained death squads ravaged the countryside, cutting tongues out of suspected insurgents, slitting their babies' throats and raping their wives.

I suppose the US's heavy military presence in Panamá since its birth nipped resistance in the bud. And Costa Rica? Maybe not having an army at all deprived the US of an excuse to invade. Honduras remained America's friends by allowing Contra troops to be stationed there while they were fighting in Nicaragua. Is Levi's the reward to the elites of Panamá and Costa Rica for keeping their populations obedient? They'll now be able to get Levi's without flying to Miami, while Nicaragua, El Salvador and Guatemala, ravaged by war, have not made it on to the 'developed' list. They are scratched off the map of the new, branded world. And would it help after so much devestation and suffering if Levi's graced their shopping malls? Would that transform defeat into development?

■

 Four days after my arrival, Jeisel insists on taking me to his home in El Chorrillo. He says if there is one thing I must do before leaving Panamá it is to see the neighbourhood at its Sunday best when the whole slum abandons its sorrows for festivity.

When we arrive in the mid-afternoon, El Chorrillo is heaving with parents and children eating the delicious fried fish and plantain from the street stalls and dancing around enormous throbbing speakers blaring *reggaetón.* Relatives and friends from all over the city embrace like long-lost loved ones, even though it was only the Sunday before that they last met. Wives brandish baseball bats as they chase their husbands who, in shirts freshly ironed by them, have made some indecent proposal to a neighbour.

A lashing of energy shoots through me. This is Panamá. The ground below sucks my feet in and yet is like a springboard, as if the layers under its skin vibrated with truth, just like in Lima, exciting me with their secrets, calming me with their familiarity. Like something that I have known, seen or felt before, but not yet peeled through. I take a deep sigh, the most relaxing sigh I have taken in ages, like a first breath.

As night falls, Chorrillo youth emerges fresh from the shower, splashed with cologne, baggy dungarees hanging off their polished and powdered torsos. The girls in mini-dresses move like sphinxes, their black skin glowing against the grim surroundings. 'Prrreeeettty,' hiss the boys as they brush past.

Jeisel leads me through the sweaty crowd of boys in string vests grinding their pelvises against barely covered booties. He spots his old mates by the stall of Super Q, one of the two *reggaetón* stations of Chorrillo, which come out on Sunday to compete for the *Chorrilleño* music market. It's *their* music, sidelined by the white business elite who find the violent and sexually explicit lyrics repellent and threatening. The new generation doesn't listen to salsa any more; the hearts once drawn to its sentimentality have seized up. *Reggaetón* is the music of a generation hardened by disillusionment.

Jeisel cocks his head towards his friends in recognition, but does not approach. He says they tease him and call him *rabinegro* because he works in a *rabiblanco* hotel and gets let into the *rabiblanco* discos, which shut their doors to his black brothers. A local advertising agent that I was put in contact with justified the door policy: 'They have to control the black quota, otherwise our places would be full of *racatacas*.' I never called her again.

We walk towards Jeisel's house, down the untarmacked Avenue of the Martyrs, a makeshift memorial to the thousands of *Chorrilleños* who were injured and killed when they stormed the Canal Zone in 1964. Their years of protesting cost them twenty interventions. In the last invasion, Operation 'Just Cause' in which President Bush Snr surgically removed General Noriega in 1989, some four thousand Chorrillo residents were killed and another fifteen thousand made homeless.

I remember watching the American invasion of Panamá on television and being convinced by the sheer ugliness of the acne-scarred Noriega in 1989 that he was indeed a very bad man and must be punished.

'Noriega put a lot money into this neighbourhood. Our

 schools and hospitals were funded when he was around,' says Jeisel. 'The Americans called him a dictator, and maybe he was, but he did not kill and torture his people like the Somozas did, whom they funded for forty years. They never removed *them.*'

From the street we can see Jeisel's mother, a big woman sporting an extravagant gown of scarlet satin with erect fans sewn into the shoulders. Leticia greets us with her big smile. She delicately perches her robust curves on the edge of a lived-in armchair, placing her hands on her tightly pressed knees as if to impress upon us her refinement. She excuses herself to take a phone call and suddenly a volcano of emotion erupts from under her princess posture. As her body shakes in fury, her tongue demolishes the caller on the other end of the line. When she is finished she turns around with an angelic 'not me' smile, perches again and continues to smooth her painted nails over the details of her Sunday frock. I ask Jeisel in a whisper who it is she is angry with, but she hears me. 'Oh, some woman my mother gave birth to,' she snaps.

Behind Leticia hangs a poster of the great welterweight champion Roberto 'Hands of Stone' Durán. It depicts the famous moment in 1980 when the born-and-bred *Chorrilleño* snatched the WBC crown from Sugar Ray Leonard, dazzling the world with his macho ferociousness and conviction. Then the champion shocked the world when, in their rematch, he turned his back on Leonard, shaking his head and saying the words, 'No more!' People said Durán was a quitter, but he came back to win world titles at four different weights and knocked out sixty-nine opponents in a thirty-nine-year career.

At thirty-eight Durán was a belt holder and only at the age of fifty did he retire. EnDuránce is a *Chorrilleño* trademark.

Like Roberto Durán, Leticia tells me she has raised her two sons to feel that they can only better themselves by believing in who they are, not trying to be like the white man. I wonder if she frowns on Jeisel for working in a white man's hotel, for bringing back a white girl to her home.

The night is young and Leticia is dressed up for dancing. Her *papi* arrives in a scarlet suit, white hanky peeking out of left breast pocket, a red-banded Panamá hat to match and a wide-collared red-and-white-striped shirt opened to reveal a thick gold chain. I gaze in awe: *that* is style. *El Caballero* (the Gent) gives Leticia a smacker on the lips before demanding his *etiqueta negra.* After swigging his glass of whisky, he rubs his hands together, swings around on his feet and we follow in the trail of his snazzy shuffle down the street. We come to a petrol station where, behind a barbed-wire fence, a soft light streams out of the crack of an almost shut garage door.

'El Boyo Florencia,' announces the Gent with a grin. Behind the garage door is a large patio, around which groups sit at floral-covered tables and plastic chairs, while *papis* with big wiry Afros cut the moves in pinstriped bell-bottoms and matching lapels.

A few drinks the better and Leticia is nuzzling up to a smooth operator in a brown velvet suit and matching bow tie. *El Caballero* appears indignantly to defend his territory. She turns to him blushing and reverts to her shy-violet pose as she lets herself be led to the floor. Her sexuality is contained in the tight, decorous movements of her large swinging buttocks. This is the generation of *pudor*: lust is implicit in the quiet pulse of the music.

I am off with some super *papi* in a nylon burgundy suit, dancing to a 1970s Stevie Wonder salsa rendition... 'Ooooh, oooh, ooooh... parr' ti' lohverrr.' With effortless elegance, my partner glides like an ice-skater. Not one bead of sweat falls. I drip with perspiration in my skimpy skirt and top.

Then the same smoky voice I heard in the taxi going towards Lima's Boulevard de Comas crackles through the speakers, waxing nostalgically about his *barrio* that hides its sadness and plays at beauty:

Like a watercolour of poverty.
But nobody speaks of its pain.
Where the true patriots lie,
It contains a desire nobody notices,
And the bitterness of defeat
It never deserved.
In its Sunday happiness,
on its dirt tracks,
lies an appeal to the heart.
It is a slum of paupers,
But of noble citizens
Whose sweating pores earn their bread.

■

Must get back to the bullet points. Switching into automatic mode I head for the state-run University of Panamá. Something robotic takes over, which must express some part of me. My Anglo part, perhaps, where my encounters must render profitable results. So I find myself in the hospital-blue admissions office. I have come to ask for permission to roam the grounds. The woman in thick-rimmed glasses smiles at me as my words are drowned by the deafening rattle of the air-conditioner. She mouths something back, still smiling.

The campus is neither smart nor new, but its humble facilities are preserved with pride. A sanctuary of cherished opportunity, like a 1950s American college campus. The girls dress in twin-sets, fake pearls and knee-length skirts, in appreciation of this hard-earned privilege, and the boys in trousers and short-sleeved shirts, clinging to respectability by professing ambitions of devoted fatherhood and faithful husbandry. Both are eager to distinguish themselves from the '*racatacas*' of Chorrillo with moralistic mottos such as: 'Tell me who you hang round with and I'll tell you who you are.' A billboard message to play on their aspirations of dignity? I'll call this tribe *los Buenitos* (Goody Two-Shoes).

I decide to make my way to the history department and enrol myself in a class, partly to legitimize my presence on campus, partly because I am curious. As I walk down the cement staircase, a boy with a shaved head and a big boar-like nose-ring shoves a leaflet into my hand. It invites me to a meeting at the 'Red House' this evening.

At the history department a friendly librarian greets me and without any questions sits me down and tells me I must learn about General Omar Torrijos if I really want to know about Panamá. 'It is thanks to him that we have our canal and our sovereignty,' he says. He guides me through the library, almost empty but for a woman tapping away industriously at a very antiquated electric typewriter in the corner, and several lonely books desperately trying to fill the shelves. He brings a pile from a back room, one of them written by an English novelist whose name he pronounces 'Grraaaahham Grrrreeeene'.

With his tanned, cigar-chewing good looks, General Torrijos had come up through the ranks of the National Guard, the US-funded militia whose role it was to keep a restless and independence-focused public in check. The Americans had little idea, when Torrijos staged a coup, that this general thought differently. 'If the people storm the Canal Zone again, my options are to either repress them or lead them. And I will not send orders to repress them,' Torrijos declared on taking power.

Torrijos loved to rummage through the foliage of the Panamanian *monte* clad in matching olive combat gear and talking to peasants, and then to lie in his hammock at siesta time. He once offended an ambassador by receiving him while lying in one, when he thought it the highest compliment. He hated wearing suits. But in 1973 he wore one as he hosted a UN Security Council meeting. It was to be a particularly important occasion, perhaps the most important in his life. To the US delegation's shock, he made an extraordinary appeal to international leaders for the return of the Canal: 'I know that deep in their hearts, the American people will appreciate our spirit of independence, for they too had the courage to throw off the hand of imperialism.'

The US attitude hardened, as did the tenacity of Torrijos: 'One day they'll get so fed up with me they'll say, "Have your damned canal then!"' Even though he considered the Canal treaty deeply flawed – while transferral was to begin immediately, a neutrality clause valid until 2000 would allow US intervention if it felt the Canal was being threatened – he also saw that the treaty was only just scraping through US Congress, and knew that if he didn't get it through with the sympathetic President Carter, there would not be another chance. He was right. The next president, Reagan, was one of the biggest campaigners against it, and then Bush did exactly what Torrijos feared and used the loophole to punish Panamá when Norierga didn't allow Contra troops to be stationed there.

The librarian finally throws me out long after dusk. I take a taxi and give the driver the address of the Red House. I get out in La Cresta, a middle-class neighbourhood of small white bungalows separated from the street by wrought-iron gates guarding the family cars. Youths, mostly wearing bovver boots, chain-draped khaki pants and torn sleeveless shirts, spill out of a half-built house, which has nothing red about it. It is unpainted but for the graffiti: 'Fuck false patriotism' and 'Resist global capitalism'. There is a banner hanging behind the band equipment with a very intricate design on it. An indigenous Panamanian is climbing into the funnel of a sausage factory and appears spat out of the other end as a gum-chewing *gringo* with television-shaped eyes and a dollar sign on his T-shirt. The character's brain, hanging out of his head on a spring, is being sizzled in a frying pan held by Uncle Sam.

Inside, the timid pamphleteer welcomes me as he runs between setting up a Che Guevara documentary and the punk band that will play after. A multicoloured crowd, *rabiblanco, mulato, mestizo* and Cuna, Panamá's biggest indigenous tribe, flickers under the screen, captivated by the whirring reels of a silent Che scurrying his way through the Sierra Maestra to liberate a people not even his own. A lost solidarity they marvel at. Their wide eyes remind me of the *Surfers* and *Desinhibidos* of Perú, building a breathing space from class and race discrimination, and from US culture, which does not seem to practise abroad the multiculturalism it preaches at home.

A Cuna boy called Rana ('frog') introduces himself. He looks more like a tribal prince, with beautiful high cheekbones and smooth terracotta skin, rings sprouting from every possible pore. His wiry figure is tattooed on every body part visible. He has come from the coastal province of San Blas, which belongs to his Cuna tribe, to sell artisan goods and patterned cloths called *molas.* Other Cunas come to the city to study at the university. Rana tells me the Red House is about defining their identity, reinforcing it.

'Every Panamanian wonders who he really is,' he says. 'But few are prepared to confront it for they fear the answer.' And yet, I point out, every car and house I've seen has the Panamanian flag flying in honour of Patriot's month. Not a day, but a whole month. How much more patriotic can you get?

'Yeah, they fly their flags all day, so they can convinve themselves that they are Panamanian,' says Rana. 'But we have no culture, we just have the Americans and a canal that's not even ours. The canal is supposed to be our national symbol, but to me it is nothing, a piece of metal to remind us of the divisions that have broken our country.' Their hardcore costumes are copied from MTV, I observe, but their ideals are their own.

I prowl around the sidelines, forgetting that embedded in my curiosity is a hidden agenda. Is this little detour on behalf of Levi's, or is it *my* interest? Despite my efforts to separate my two journeys, the lines between them seem to blur more every day. Roaming around in and out of lives and situations seems so accidental sometimes that I almost believe I am on a personal adventure, not a commercial one.

It feels like I'm spying. Is it ideals that Levi's has sent me to root out from these kids? Or weakness, vulnerability and doubt, as they find their footing in the world? Ideals begin when one confronts one's fears and weakness. Brand indulgence is surely to escape them. And yet to combine ideals with brands must be the gold of marketing. Is this the stuff of my job? To tap their search for the sacred flame within? To understand the rationale behind admiration? To channel this crisp budding of youthful self-discovery into blue jean aspiration before their hearts have closed?

I think about the old days of espionage, in the Cold War or in Central America, when governments would send spies to infiltrate groups whose ideals dared defy the established truth, law and order. They had to be kept tabs on. Perhaps now it is different. If a cause can move people into action and loyalty, surely that is what brands want. There's no need to bomb deviants when you can brand them. Will this research help to control consumer subjects, keep them loyal to brand empires? The thought makes me shudder.

I stalk the backstreets. A voice in my head reassures me this is just about getting to know the market. All innocent enough. What has Levi's or I got to do with the injustices of the past? Levi's is just riding the global economic wave.

Suddenly I find myself under a spotlight staring into a television camera. A voice from behind the camera insists I give my views on global capitalism. They beg me: 'It takes a *gringa* on our side to get us noticed.' I try to mumble a few words, but my thoughts are swirling round my head, they are unclear, contaminated. I do not have the clarity, or hold the secrets they think I have. Maybe I should.

■

I am two weeks into my trip, and the American photographer and his canal obsession are still hovering. I try to seem engrossed in the newspaper, but there is no escaping an evangelist, and he asks me for the fortieth time if I have gone to the Canal yet, the country's 'only major attraction'.

I decide to visit Punta Paitilla where the *rabiblancos* live, or, as Jeisel calls them, *los Yes-Yes,* because they say 'yes-yes' to everything the Americans want. During Operation 'Just Cause', the inhabitants watched the bombs pound Chorrillo from their high-rise balconies and celebrated the fall of Noriega with champagne. Bush said he was freeing the

Panamanian people, but really he was saving the elite of Punta Paitilla since Torrijos's National Guard had taken away its political grip over the country and built a platform to incorporate the *mestizo,* black and Cuna population into political decision-making for the first time.

Alberto, Cristian and Antonio are sitting on a wall in front of a sky-high apartment block identical to those you find on North Miami Beach. They are watching the swirling brushes of the pavement-polishing machine, which has been going back and forth over the same piece of pavement for the last half-hour. They can afford to be relaxed; they are waiting for their moment. Next year they will attend Florida State University, a branch of which is stationed in the Canal Zone.

Cristian tells me he will be president of the country one day. As such he is already riddled with deep moral concern about its condition.

'All Panamanians do is think about sex, you can tell that from their *reggaetón* songs, so it's no wonder they are as poor as they are,' says Cristian. He tells me that family structure is fundamental to civilized society. 'The trouble with the Panamanian people is that they don't respect each other,' says Antonio. 'They don't like to work, they are not like us. You go to Chorrillo. No family has a father. That's the problem with Panamá.'

Why is it that rich people always blame social ills on some morally deviant group or race, like social workers or taxi drivers, or here, *Chorrilleños,* who only dream they had the power to make such an impact? And what do they mean 'not like us'? Are they not Panamanian too? In their imagination these boys live in a more civilized place, VIP land where everything is bigger and better, and yet they are stuck here, their only loyalty to an abstraction, a flag, a country, rather than the people in it. Alberto tells me he will build a company and expand it throughout the whole of South America, an ambassador for a nationality he is so unhappy about.

'Everything takes so long here, people are so backward,' he says. 'I can't wait till I get out of this dump and get on with life.'

They sound like tourists complaining about 'the locals'. I notice Alberto wears a T-shirt that says 'My Name is Panamá', like ones in the tourist shop at the Intercontinental. 'Why are you wearing a tourist T-shirt of your own country?' I ask. Alberto answers that the 'My Name is Panamá' clothing company is the coolest company in Panamá, run by whiz-kid entrepreneurs. Branding identity crisis. Wear the T-shirt, relieve your burden!

He desperately wants to show me the new jeep his dad recently bought him. He disappears and in seconds the powerful engine roars up from the underground garage, accompanied by that familiar thud of the *reggaetón* bass. He turns the volume up and Cristian and Antonio immediately go into a bad imitation of Chorrillo-style dancehall pelvic thrusting. So much for their complaining about *reggaesero* depravity. 'Jump in,' shouts Alberto. 'I'll take you for a ride round the hood.'

As we coast along the rather well-kept ghetto, my rude-boy escorts roll up their sleeves to show their tattoos to elegant disapproving housewives, wrap bandanas round their heads and pout the badass pout, nodding to the *reggaetón* beat.

They've been practising their gangsta poses in front of MTV, but Antonio, the skinny one with glasses, swears he's been to Chorrillo on a Sunday. 'You never did, you liar,' the others cry.

Wanting to compete, Alberto tells us how he turns his Super Q *reggaetón* to full volume in his bedroom, and waits till Mummy screams through the house: 'Turn that black music down! People will think we've got niggers camping in our house!' This has Cristian and Antonio on the floor of the car holding their ribs from so much laughter. 'And then, get this,' Alberto adds, 'I say, "But, Mom, I *am* black. I may be white on the outside, but I'm black inside!"'

■

Rana invites me to go and visit his family in the archipelago of San Blas. His tribe live on one of the 365 islands off Panamá's Caribbean coast.

It is the first trip I take out of a capital since I have been in Latin America, apart from my adventure with the *Ricoteros* in Argentina, and it is the first time Rana has been back to see his family in ten years. News has come to him of a cruise ship and he wants to sell his jewellery to the three thousand tourists who will flood out to stare at the straw huts of his old shore.

We fly in a rickety eight-seater back towards the Caribbean coast over the Darien jungle, which covers Panamá south of the Canal all the way to Colombia. I cannot keep my eyes off this massive green breathing organism below, like a giant broccoli expanding and retracting with all the life it contains. I imagine its panthers, butterflies and alligators, a million medicinal plants and trees, a world so alien to the one I am living inside people's heads. Down there the sun, moon, earth, mountains and trees are worshipped for the wisdom accumulated in their years, rather than the projected meaning of life on a disposable Coke can. Then we come to the liquid mosaic of fluorescent turquoise, speckled with perfect desert islands, whose bright white linings burst out of the blue like radioactive bacteria.

The plane screeches to a halt just as we are about to fall off the end of an island. The pilot jumps out first, reaching for his fags. I grab some shade in the palm-tree waiting room while Rana negotiates for a boat to take us to his island. As we wait for someone to pick us up, Rana tells me about his culture, how his people live, what they eat, what they wear. The stress he places on *my* shows he is full of pride. He tells me of life on the water, the fishing tradition. He tells me tales about hunting the seas, battling with sharks and other monsters.

It is late afternoon when a boat comes, a good five hours after our arrival. I had suggested we swim the distance to Rana's island, which must be only three hundred metres away, but he reacted with intense disapproval, as if it were an insult to local custom. Our arrival is met with little more than a few grunts of recognition from Rana's relatives, not the welcome I'd imagine after a ten-year absence. He tries to shrug the rejection off, but I can see in his subtle flinching the pain and insecurity it has caused. Rana, like a Seattle teenager in his baggy khaki pants and vest, looks so different from the islanders in their traditional *mola* garments embroidered with fish and birds. He shows me our hut and I can just about make out the silhouettes of a bed, a sink and a dish of fried fish in the corner. The sun has gone to bed and there is no electricity to keep us awake.

I am woken up the next day as a laser ray of sun operates on my eye through a gap in the wooden boards. I lie in the hammock on the balcony that hangs over the water's edge. Rana soon joins me and begins his commentary on the traditional morning activities of *his* people and *his* culture. Is he trying to play that Cusco trick on me?

I convince Rana, despite his reluctance, to take us out on one of the two unused boats in the small harbour. He tugs at the engine so hard it shudders and wheezes until it gives up, and he confesses that he doesn't know how to work the boat and cannot swim. A small group of children are standing on the tiny pier giggling. One of them has called an old man who comes running and shouting in despair. He jumps into the boat and, after shaking the tank, pulls the starter and fires the motor.

Rana wants to speed off as quickly as possible and stalls the engine several times. Only when we are out of sight does Rana collapse exhausted, sweating from the stress.

'How embarrassing, how embarrassing!' he cries and asks me worriedly: 'Do you think my uncles saw?'

I suddenly pity him, and tell myself off for forcing him to expose the gaping hole in the identity he so fiercely defended in his *my* people stories.

But I am in paradise, bathing in the crystalline waters, teasing the leering barracudas. We soon shore up on a white sandbank, the most perfect desert island you've ever seen. An old man shuffles through the sand to greet us with his hand out, which is not presented to be shaken but to collect the dollar fee for stepping on *his* island. The signpost he stands next to says 'Dog Island'. The man tells us it is named after the creature his grandfather found on it when he first landed there a hundred years ago, and, by the way, for another dollar he can offer us a coconut.

Underneath the name of the island are two other words in English: WANT WIFE.

'I will die soon,' the man explains, 'and if I do not have children to inherit my island, my people will take it back from me.'

He disappears, returning two minutes later with a photocopied sheet listing the qualifications for the position. They include cooking, cleaning and three hours of lovemaking a day.

'Once she is here she will never be able to leave!' he says, holding his finger in the air triumphantly as if he has just announced a five-year economic plan for the nation.

One American woman, he tells us, professed her love for him but after a month would refuse to make love to him and then left him alone while she visited her family in Virginia.

'What kind of commitment is that?' he asks.

We watch the sun settle over the Caribbean, and the island owner's *reggaetón*-free radio station plays a salsa by Panamá's own Rubén Blades. Within its happy Caribbean rhythm, his story rings like a siren, shaking the stars above.

> … *The moon lies cushioned in the silence*
> *Of the great resting Caribbean*
> *Only the shark stays awake*

Only the shark keeps searching
Only the shark remains restless
Only the shark watches your every move
'Hmmm, what a nice little flag'
Shark, if yours is another sea
What are you doing here?

The song ends with a shout to '*nuestra hermana* El Salvador', the cry of another era. It makes me think of Marcel, Alfredo and César in Perú who hated salsa but for Blades because his songs embodied the spirit of solidarity that Latin Americans extend to each other, when their governments fail them or are slapped down for trying to do so. These common ideals that run like blood through the veins of the continent are never mentioned on Cisneros channels or on Latin America's branded streets.

The man on the island has to take us back because Rana is too scared to row at night in the shark-infested waters. But throughout the day he has acquired a new determination to prove he is a Cuna. The next day the big shark arrives, in the form of a cruise ship about the size of twenty islands, its shining white impenetrability charging through the serene waters as if fearing attack. The tourists bundle off the boat, their dollars falling out of their pockets into the ocean, looking for things to buy, but Rana has gone out fishing with his cousins, having left his bracelets in the hut. I make my way back to Panamá City alone. Rana has decided to stay in San Blas. Perhaps his ideals compensate for some of the identity he lost.

■

 There is no Chorrillo to give me the send-off on the Sunday before my departure. Blaming the increasing violence in the area on the weekly festival, the authorities issued a ban on Friday. Jeisel was upset. He wanted it to be my last Panamanian experience. We have formed a bond I am not yet sure I'd call friendship. We argue endlessly, for neither of us is scared of saying what we think, and both of us prefer to criticize than expose our doubts, but there is an underlying empathy. We share, in different ways, similar ideological conflicts of conscience: his between rebellion and ambition, dignity and necessity, mine between the truth and the contradictions I am beginning to realize lie at the heart of my job.

By Sunday, however, another plan is announced by Radio Super Q and Radio Fabulosa. Everyone is to meet at four o'clock with their cars and stereos down at the long key in the Canal Zone. With Jeisel at the wheel and *reggaetón* blasting out, we drive alongside the green lawns and the deserted army barracks in our battered brown Ford.

Towering behind us, a few posh jeeps are also on their way to join the party. Jeisel grins. 'See? They despise us, but they copy us because they have nothing of their own.'

Twenty years ago Jeisel and Co. would not have been allowed in this area; now they lead the pack. Whatever Rana says, the Canal's return *is* significant. Jeisel's ancestors shed blood, sweat and tears to give them this moment. The spirit of Torrijos's irreverence echoes in this generation. 'I don't want to enter the history books,' he had said to silence US accusations that he was a dictator, a populist, a fame-seeker. 'I want to enter the Canal Zone.' Whatever it was before, the Canal now represents a freedom that was clawed back.

And it was not just the Canal he won back. Today the pride Torrijos fought to reclaim resounds like never before in the young. You can feel it in their music and in their attitude – a kind of graceful arrogance, not the aggressive bullying one we know, but one that expresses pride and the determination to overcome. Like its famous boxer, Panamá is burdened with a past of forced dependency, but it has the fighter spirit. Durán says: 'Other fighters say, "I was, I did." I say, "I AM."' That is Panamá.

5

BULLET POINTS AND MEMORIES

Yoel picks me up at Miami airport. He says he thinks it's a crime for me to be paying for the shoddy room at the Mermaid and insists I move to his house.

'Man, ees jus an ole wooden hut, you see how ees fallin' to pieces? Why you wanna pay for somefin das all improvise, when you can ha' brand new, like the Hilton or Sheraton weed all dose waterfalls, sliding doors and elevators. Das nice. Seen enuff crumbling ole buildings in Havana, man.'

No matter how colourfully it is disguised, Yoel says, old is old. Old, like the chewing gum he had to put in the fridge every night in Cuba so that it lasted a week. Yoel has lived his entire life improvising. Everything he had in Cuba was made from something else. A motorbike was a bicycle with an engine stuck on. A football was rags tied with string. Finally here in the US Yoel can have things that are built for their purpose. A car that is actually built in a factory, not in some makeshift workshop that produces moving miracles from a scrapheap. A hotel that is actually built to be a hotel, not some converted home.

Yoel's cheap and clean two-bedroom bungalow near Calle Oche, five miles inland from the beach, where he lives with his parents and brother, could not be further from rustic. There is no spare room (I will sleep on the sofa) and I wonder how I am going to write my reports without getting in everyone's way. But as the salsa song goes: 'If the skies rain lemons, learn how to make lemonade.'

My main problem is getting around since there are huge distances between everything, and using public transport is tantamount to being a communist around these parts, which is probably why the Cuban-American municipality has rendered buses virtually obsolete. Once, when I was working here, a half-hour car ride took me two hours by bus. The South Beach, for all its faults, was the one place where everything you needed was within walking distance. Yoel promises to lend me a bicycle (primitive, but not subversive, it seems). With my computer on my back I'll ride in the heat across the motorway bridge to the library, the token public scourge of the Beach.

Yoel introduces me to his friend Victor, a bulging-biceped Miami cop. They met for the first time a year ago, when Yoel arrived in Miami. Though both consider themselves Cuban, they are worlds apart. Miami-bred Victor, just turned thirty, is a child of the anti-Castro generation. His upbringing, thanks to the South Florida Military Academy, a high school started by the first post-Cuban revolution exiles in order to train their children to fight Fidel, has given him the American square jaw and military-style respectability – short hair, side parting and a meticulously trimmed goatee.

We are in the pink shade of the Club Mystique bar. Seized by the salsa rhythm, Victor shuffles in anxious excitement, as if something from his past is calling. Looking at me doubtfully, he asks: 'Do you dance?'

After watching the Britney Spears fiasco last time, I understand the seriousness of this question from a born-again Cuban, but not wanting to miss the opportunity, I shrug. Victor puts me through a little test to see whether my feet will remain in the right place when he tries to move me, then he drags me to the dance floor. As soon he begins to pull me in his firm embrace, I understand why Britney was so enthusiastic. There is something about having your will wrenched from you, being moulded into a dough of floppy limbs, that is perversely alluring. And my partner's particularly hard-line determination to impose his regime gives the experience an exciting edge. This firm hand might have been what Britney craved, but it is not something a woman can seek of her own volition, just like you cannot choose to be loved.

We stay the night at Victor's. He gives me his bed while the two men sleep in the living room. When I wake up the first thing I spot is a swastika on the sleeve of a leather jacket. 'It's from my rebellious days,' Victor admits, laughing. As a teenager he had ran away to New York, where for three years he sported a silver-studded dog collar, black drainpipe jeans, matching torn T-shirt and spiked hair. He squatted in crack houses, shot heroin and stormed the streets of Queens queer-bashing, all to vent the frustrations inherited from his authoritarian father who had never come to terms with starting life again as a penniless immigrant after Fidel had confiscated all his belongings, the foundation of a self-respecting breadwinner.

'Yeah, I kinda did a 360,' says Victor of his conversion back to this side of the law.

■

Yoel's mother watches me draw big coloured circles and disappears shaking her head. Yoel chuckles when I show him my bullet points and try to explain their relation to the circles.

But look! I urge, and tell him how proud of the same neighbourhoods the *Reggeseros* are. That they are never defeated. How, nevertheless, the *Buenitos* are terrified of being confused with them, for it might taint their prospects, that the *Yes-yesitos* may want to be like them, but curse them all the same. But Yoel does not want to share my employer's interest in the reality represented by the grid, perhaps because it is what he's left behind.

He ruffles my hair like this job is a joke I've invented. It is no laughing matter. Reputations are at stake! Identities waiting to be reconfigured!

It could be made into a game. Youth Tribes: chess for the consumer generation. One must match the figurines and place them in their proper tribes before taking them off the board of chaotic reality into the safety of consumer homogeneity. Youngsters could test their skill in psychology and social strategy, their knowledge of worlds of lifestyle and virtual desires.

Is this really any use? Maybe I exist to cover the *culos* of marketing managers so that when sales don't meet targets they can point to my silly reports and say: 'See? It's all in there. It wasn't my idea.' I hope that's all they're being used for…

■

When my father returned to England from Buenos Aires, he gave up his bright future in Reuters. Why? Later, when I call my mother, she tells me that it was true: his ambition was not the same when he returned from Argentina. 'Climbing the ladder of a multinational corporation seemed irrelevant, distasteful even, in the larger scale of things. I think he realized that as long as countries like Argentina depended on Western media agencies for information that was subtly imbued with others' values and interests, they would never be free to find their own path of progress.'

Control of information was not some sort of big brother mission, just business expansion. But multinationals benefited from their governements' foreign policies in the region. In 1976 US Secretary of State Henry Kissinger had given the Argentine military government the go-ahead with their disappearances. 'We won't cause you any unnecessary difficulties. If you can finish before Congress gets back, the better,' he told the Argentine foreign minister Admiral Guzzetti in 1976. After Chile's Pinochet, the Argentine military junta was the next government of Latin America to open its markets to foreign goods.

I don't think Yoel's mum sees much future in me as a daughter-in-law. She keeps telling me that I'm too anxious, that I should be more comfortable at home. She is what they call a '*mujer de casa*' as opposed to '*mujer de la calle*' (apparently a woman can only be one of two things). But Yoel complains that whereas before she stayed at home to look after them, now she just watches soap operas. 'When we were in Cuba, Mama always complain she don' ha noffin' to cook wif. Now we ha everythin' but she don' wanna cook. She say she wanna watch TV and we go to Taco Bell.'

Yoel's mother has recently been indicating a desire for another TV, so that she can watch the soap operas in her bedroom, and this has got Yoel in a panic. His father's heart operation already set him back. He already works eighteen hours a day; after his telephone technician job, he works four hours setting up or cleaning operating theatres in a hospital, but he can never keep up with the bills. 'Why do you have to buy a second TV?' I ask.

'I wanna make Mama happy, yoo understan'?' He did not want to discuss the matter further.

Yoel invites me to go on a camping trip to the Florida Keys, with Victor, and other Cuban friends. We set off early one Friday morning on what feels a bit like a family outing to Bognor Regis but with palm trees. When we reach our key, we pitch four tents in the allocated slot of 10 by 2 metres and begin the barbecue. The girls all sit on one side and the men on the other. I do not know where to put myself. Maybe if I stray from one group I will turn from '*mujer de casa*' to '*mujer de la calle*' and be eternally condemned.

'Which am I?' I ask Yoel.

'I don't know,' Yoel says. 'You're strange. I suppose you're neither.'

The next day we take a little trip through the Keys. Yoel is enjoying the American newness of the white-padded boat, lying with his arms behind his head and his fishing rod dangling in the water. He describes the night he floated in these waters huddled on his sinking raft, staring at the black sky and an unknown future, his fingers stuck in his ears to block out the sound of the sharks. Three people died out of twenty-five on that trip from Cuba.

Yoel is so relaxed. Nothing can stir him from this indulgence, not even the fish that tug relentlessly at his rod. Everything in its time, he says to himself. He knows how to wait. He waited a long time for this and nothing and nobody is going to rush him.

Victor, meanwhile, sits erect wearing a strenuous grimace. His squinting eyes reflect someone troubled by more than the sun. He watches his rod intently, nervously, and scrambles to wind up the handle at the slightest sign of activity, eyes bulging. When after each frenetic moment he whips out an empty hook, his gleaming face drops.

The others laugh and implore him to relax. Victor ignores their protests, only shifting up the gears of his determination. 'Those little bastard commies!' he cries. 'You fuckin' little scum-bearded Fidelitos, chew fink you can get away from *me*?' And as he visualizes this metaphorical challenge, shouting, 'I'll getcha you… you shit-eaters, *come-mierdas toditos*… you fucking gonna DIE!!', we almost fear he'll grab his pistol and start shooting into the crystal Caribbean.

Now Victor is Tony Montana, mad with rage. The boat jumps about and we beg him to stop, but while Victor is waving his gun in the air, his face alight with retribution, the adrenalin pumping through him, nobody dares go near him. He is his father attacking the shores of Cuba.

'*Coño!* Yooo fuckin' creisy, yooo creisy man!' screams Yoel and, breaking the paralysis that has gripped the boat, he grabs the gun and throws Victor onto the bench behind. Victor sits back panting heavily, looking notably frustrated at not having emptied his gun on the fish.

The sky has become overcast. On the horizon black clouds are gathering. We charge back to land, trying to beat the storm. At the harbour we meet full-scale torrential rain.

Later, we busy ourselves preparing for the barbecue. My job is to lay the table, but I am interrupted by Victor's post-mortem on his fish, which he is determined to hack to pieces, this time with a machete on the table.

'They are not good for eating, anyway,' he says. 'They're only catfish.'

■

Each day I feel more aware of where I am and each day that feeling conflicts with where I want to be. Maybe, like Victor, I will explode and bear the angst of my displacement and my search. I wonder what form it will take? I don't want my revenge, like Victor. I don't want to pummel my past, like a punchbag, strike it until it gives me back what it has taken away. I want to seduce mine, maybe because it did not eject *me* from its bowels. I left.

I am determined to learn to dance properly. Salsa lessons are given every Tuesday and Thursday on the ground floor of a shopping mall in Coral Gables by Ricky and his teenage crew. Hundreds of men and women flock there to unite under the religion of romance. For our priests, who look barely over thirteen, delivering sentimental sacraments is a question of pocket money, but Miami's most successful professionals are dependent on these mini-mentors for salvation. Even the kids' dating sagas seem to captivate the forty-something power-dressed pupils. 'Who's broken up with who?' they whisper as they observe the new combination of hand-holding and dirty looks across the dance floor.

The lesson goes beyond the dance steps. With their chewing-gum breath and deodorant dew still drying deliciously, the teenies are role models in *detallismo*, while some of their adult Waspy pupils, in their emotional inebriation, often neglect the details of hygiene so essential to this intimate activity.

There is one who goes through two changes of shirt during the two-hour lesson. Every time he spins you get a face spray. Then there is John. But it is not the musky patchouli vapour that makes him the most dreaded partner of all: it is the military approach with which he pursues Travolta glory and the sexual conquest of Miami. He counts every step in every move and notes the numbers down on a little pad, and then takes his pad with him to Club Mystique where he prowls sheepishly on the sidelines.

There are also the female equivalents of John, whom, I imagine the men must be equally terrified of, because dancing with them always ends in an argument. Usually she is the executive type, so set on not being bossed about she ends up blaming her partner for blaming her for not doing it right before he has uttered a word. She usually has short hair, glasses and an upright posture that stiffens with every turn. Whenever there is a move that involves many turns, a frown creeps over her face and then she will stop in the middle of the music to inform her partner that he has done it wrong. She then proceeds to show him how it should be done and turns the ordeal into a public humiliation.

One wonders why these women persist in an activity that requires a submission so objectionable to them. Only in the arms of the adolescent teacher does she turn to putty and smile adoringly at her master, who is probably no older than her own son. These suave and savvy teens humour the inadequacies of their elders in order to make them more dependent on their tutoring. Far from encouraging John to relax and take a more intuitive approach, Ricky, the head of the school, helps him keep count of the steps and writes the number down alongside each name on the list like this:

Dilequeno 46 steps
El Zorro 52 steps
El Adios 48 steps

Ricky is the salsa sales king. He has made salsa and dysfunctional *gringos* a unique business combination, and he relishes it. Levi's should employ him. His best trick is to constantly add new names to the list of Ricky moves – the spin in the Dunkin' Donut accentuates the hole effect – even though the 'new moves' are just different combinations of the same steps, so that the 'course' never ends. Perhaps it is a good thing, for I have the feeling that the Ricky therapy is relieving Miami of several potential psychopaths. One could say he is providing a service to society.

Ricky advertises his classes on Sol 95 FM, Miami's favourite radio station, where squeaky voices will annoyingly interrupt a salsa tune with messages such as:

'Ay, HONEY, quiero hacerme más SEXY para ti. Sabes? He encontrado la solución. Dicen que me puedo conseguir un BREAST IMPLANT por solo FIVE HUNDRED AND TWENTY-FIVE DOLLARS TAX FREE!'

Or a deep, commanding fatherly voice:

'Ven con toda la familia a… RED LOBSTER! Steak house and seafood grill. Los Jueves y Viernes es ALL YOU CAN EAT por FIVE NINETY-NINE!!!'

Ricky says being a Miami Latino is God's blessing: 'I am what Cubans would be if they had the chance. Everyone in Latin America wants to come here to Miami. They wanna be Latino, but Latino in heaven, not hell.'

'He no Cuban!' says Yoel. 'We speak de sa'e language, we ha de same colour skeen, but we tink different, so different. He American who wanna be Cuban again!'

But the longer Yoel stays, the more he becomes one of these hybrids, and he knows it. There is no option, for chasing the American dream is a full-time occupation and it changes you. Yoel arrived on these shores with his Cuban manners, always ready to help a woman with her shopping bags. The women offered him a tip when he helped them and he would think that strange, slightly offensive.

'I tink... she don' tink I'm nice? She tink I a servant?' Then he forgot dignity and began accepting tips. After accepting, he began expecting, and through expecting he began getting annoyed if a woman only gave him a dime instead of a dollar.

'The way life ees here, you cant afford to be helping everybody. You don' have time. In Cuba we didn' ha money but we had a lotta time. Here, there ain't nough hours in de day. Dare ees no halfway. De seestem too rigid, man. You have to forget where you came from to be able to live here. You have to forget your broderhoo' values to be American. You can't ha bote. I ha to accept my choice and my loss.'

In this transitory city, the place I hold no love for, I am still looking for something. Perhaps a solution to loneliness: an embrace, a kiss... warmth. I am lost in a midway station, between London, that holds the memories of growing up, and Buenos Aires, my birthplace, my other home. I have tried to find my place here, but I can't.

■

Panamá's youth has been packed into their bullet points and axes and sent off to a Levi's office on the other side of the country. And I am now coasting freely along a smooth four-lane highway in a Toyota jeep, the Caribbean sun sizzling on its shiny black coat. I'm a little confused as to my whereabouts. I see the familiar Spanglish billboards advertising a new US-

Venezuelan youth internet portal. 'I am El Presidente,' the very MTV-funky-short-spiky redhead Latina shouts. My driver blabbers the usual Miami English inanities.

We arrive at an office in a business park, could be anywhere, but in the maze of dividers the Caribbean Spanish squawk dominates. Am I back at the Cisneros office? Is this a bad dream? Finally I am shown into an office where a sunburnt Miami Cuban, with a kind of Venezuelan accent, sits behind a desk in a Hawaii-style shirt that bares chest hair and a medallion. He welcomes me with palm-rubbing enthusiasm as if we have cracked the route to the treasure. He wants to talk money and hands me a wad of cash to cover my expenses. No, Carlos Cisneros would never be so crude; his Cuban roots had been assimilated into Venezuelan aristocracy, while this man has that Miami hunger still. I am not in the Cisneros office that had surpassed aspiration and was well into the dynastic. I am in Oscar Cerallo's: Cuban-fled, Miami-bred and now Levi's man in Caracas.

The name Chávez is mentioned, which also reminds me of my last days at the Cisneros when the very name was making nerves jangle throughout the office as election neared. You could hear Carlos's fits from the floor above. It was not just the striking indigenous features of the Venezuelan president-to-be, Hugo Chávez, that was worrying the Miami business community, but his revolutionary talk about wresting Venezuela from its dependency on the US, international monetary agencies and the country's business elite. Then a week before the election, everyone calmed down. A deal had been struck: the

 Cisneros would not use its media influence or Gustavo's contacts in US political circles to sabotage the election, and Chávez would leave the private sector alone.

We are a year on, however, and Chávez's land reforms and corporate tax increases to compensate the 80 per cent of his people living in poverty has sent investors running in panic. In the space of a year the government has raised public spending by 46 per cent and forced banks to lend 15 per cent of their money to agriculture. But Caracas is now officially the most crime-ridden city in Latin America and the media is blaming it all on Chávez.

'It's terrible, terrible,' says Oscar, visibly distraught by the year's events in Venezuela. 'We used to be a stable country. The poor did not hate us. Chávez has stirred them up against us, created so much resentment. You cannot walk the streets any more. You cannot walk into your house without watching your back.'

Forty years after his participation in the failed Bay of Pigs invasion to oust Fidel, Oscar's supreme sales figures have made him Levi's model licensee, the king of Levi's Latin America. He had cracked the women's market with the tight Lycra fit that flatters Vene-curves. Yet his pale shaking face reflects the spectre of old phantom Fidel, whom the Venezuelan president already claims to be his comrade-in-arms in the fight against American imperialism, threatening to turn his world upside down all over again. The dreaded F-word has been replaced by the C-word.

On the highway again, still so Miami-tainted, my companion José Luis, marketing director of Levi's Venezuela, is inviting me to the launch of a music channel owned by El Puma Rodríguez, the leathery crooner frequently seen in Miami magazine shows. We pass billboards of ecstatic youngsters keeping their cigarettes dry and wetting their jeans in the Caribbean. Of course, we could not be in Miami. It's been long frowned upon to advertise death sticks to children in the US. The future of Philip Morris now depends on countries where governments are desperate enough to sacrifice the health of their children for investment.

José Luis points to one billboard with Michael Jordan and informs me, 'See, it's Michael Jordan, it's a sports product so that's OK, but as a rule we don't use black people in our adverts. I know in the US they have more liberal ideas but here we don't like that.' And then he gives this nervous little laugh. No, we are not in Miami, where brands would still be under the confines of political correctness.

Above the billboards, the slums cling to the mountain range, like stacked humans clambering to heaven. I scan the hillside to see where they end, but they don't. All the way round the *ranchos* hang, as shameless as Oscar's hunger for commerce, glaring down into the clean, glass-skyscraper Caracas below, threatening to fall and contaminate its modernity with their brown backwardness. However hard we've tried, we are not quite Miami. Not quite.

6

A PROMISE THAT NEVER ARRIVED

'Life shouldn't be about having and getting
but being and becoming.'
LUCIA, 16, CARACAS

My dad says that when he used to come to Caracas thirty years ago there were no *ranchos*. Caracas in 1972 was a safe and beautiful city, like a modern tropical Buenos Aires. Rather than flirtatious mutual psychoanalysing in the bars of Madrileño style tree-lined avenues, *Caraqueño* coquetry bloomed in the night breeze under the palm trees of the curvy, modernist urban spaces with mosaic designs. The Caribbean smells and sensations were more similar to those Dad had been born with in Cuba, as a diplomat's son. The soft, dark *Caraqueña* curves must have reminded him of his first nannies, whose bosoms he'd spent his first months cradled between. He was struck by the absence of aggression in the people, the Caribbean ease about everything. *Las Misses,* the reward for Venezuela's mastery of *detallismo* that created an endless string of Miss World successes, was the only brand name that mattered.

In 1973 Caracas was the place to be. Oil prices quadrupled, making the freedom many were dreaming of in Latin America seem even more attainable. Carlos Andrés Pérez, the new president, was determined to create Venezuela's own motor industry, rather than just produce oil for the US. This way Venezuela would build a future of skilled employment and technological independence. Pérez even convinced voters to accept high car prices in the short term (as a result of protective measures) to achieve this long-term goal. His target was to produce 90 per cent of each car made in Venezuela by 1985, with a national industry that added value to the economy, rather than be the assembly-line economy most Latin American countries were limited to. It was as if God had created a second chance to build the 'Gran Venezuela' of Simón Bolívar's dreams.

In the lobby of the Miami-style Eurobuilding Hotel, frenetic little men with clipboards are rushing round screaming at people and doting on sulking curvaceous women under flashlights. I talk to what I thought was a bellboy and discover that the lobby has been temporarily converted into the set for a Latin American soap opera. The soap-opera bellboy is a Germanic blue-eyed blond; the real one is dark and mixed race.

Outside, the porters chuckle as an old banger chugs up the

luxurious driveway and pulls up under the white pillars. It is my second day in Caracas and I have called for a taxi from outside since I can't see myself stepping out into Petare, one of the *ranchos* on the hill, in one of the hotel's Evita-style limousines. The driver of the battered 1970s Ford is no more than nineteen, as if emblematic of the new generation still stuck in the old promise of Saudi Venezuela.

The protective tariffs proposed by Pérez's government were a direct threat to US car manufacturers who needed Venezuela's hungry market in the global recession. Ford launched a furious campaign to change the public's and industrialists' minds about building its own motor industry, printing full-page adverts stressing Ford's importance to the local market, lobbying US Congress to favour Venezuelan trade if industrialists switched to import rather than production. Finally, when persuasion did not work, Ford set about pressurizing other countries in the Andean Pact to adopt neo-liberal measures. The government's surprise defeat in the 1978 elections was the fatal blow to plans of industrial independence. Still embroiled in motor contracts, the government had not managed to get its show on the road in time to convince the electorate.

Subsequent governments reversed the production-based policies and protective tariffs and began deregulating prices to favour imports. Parts production was swiftly subordinated to oil rents. When Andrés Pérez returned to power in 1988, he too followed the neo-liberal prescription already in place. Instead of real progress, oil money served only to perpetuate an illusion of the progress while spawning two unequal twins:

 one over-fed bully living off oil profits, and a runt scavenging for the crumbs off his brother's table.

'You want to go to Petare?' Eliécer, my young driver, squeals incredulously as I get into the seat beside him. We head west and after a five-minute silence, he sneaks a look at me sideways and says, 'You know, I'm not taking this car up there. I already got assaulted this month.' He points to the knife scar on his face. 'They wanted to steal my car radio and mobile. No one is going to take them away from me. We feel the things we own. We kill for them.' Then he sits back in his seat, still slightly ruffled.

As we drive closer, I see windows and aerials, signs of human life in the giant brown pile of Petare. My stomach tightens. But with fear lumped in my throat, I know it is something I must do, even though I am sure in Petare there will be no market for Levi's.

Eliécer drops me off on the highway at a petrol station, next to a baseball pitch where portly men vent frustrations in a Sunday swing. The audience in the stands takes its eyes off the game for a moment to watch this alien. I feel so self-conscious I pay no attention to where I am walking, and from one minute to the next I find myself on the other side of the footbridge, standing at the foot of a mountain of shacks. It seems a giant haystack that a single dislodged straw could bring tumbling down. Last year heavy rainfalls sent the other side of the mountain sliding and forty thousand people died. Today, a human river pours out of its estuaries, and I am suddenly lost in the crowd.

I need to look purposeful, like I belong. To my relief, on a low wall by the footbridge I spot a group of boys. One of them is already getting up to give me his place. He has a growth on his cheek, which makes half his face look twice the size of the other, and swamps his right eye. The boys say they are resting at half-time in their weekly basketball match with another sector of Petare. They are very shy, and just stare at me. Freddy, the referee, talks. He is slightly older and has intelligent eyes. He is the one who organizes the basketball tournament between the *barrios* of Petare. It's to keep the boys off drugs – a new government initiative, he says.

'I don't care what people say. At least Chávez is giving us hope. He is one of *us*, he is not a *plástico.* Those people hate him because they are scared of losing what they have. But we have nothing to lose and things can only get better. Chavez can't undo thirty years of injustice overnight; he must be given a chance.'

One boy called Richard, who has sad eyes, wants to speak but he stutters and stops. Go on, I urge, you were going to say something.

'It's just that... I wanted to say ...' He speaks so quietly I have to strain to hear him. 'I don't have anything against rich people, but they think they are more important than us. But if a rich person suffers from flu, he feels the same pain as I do. If he is in love, he feels the same as I do.'

'They say we are robbers, but that is not true,' says Rodolfo, encouraged by Freddy. 'If we were thieves we would have money. The real robbers are the ones who have kept all the money from the oil we produce. We all belong to this country.

 Why should the oil be taken by just a few people? They have stolen what belongs to all of us.'

'Look, we have to go and play,' Freddy tells the boys and invites me to watch them.

Inside the high fencing, the ghetto blaster is playing salsa. Beer billboard sponsor the surrounding poverty, tempting the players as they slalom through the bump-and-grinding crowd in search of a route. 'It's good for the boys' reflexes,' laughs Freddy.

Outside the fence a score of military police patrol. They are looking for a delinquent, but they don't dare enter the *rancho* above. They ask people around the court but everybody shrugs, nobody is going to snitch. Their heavy artillery makes me nervous but everyone else ignores them. Then I see two men from my world, white and blond, wearing short-sleeved shirts and ties and carrying briefcases, like door-to-door salesmen in Pleasantville. 'Missionaries,' Freddy says. Of course, only evangelism – theirs, mine – could bring a *gringo* into these parts.

The boys have won their basketball match. I want to leave. 'When will you come back?' the boys ask me. 'We have a party next Saturday in the *barrio.* Do you want to come?'

Richard sees my hesitance. 'You're scared to come, aren't you?'

'Scared?' I laugh. 'I'd be honoured.'

We arrange to meet up at the top of the bridge at ten o'clock on Saturday. They give me the directions, the last exit off the Urbina Two. As I leave, the entire court waves goodbye. I feel embarrassed, but happy. The fear has gone.

■

Down in the city, *Caraqueños* boast that their Sambil shopping mall is Latin America's largest: five floors and more than five hundred stores. Like Petare, also allegedly Latin America's biggest slum, it is a world unto itself, only that its ensnaring labyrinth is made of chrome, not dust. I've come to meet a girl called Vanessa and some of her friends whom I met at the Catholic University, one of Caracas's most expensive, where the *ranchos* are so close they look like they are about to spill onto its lawns. 'We need another natural disaster to get rid of them,' said Gerardo, Vanessa's friend.

I have spent an hour trying to find the food hall, slowed down by my fascination with the sublime specimens all around: the precision curves, the perfect teeth, and a parade of hundreds of little girls in swimming costumes and silk sashes. One proud father tells me that perfection is a labour of long-term love and an early start is imperative.

I notice that everyone in this metallic indoor world wears identical clothing: Levi's jeans, Tommy Hilfiger shirt and Timberland boots. Brands couldn't have wished for a better conformity if the uniform were obligatory. Perhaps they are compensation for a greatness that never came. Security guards carry off those who are suspiciously scruffy or brand deficient.

I finally spot Vanessa on the recreational floor at the top of the mall with her *pavito* friends. *Los pavos,* 'the turkeys', recognizable by their puffed chests stuffed into tight black D&G T-shirts, drive the right cars, date the right girls, know the right discos. In the background, a techno anthem blares out of one of the discos – 'Pump up the jam, pump it up...' – in praise of gym satisfaction and the results on display. 'Wuperoh, wuperoh!' the pumped-up crowd imitates. The hall is full of Caracas beauties, dripping in glitzy garments, jewellery, nose dressings. One, two, three, four faces are bandaged. Terrible, I think, the price of car culture. Vanessa laughs. The only affliction linking these ladies, she says, is post-cosmetic-surgery stress disorder.

'You have to wear the bandage, otherwise what's the use in having an expensive operation if nobody knows that you've forked out for it?'

■

Saturday comes, the day of the party in Petare. At nine thirty I put on my jeans, trainers and a T-shirt, grab the bags of liquor and ring Eliécer.

'Ha! Sucker for punishment, eh?' he says as I jump into the seat beside him.

Petare rises above us like a medieval hamlet, the highway below the moat that protects it from the outside world – or vice versa. A checkpoint awaits us on the bridge. The military police ask Eliécer who I am and where he is taking me. He keeps repeating that we have come from the Eurobuilding Hotel, as if this should reassure them of my legitimacy, but they do not look convinced. 'Why is she coming here?' they ask, and they take his documents and gather in conference over them.

'It's no big deal,' Eliécer reassures me. 'The curfew is not to stop us going in, but to stop the *lavaperros* coming out.'

Petare was just another of the slums that had been multiplying around Caracas since the 1970s, until one day in

February 1989 when it exploded into a two-day riot. Bus fares had suddenly doubled after the bankrupt government had been forced to raise petrol prices once the oil boom had deflated. The uprising was short-lived. The military repression to continue IMF-prescribed economic 'reform' and 'stability' cost Petare fifteen hundred lives (unofficial reports said three thousand). Now it is like any other Latin American slum, filling the Monday papers with figures of weekend deaths, heavily policed to contain the crime.

At the end of the bridge we turn left and head for the little wall where I first approached the boys. They are nowhere to be seen. As I open the door to get out, a navy blue van screeches to a halt beside us and armed men pour out of the back. One of them points a rifle into Eliécer's window. 'Get out!' shouts a voice. He pulls me out of the car, tells me to put my hands on the car roof and begins sprawling his hands all over my body, the insides of my legs and down to my feet. He orders me to take off my shoes and shakes them.

Richard, Rodolfo and their friend Elvis come running towards us. Other officers get them up against the wall, jostle their rifles into their bodies and insult them. 'Haven't you got better things to do than to bully people?' I ask the man going through the contents of my bag on the car roof. Richard, who stands with his arms in the air going through the motions of being searched like it is something he does every day, tries to calm me down. 'Amaranta,' he whispers, putting his finger to his lips, a diplomatic way of telling me to shut the fuck up. 'Don't worry, nothing will happen, everything will be OK. Just be calm.' Finally, the officers climb back into their van. One of them grins at me and nods his head. They speed off, leaving Eliécer's car a wreck.

'I'll be going now,' he says.

Richard and the others take me up through the winding alleys above. All is alive in the darkness: laughter through the windows and salsa tunes floating into each other as we pass crowded living rooms, their TVs flickering behind iron bars. Everyone here seems to have cable TV and mobile phones, even though there is neither tap water nor sewage collection. We reach a little open space, about the size of a penalty area, which Richard tells me is *la plazita* (the little square).

In the corner there is a nativity scene made of sawdust. People have stuck monopoly money around Jesus' manger to bring good luck in the new year. On the wall the word MAGALLANES is painted, the name of the baseball team they support. Richard points his house out to me opposite. I ask him about his family. He had two brothers, he says; one died last year, the other this year, both caught in crossfire.

He takes me through an alley and the city appears before us in flickering blips. The lights of Petare envelop us, and for a minute we can dream of being in the turret of an enchanted castle in a sky of stars, looking over the kingdom below. For a minute we can forget that we are somewhere in a pile of paper-thin buildings which one heavy rainstorm could send tumbling down in a mudslide.

The other boys arrive, all spruced up, their Levi's and T-shirts freshly washed, ready to impress the girls at the party.

We come to an alley where people are spilling out from a house. Faces come to greet me – an ear half bitten, an eye missing, an absent upper lip that a simple operation at birth could have fixed but no amount of *detallismo* can cure. I have to cover my shock with a smile as my stomach heaves. Then, all of a sudden, in the middle of the crowd, against the brick, loose electric wires and washing lines, an angel appears, dressed in a long white gown and a headdress of white lilies. She swans around nodding to her guests; they look at her in wonder. The Princess of Petare. Someone puts on a waltz. An old man in a chequered shirt, a cowboy hat and a smiling face of brown leathery skin steps forward to take his fifteen-year-old treasure for the last time before he offers her to the world. Then each boy in the circle takes it in turns to dance with her. And the party begins.

I dance with all of the boys in turn, squeezed between all the other bodies in the tiny room. The heat is suffocating, but I don't care. Everyone guzzles down bottles of Coca-Cola. A perfect advert for ghetto happiness? Not much option in the absence of clean drinking water, they tell me: Cola is cheaper than bottled water. The feeling is good and I am happy. Then, curiously, from the warm, tender and romantic melody of the salsa, strange words escape:

Simón, Don Simón…
Our eternal lament leaves you restless,
You never imagined that
For all the blood and love you gave

For all your pretensions of liberty
You'd be rewarded with a
Privatised America,
With false politicians,
foreign owners,
thieving governors…

Under the umbrella of romantic escape stands the stubborn Simón Bolívar, the great liberator. Petare still awaits the liberation he promised. Bolívar in Levi's, the second coming on a horse over the horizon. That's an idea.

■

'Ah, here comes Mother Teresa of Petare!' mocks Carlos, the barman, when I arrive the next day for my early evening Mojito. These days I am exhausted. I do more interviews every day, and they are longer and more intense. I have become obsessed with finding the truest possible picture of the city. I am no longer shy in approaching kids, or waste time hiding behind trees and prowling like a stalker, wondering who to pounce on next. Now I march straight in and I can see the kids are sometimes stunned by my audacity. Sometimes we spend hours sharing experiences and ideas; they confess things they say they have never told anyone. They don't want me to leave. Of course they don't – I am taking their secrets with me.

Strangely, they say they cannot trust anyone with the things that matter for fear it will be used against them. After we have talked, they panic and make me promise I am not secretly hired by their 'enemies'. What paranoia! What 'enemies' can lurk in a fourteen-year-old's mind? They are so dramatic about it I have to promise.

I love working on the streets. It makes me feel that my work belongs to the real world, rough, raw, unprotected, imperfect. I felt grateful for this opportunity at first. And yet I can't help feeling that as I tread in this reality I taint it, for my job is to sell this *real* world, with its *real* aspiration for a better life, to a corporate marketing machine that converts real hope into consumer fantasy. Like the man at the altar who can turn bread and wine into Christ's body and blood, Levi's jeans are received as something else. With this cloth pieced together with orange stitching comes an imaginary ticket to a better world. Levi's has sacramental power. Surely then, I am the priest listening to confessions. I do not make lives better, I just help deliver a false remedy. But what is this dream machine I have become a cog in? I am part of it but I have no real knowledge of it.

The bar is always full of unattractive men in suits whose roving eyes I am eager not to meet. I can tell they are craving for company, for humanity. It must be the effect of talking figures and strategies all day. They impress me with philosophical convictions such as 'there is no such thing as injustice. The world is just a struggle between those who have power and those who want it', or 'Greed and power are human nature. Everyone wants to be better than the next.' How convenient. But maybe some just want to be equal.

They try to engage Carlos in conversation too. Unlike me, it is his job to humour them. There's an Englishman who works for some pharmaceutical company and likes to boast about how well he knows the region. 'You don't like to rush things down here, eh? A little lazy,' he sniggers, unaware of the patronizing tone. I think he confuses knowledge with the length of time he's been here. Carlos gets up at four every day to get here by six, and, when he is not doing double shifts, goes straight to the university to study and never gets home before midnight. Today, the Englishman waxes lyrical about his love for Latin America, and is laughing about the *ley seca*, a 'dry law' they implement to stop people drinking for twenty-four hours before a general election. 'Don't you have the dry law in your country?' asks Carlos.

The Englishman sniggers. 'Young man, in civilized countries, we don't waste time with that kind of nonsense.' Excuse me, is this the same civilized country where fat louts get so plastered they rampage the streets with their trousers round their ankles, pissing on tramps and smashing up strangers?

I go up to my room. Poor Carlos cannot escape so easily. If it isn't the English guy there's always someone else. I ring the boys from Petare to invite them out somewhere, but they say they cannot come. There has been a shooting and a curfew has been imposed, and anyway they have to get up early for work.

■

One of my favourite youth-hunting spots is Parque del Este, a working-class neighbourhood on the east side of the city. The houses are bland cement blocks with railed windows, and the main road, Avenida Sucre, is a twenty-four-hour traffic jam, but it's not as bad as Petare. On the *avenida*, there is a school and some sort of technical college. They share the playground with each other. I swear they are Caracas's most gorgeous teenagers; a fusion of glowing *café con leche* complexions, indigenous cheekbones with European eyes of pale blues, greens and greys. The boys play basketball and the girls play volleyball, others sit around flirting and laughing, and a faithful few run towards me to claim their stake in the afternoon chat. The mysterious interrogations seem to have become notorious, and now they all want to take turns.

The first day I arrived, the kids proudly introduced themselves as the *guaperó*. 'Wuperoh!' they shouted. When they saw I didn't understand, they began to sing: 'Pump up the jam… pump it up… wuperoh!' and I recognized the phonetic translation of the same Belgian techno lyric the *pavos* were dancing to in the Sambil. 'We wear brand names, Nike and Levi's – they are the best – and baseball caps. We look cool, we're the biz' was their definition of a *guaperó*. And the song? The anthem of their desires, I assume: the *pavo* lifestyle, the pumping up… of their muscles, their confidence, their mood, their life. Perhaps the song represents all the things the *pavos* have and they don't: the jeeps, the *misses*, the money, the real brands, not the counterfeit.

If there were ever a competition to find the ideal consumer aspirationalists, the Venezuelans would win it. They say when a Venezuelan dies, he doesn't want to go to heaven, he wants to go to Miami. The oil boom strengthened the Venezuelan currency and provoked mass shopping sprees to Florida. The Venezuelans became known as *los dame-dos* (the gimme-twos) because they could always be heard in Miami stores shouting, 'Jesus, that's so cheap, *dame dos*!'

 Now all that is left of Saudi Venezuela are the motorways and their billboards dangling the distant memory of consumer heaven to an impoverished majority.

In Parque del Este the kids talk a lot about their heads – that they are their weak spots, that they hurt, that they are vulnerable.

'What do you mean you have a weak head?' I ask.

'They mess with your mind,' answers Elisarde, his enthusiastic fourteen-year-old face twisting into a geriatric bitterness. 'The mind games, the trickery...'

'What tricks?' I insist.

'Treachery. This world is full of treachery,' growls Elvira, a girl with luminous bands intertwined with her long black locks. She spits the last word out and distorts her pretty face.

'If someone wants to get at you they never do it to your face,' Marvie explains. 'They'll do it through someone else, like your mum because they know that hurting her is worse than feeling it yourself.'

'Why would anyone want to hurt you?'

'They do it without even knowing why they are doing it,' Elvira says. 'Even people you know well and you like. One minute they are your best friend, the next they are stabbing you in the back. It's our nature.'

I remember something Eliécer said: 'Envy is bringing this city down. There are so many people who resent you just because you have a car. You can be sure there is always someone who wants to do you in.'

Marvie says that one day he's going to invent a computer

chip to get inside people's heads 'to read their thoughts and know when they are lying'. These kids are only fourteen and they already sound like conspiracy theorists.

'The only sure way of protecting yourself is not to open your mouth,' Elisarde advises me, proud to have cracked the formula. 'It is better that no one knows what you really feel.'

Marvie nods: 'Always remember: you are the owner of your thoughts and a slave to your words.' I can see it in a campaign somewhere. Branding paranoia. With humour, of course. Marvie, Elisarde and Elvira are easy prey. They are desperate to capture that moment that was there, just there for the grabbing, when material comfort and glossy, shiny first-worldness flashed by. They can grasp this moment in a sugary caramel taste, a swoosh on their shoes and the sensation of a denim, wherein lies the 'original' bright future where everything is possible. Branding nostalgia. Does it matter that this well-being only comes in symbols that make money for others?

'What happened to Bolívar's dream,' I ask, 'of a united Latin America?' Three hundred years ago, Venezuelans died fighting for the ideal of a unified Latin America drawing on the strengths of indigenous culture, for their right to an identity.

'Aaaah. We don't believe in that any more,' Marvie says. 'The only the thing I believe in is whatever occurs to me in the moment.'

'It's that... we don't belong to ourselves any more, we belong to the US,' says Elvira.

It is not a judgement, just a matter of fact.

■

 So will my report chronicle this perfect consumer nation: the gadget-obsessed, emotionally driven, frustrated children of the '*dame-dos*' era, ripe for temptation? If I write that they are scared to express themselves for fear it will be used against them, will the bells of irony ring in Levi's head office?

Will I describe how hyper-consumerism feeds the *arribismo* and gnaws at their vulnerability, hindering their chance for real long-term progress? I don't think Levi's analysis goes beyond decoding the emotional facts in their laboratories of advertising formulae. Deconstruct, to reconstruct in blue denim image. Levi's wants reality in a useful booklet, emotions broken down into bullet points. Not active, living, breathing reality that shakes consciences.

Sometimes José Luis asks me how I'm getting on. If I talk about the kids' experiences as things of value in themselves rather than about their significance to boardroom strategy, he nods and smiles blankly. He has switched off.

Today's session in Parque del Este ends on the subject of Palestinian suicide bombers. There was something on the news about them and Marvie asks me how much I think they get paid.

'I don't think they get paid,' I say.

'But why would you do that, if it was not to leave your family wealthy?'

'I think it is more a form of protest, for their right to self-determination, to land and sovereignty.'

'Aaaah,' they say and fall into silence. They look stunned, as though trying to grapple with the concept. Then Elvira speaks, sullenly but with conviction. 'If we could only feel for

Venezuela the emotion that we feel for the material things,' she says, 'we would be a great country.'

■

I decide to give Petare another call. Since my night there I've been wanting to return their hospitality but every attempt has been thwarted by a curfew that prevents them coming out. This time I get through to Richard and I invite the boys to some hotel luxury for the day. I am not sure whether it is a good idea to tempt them with something they cannot access after I leave, but it is the only hospitality I can offer. Besides, it's not as if they don't know what the rich hoard behind their security gates. The *telenovelas* show it all the time. Their world would also be inaccessible for me without them. Despite Richard's reluctance, we agree on Saturday.

Carlos the barman laughs when he hears my idea. 'The management will probably sterilize the pool when they leave. Make sure you get them visitor's passes, because the bosses will find any excuse to chuck them out.' I have a dreadful premonition of my reluctant visitors being humiliated by the management.

When I arrive in Petare to collect the boys there is nobody to meet me. I spot Freddy the coach, who tells me he thinks they are all still asleep and leads me up to Richard's house. We pick up Rodolfo and Elvis on the way. But Richard is nowhere to be seen. His mother tells us he has gone to meet some girl for a date and won't be coming. My plan is falling apart. Rodolfo tells me that some of the boys don't want to go where they are not wanted. They have no illusions:

 they know the only black people in the hotel speak in a foreign language.

After half an hour of umming and ahhing, Richard stumbles through the door in a horrific mood and slumps on the couch beside me. His date has stood him up. Rodolfo, Elvis and Noel all laugh at him and soon Richard can't help but share their amusement. 'Come on,' Rodolfo says. 'Let's go with Amaranta. It'll cheer you up.'

Twenty minutes later we are walking through the sliding doors of the marble and gold palace, where a magical mountain of brilliant white covered in flashing Christmas trees glistens before us and the soap-opera stars fidget under the fuss of the make-up artists. But before the new reality has sunk in, the boys have already scampered into the toilets.

■

I've been lying by the pool for forty-five minutes and the boys are still in the toilet. I wonder if I should go and see if they are OK. Or perhaps they've sneaked out without telling me. Oh, to hell with them then, the cowards. I spot Rodolfo. He is walking up sheepishly, peering out from under his bowed head at the white faces that stare at him. He sits on the lounger beside me and I look at him over my sunglasses.

'Uuuhh, they don't want to come out. They are too embarrassed,' he says.

'Oh don't be ridiculous. Why are they embarrassed?'

Rodolfo shrugs.

'Well, they can stay in there for all I care,' I tell him. 'I'm not going to go and hold their hands. If they don't want to come, then they can go home. But I think it's pathetic, you can tell them that.'

Rodolfo heads off to pass the message on and ten minutes later they appear, six of them in single file, like scolded children, trying desperately not to look at anyone and to sit down as fast as they can on the loungers. I have to laugh, and so do they. Despite their monumental efforts at discretion, the boys have been noticed by the poolside babes, who now have something more pleasurable to look at than the flabby bellies and hairy backs of Italian executives.

'Can we take some of them off your hands?' I hear giggling voices ask from above. Standing over me are some busty false blondes who could be nothing else but Argentine air hostesses.

'Are they American, are they rappers?' they ask.

'SURE!' I cry. 'Don't you recognize them? They are *really* famous. You want to talk to them?' I call Rodolfo and beckon him to come. 'I was just telling these girls about your new album, what a big hit it is!'

Rodolfo looks at me suspiciously, but luckily the girls are already busy nuzzling up to him and yapping away: 'You really do speak good Spanish!' Slowly, curiosity lures the others from the pool and they gather round. Richard urges me to take a picture before it all goes horribly wrong so that they can prove it to their mates in Petare. Rodolfo makes me wait while he takes off his basketball shorts to reveal a pair of tight, 1950s-style brown-and-white-striped swim shorts, last seen on his dad in 1979. The boys laugh so much they have to hold their stomachs.

So the day goes on and Richard forgets about being stood

 up. We drink cocktails in the pool; we go to the luxury buffet for lobster and caviar. The boys order pizza. I take them to the business centre to teach them about the internet and set up an account so we can keep in touch. The secretaries stare in disbelief. 'It just goes to show they are not all *malandros,*' one of them says. 'It's nice of you to bring them here. You must be a very good person.' She touches my arm and looks at me misty-eyed, filled with emotion at my philanthropy.

I want to accuse her of misunderstanding me. Tell her that I am not 'Mother Teresa', as Carlos teases me. Is this what our inequality has reduced our relationship to, a charitable gesture on my part? I feel insulted. And yet, if I want the truth, I cannot stop halfway. I cannot believe in a Benetton advert.

As I show the boys how to surf the net, I find myself in the Levi's site, perhaps looking for answers. The words 'empathetic marketing' in bold letters catch my eye. That's me, I think.

We walk in our consumers' shoes... appreciating and meeting the needs of those we serve.

I learn that:

being empathetic also means that we are inclusive. We reflect the diverse world we serve... it means engagement and compassion, giving back to the people we serve.

That's me, earnestly communicating with my kids in the streets, hearing their confessions, even giving advice sometimes.

Originality is the symbol of frontier independence, democratic idealism, social change.

Oscar doesn't seem too happy with democracy at the

moment. I don't think Chávez is the kind of social change he has in mind.

Courage: it takes courage to be great. Courage is the willingness to challenge hierarchy, accepted practices and conventional wisdom... Levi's had integrated factories decades before the federally mandated desegregation... Our values are fundamental to our success: Empathy, Originality, Integrity and Courage.

I feel sick. How can they throw me into the real world and expect me to espouse such sentiments? Did Levi's make a stand when, following the destruction of opponents, the US pressured financial institutions to attach structural adjustment conditions to loans, destroying local industry and widening the gap between rich and poor? Did Levi's local subsidiaries challenge the crooked governments that have invited multinationals into their own pockets? Has it made a stand against racism and prejudice? Some of their marketing campaigns seemed to me to play on the fears generated by racism and prejudice, rather than try to break them down.

Perhaps it is not the company's fault that the sacrament of a pair of Levi's is the closest a kid can get to the American dream, just like Philip Morris and British American Tobacco cannot help it that Latin American governments have the world's worst record in setting restrictions to protect their young against cigarette advertising. But they ride the neo-liberal wave nevertheless.

'Throughout history,' the website says, Levi's reached out to 'often-neglected consumers... We will clothe the world.' I imagine little children cheering as denim rains upon them from the back of a lorry, liberating them from brand deprivation. But what real chance does one little boy have to break out of the planet of rubble that is annexed to Lima or Caracas and which is marked on his face, condemning him for life? Perhaps this boy should be thankful for the billion-dollar marketing strategies that help to transform perceptions so that the omnipresent fantasy of well-being on billboards and on TV can become a kind of reality in which their own grim reality dissolves. Brand culture helps them to forget.

We are honest and trustworthy... The Consumer can trust us.

Philanthropic rubbish. And, perversely, charity is what my perceived power has reduced my every relationship to; it taints my experiences and my supposed friendships. Only if we were equal could they be real.

I am hearing voices, echoes from Parque del Este: 'If people didn't interfere we would be able to think more clearly,' the little girl said. 'And if we could all find what we have in common rather than treat each other with distrust, maybe we could start to make things better.'

7

IN BETWEEN WORLDS

María, a large forty-five-year-old woman who looks older than her age, is happiest when sitting alongside her husband Rafael on the edge of their bed, each with a joystick, playing Pacman on a black and white screen in their pyjamas. She wears a too-washed nightie that bares her thick rough arms and a sunburn line so entrenched by years of wearing the same blouse that it is now permanent. Rafael's leathery brown face peers wide-eyed, like a tortoise's, out of his white *guayabera* shirt. In the background Fidel is ranting as usual, about what nobody knows – his words have long ceased to command attention. The rattle of an air-conditioner would be a more welcome Pacman theme tune.

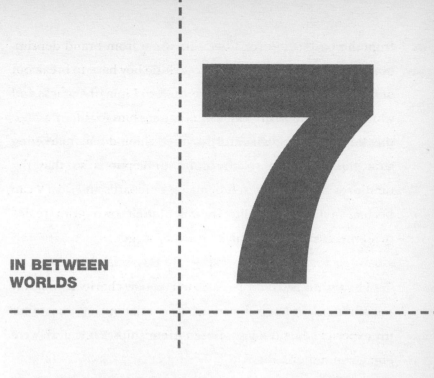

Grandmother, who has not uttered a word since I moved in, sits in her chair in the living room for her twelve waking hours. The shelves above display a variety of decorative treasures: an empty Pringles tube (original green), a carton of Tropicana orange juice and various sizes of Jack Daniel's bottles. Lázaro, the son, is fidgeting on the sticky sofa. His girlfriend, Elisa, is in the cupboard-sized kitchen separating the grit from the state-supplied rice, an intricate daily chore that takes at least an hour. Daughter Teresa is out back with her boyfriend hanging up the washing.

Just another day for the González family.

I, the intruder, sit crouched on the doorway step. The sun is blasting down on the dusty streets of Havana, the kind of heat that melts your will. You can't go out, you can't move.

Three nights ago I arrived from Caracas to write my Venezuela report. No investigating here. Cuba is invisible on the Levi's map. Perhaps this is why I have come. I couldn't make the leap up to the calculating north; even Miami seemed too far. My legs are heavy, sinking into this continent. My other existence up north more remote by the day.

I think of my mother, whose doctorate in pre-revolutionary Cuban writings had brought her here for six months when I was about nine. My brother didn't speak to her for weeks after she returned. I only remember the pictures she brought back of schoolgirls just like me, but their teeth were brilliant against smiling brown faces and they wore little red scarves round their necks and matching red pinafores over white blouses. Mum began plastering posters of a dark, scrawny-bearded man in a beret, whose soft, intense gaze was to look over us at meal-times ever since. They called him 'Che', just as the Argies in our house called each other 'Che', because he also came from the land I came from, where everyone called each other that. He had fought for a united Latin America, free and independent from foreign interests, a mission Mum said was guided by love. My father was born in the British Embassy in Havana, nineteen years before the revolution. Then he was taken to Ecuador until he was six. He says he remembers leaving the port for England for the first time, sniffing the burning cocoa, fresh for export. And then to a life of cold grey drizzle. Yes, here the moist warmth envelopes me as would a womb, here it's bright and glistening like that place in my imagination that I used to reserve for sad times in my Highgate playground.

The man at the airport convinced me to book a room at the luxurious Havana Libre Hotel. In the morning I phoned Lázaro, to whom I was ordered by an acquaintance in Miami to take presents (Nike and Levi's only). We arranged to meet outside the zoo and from there he took me to his house, where I unleashed the products raided from the cupboards in Levi's Venezuela. When the family heard I was staying at the Havana Libre, they were outraged, as if it were an offence that I was wasting money on the state when it could help someone they know. A day's room charge at the Libre would pay for us all to eat like kings for a week. I agreed and the whole house decided to accompany me back to the hotel to help me pack (and to make sure I didn't change my mind).

A neighbour who looked too old to be driving came round in a black 1950s Dodge, with which he had proudly provided the first ride for three newly born generations after him. They squashed me in the middle to hide me from the Revolutionary

 Defence Committee, who snoop round the *barrio* looking for transgressors of Fidel's rules, one of which is not to make personal profit by using your car as a taxi for tourists.

Inside the hotel lobby, something was not quite right. I heard the nasal boom of too many American voices. As I waited to pay my bill, the Americans discussed property development, casing the country with a local expert in preparation for Fidel's fall.

I paid my bill. Shit, no cash left, must get some out on my Visa card. I gave the woman my card, which she swiped three times. Then she shook her head. No, not possible. 'Your bank is American. American banks don't deal with us.' How could I be so naive? Me, the world traveller!

I had to break the news to my eager escorts: 'I only have a hundred dollars. I can't stay here. I might as well leave Cuba straight away.' One hundred dollars doesn't last you a day in tourist currency, but they said they weren't letting me go and proceeded to carry off my suitcases, leaving me with no choice but to follow. Back in the Dodge everyone tried to work out ways I could get money. Lázaro said he had a friend whose brother-in-law had invented a special machine that connects to the American banks. María said she had a cousin who works in a bureau de change. Everything would be all right, they assured me. They're living in a dream world, I thought.

The next day we tried all the miracle formulas and got nowhere. In the end they decided that I should get my dad to wire me some money and stay with them while it arrived. I almost died at the suggestion. I could just hear my dad's when-will-she-ever-learn sigh on the other end of the phone. And then there was the thought of another night in that sweaty bed with roly-poly Teresa and her boyfriend, listening to the whispered groans of Lázaro and his wife-to-be in the other bed half a foot away. There were eight of us in two tiny rooms and Grandma's snoring sounded like an all-night bombing raid, but after all the effort they had made I couldn't very well refuse.

My dad was fine about the transfer. It'd take a week for the money to get through. Meanwhile I am being held emotional hostage. Just the look on Maria's face when I threatened to leave was like a dagger in my heart. She has this way of looking at you.

This is not how it's supposed to be for tourists in Cuba. Usually it is the locals who latch on to the visiting rich, hoping to be treated to a meal or a night out, perhaps a life abroad. If I want to leave the house for a walk, Maria looks at me as if I'm committing the most devastating act of betrayal. She will follow me to the front door and demand to know where I am going. Lázaro won't let his girlfriend leave the house on her own either. He is out all day and she stays in doing the housework. 'You too crazy,' he takes it upon himself to inform me one day. 'A woman should be at home looking after her man, not travelling the world.' You cannot have a conversation with the men. They just tell you things. When the men talk to each other there is no discussion or debate, just an exchange of proclamations. Maybe it comes from watching too much of Fidel on TV.

But then there is the affection, the care and the tolerance. Here we have eight people living virtually on top of each other, twenty-four hours a day, day in day out, and nobody gets irritated. Sometimes the intimacy gets so intense I can't stand it. I find myself hating them, but they take the lack of privacy in their stride.

■

This morning Mama (María) and daughter Teresa have been trying on swimming costumes. They are so fat from eating rice and fried pork all day it takes them half an hour to squeeze into their respective fluorescent Lycra. Mama has already cut a hole in the middle of one to make room for her tummy. It looks like a wrestler's outfit. Teresa has got hold of a luminous lemon-and-lime tanga bikini, which is about ten sizes too small for her. Her buttocks bulge on either side and her enormous breasts keep popping out, to the right, to the left, according to which way she tugs the fabric. Elisa and I are on the bed and we can't stop laughing. María frowns as she tries to get the hole in the right position, but it ends up to the side of her pot belly. She keeps saying, 'This isn't right, it's strange,' and Elisa says, 'The suit is fine. You're just old and fat!' and bursts out laughing. I can't stop myself either.

María leaps onto the bed and rolls on top of us, spreading her flabby arms and legs and smothering us. 'See how fat I am?!' she screams. 'See how fat I am, I'm soooooo fat it's unbelievable!' Then María wraps her legs and arms around her daughter-in-law while her daughter stands by the door in her ridiculous bikini, half a breast hanging out, hands on her hips and with a pout that spells danger. 'I'm getting jealous,' she warns, crossing her arms and tapping her fingers on each elbow. 'I'm getting very jealous. I'm going to have to defend my territory' and she takes a huge dive and flies across the room, landing on top of us with a thud. 'Aaaaaah!' she screams. 'Fat is might and might is right!'

■

Friday is the first day I get out of the neighbourhood. We are all going off to what they call a *campismo* (even holidays are ideological!), communist Cuba's version of Butlin's and the yearly holiday provided by the state. Foreigners aren't allowed to go, and Cubans are banned from going to the tourist resorts to avoid the temptation of 'dollar life'. But they have got me a ticket, and will say that I am Lázaro's wife if questions are asked.

We go to a meeting place in the *barrio* of Vedado, where there are hundreds of people waiting to get on the buses. Men in tracksuits with clipboards call out the numbers of buses and we see if they match our tickets.

The Cuban motorway is the emptiest I have ever seen in my life. The nearest thing I see to a vehicle in our four-hour journey is a cow standing in the middle of the road. Sometimes you see people selling cheese. As they see the bus approaching they stand in the road holding the cheese in the air, then dive into the grass just before they get flattened. The Back Street Boys is the music of choice on the journey, a strange soundtrack to a route lined with revolutionary billboards with catchphrases like: 'A revolutionary is guided by great feelings of love.' In England love sells mobile phones. 'You get £20 off a Nokia 3310 when you buy £20 of airtime. Now that's true love!'

By the looks of it, the camp has not been touched since Señor Butlin opened it circa 1945. We install ourselves in one of the huts, which contains a bunk bed and mattresses that we dress with sheets brought from home, then head for the pool with bottles of *Chispa del Tren*, the Spark of the Train, on sale at a Cuban petrol station near you. Its name is supposed to be indicative of the sensation in the throat, but I feel no spark, only that my throat is on fire for half an hour.

A Butlin's redcoat would have a hard time with this crowd. If there is one thing Cubans don't need organizing in, it's how to forget their revolutionary duties. The only external factor required is a sound system. They dance and sing and save each other from drowning. They are in their element.

When it's getting dark, we head back to our hut to eat spaghetti and mayonnaise, the regulation dish in *campismos*. The night is filled with the sounds of competing stereo systems. Men in military uniform roam about for the sake of social consistency, but they let everyone get on with enjoying themselves. After dinner we join a barefoot crowd in torn T-shirts and shorts drifting towards the fuzzy sound system under a straw roof – a world away from the mirror-walled Club Mystiques of Miami. The music is the same, the people are the same, the dance is the same, but the movement is very different. Here there is none of the mechanical synchronicity: it is a throbbing, pulsating heartbeat, a mass of bodies heaving up and down like a single giant organ. Ba boom, ba boom, ba boom. The components – limbs, muscle and bone – are loose, sensual and free, but each individual movement fits into the next like a piece in a jigsaw puzzle. Cohesion out of chaos; the order and anarchy that coexist in Cuba.

You could imagine it on a London stage, mesmerizing a pale audience with its writhing agility and sensuality. The dance critics would analyse its complex artistry, layers of movement and measured harmony. But in flip-flops, within the confines of the *campismo*, it is just a way to relax. Of course, art doesn't just appear. They have dedicated as much time, energy and ambition to this skill as we do in making money and building careers. It is their study, their labour.

There is no real beach at the *campismo*, just a couple of rocks and the odd bit of sand between them. The next day, I want to investigate. María and Rafael insist on accompanying me on a walk along the coast. After a short while we come to a beautiful white sandy beach where waiters carry trays of Mojitos to Italian tourists on cushioned sunbeds. They also ride bananas on the sea. Officially, this is the place I should be, but, with María and Rafael, I am now an intruder. The security guards are far away and I find María and Rafael a space on the sand. Last night they were lost in a pulsing crowd of Cuban dancers. Now they sit quietly on foreign ground like two lost puppies.

■

On Sunday afternoon we head back to Havana. I must be burned to a frazzle, but I do not have a mirror to check. In fact, it has just occurred to me that I haven't looked at myself for a week. Now I know why I've been feeling strange, detached and slightly uncomfortable, deprived of the reassurance of checking what I look like, reminding myself who I am. Here the need to see yourself is not so crucial. If anything, music is the mirror. To feel is to know who you are.

 The day after we get back from the *campismo*, my money comes through. The whole family celebrates. The first thing I do with it is hire a couple of scooters, one for me and one for Lázaro and Elisa. Lázaro has to hide round the corner while I do the paperwork with the hire company because, being Cuban, he is not allowed the luxuries reserved for tourists, even if money permits. Since he is white, he reckons he can pass as a tourist once he's on the bike.

Riding into the *barrio*, we get a hero's welcome. All the kids in the street run after us and want to have a go. After half an hour they crawl back sheepishly to tell me that someone has crashed mine and the whole side has been scratched. Lázaro does not let anyone have a go on his.

I want to see Havana Vieja. The core of the old colonial city has been dolled up for foreigners – most Cubans who filter through get picked up by the police under suspicion of being hustlers, *jineteros* – but much of it is still inhabited by the Afro-Cubans who live there. The streets are electric. They buzz with the energy of errand-running, socializing, scandalizing and whistling up to windows from the street – the communication of choice in the absence of fibre optics. In our cities, technology keeps our heads down, but here the culture of inconvenience makes people expert in managing the unreliable world of contact.

The city rumbles to the sound of Cuba's heavy industry: *rumba* and *son* – the origins of salsa. No McDonald's signs, no ad pitches, no visual contamination and nowhere to shop. As we zigzag through the crowded streets, I hear the raw sound of salsa coming out from one of the houses: the horns, the percussion, the voices. People are standing in the doorway. Lázaro doesn't want to stop. He is not interested in this world. I beg him to leave me and take Elisa on a romantic ride along the Malecón. It is a relief to see him go. You could say we don't quite see eye to eye.

His worship of brands makes me feel uncomfortable. This is Cuba, for God's sake, the only Latin country saved from Levi's espionage, and I end up living with branding's most self-loathing victim. Lázaro does not know what branding is. He knows of no propaganda that is not Fidel's, and is convinced Levi's symbolizes freedom. I tell him capitalism has also become oppressive; like Fidel's, the power of big business is close to absolute, controlling governments and democracy alike. People hardly count as citizens, only consumers. And in their wish to control our thoughts and desires, corporations spy on people, track their irrational impulses and manipulate them in order to make them better consumers. It is another kind of dictatorship. But he only cares that I can get cheap jeans.

The band members smile when they see me sneak in, and get me a rum. I am finally left to my own devices, without Lázaro controlling my perceptions. I can just watch and wait, like everyone else on this island where time just exists, without justification or reason, almost standing still. Here Time doesn't have the rats of progress scrambling in her entrails for an opportunity, panicking that someone else might get there first. No, here Time is a friend that lavishes her attention on you. 'Here I am,' she says, 'take me, discover my secrets, savour me.'

 She offers another face of humanity, poor and dependent on solidarity, yet never looking back over her shoulder in fear. She throws her chest out to the ocean. She is alive.

■

Lost in time, I am dancing with one of the younger singers. His name is Harold, the same name as my diplomat grandfather in pre-revolutionary Cuba. Harold is very friendly and introduces me to the entire band. They are rehearsing for their European tour. They ask me to contribute to the cost of more rum, to 'keep them going'. Tourists have warned me of Cuban 'scroungers'. 'They assume you are a millionaire just because you are foreign,' they say. 'They don't realize that we have to work hard for our money. We don't slave away all year to spend it on them.' Yet they don't see that this island's uniqueness is also worked hard for. It doesn't grow on trees. The feeling, the music, the culture are all fruits of a process that also suffers its own winter. And surely not just so that it can be picked over by vibes vultures hustling for humanity.

Harold sings salsa, Cuba's biggest-selling export commodity, but his passion is hip-hop. He sings in this band for money, but rap is the future, 'the expression of the new Cuban generation'. He wants to be a world-famous rapper, if Fidel allows.

The next day Harold calls round the house and asks me if I want to come to the beach with him where his first video is to be shot. We scoot around town, shouting up at windows in search of a camera crew, and find the friend with a camera and a turbo-charged bicycle, which packs up on the outskirts of Havana. After returning to pick up the other scooter (Lázaro is not home), we finally get on the road to Baracoa, where the police stop us. That costs us another hour. By the time we arrive, there is hardly any light to film by. Nobody seems to be concerned that the day's objective has evaporated in the complex process of meeting it. The journey seems to be the focus, not the goal.

Bare-chested and bursting out of a pair of Cuban-flag trunks, Harold begins his hip-hop dance on the sand, mouthing the words to the tune from a portable stereo. In the background little blond Russian kids run around. 'They come from Chernobyl,' the cameraman tells me, 'to get cured of leukaemia.' They are happy and tanned, and I imagine them pale, thin and pasty back in Russia. I am told to sit in front of Harold with the bottle of Havana Club and the tourist scooter – the token bling bling. 'What am I supposed to do?' I ask the cameraman. 'You just sit here, doing your own thing.'

Harold's rap is called 'All For One And One For All' and is about three Cuban Musketeers and the spirit of Cuban solidarity: 'I choose Cuba, as it is, with all its faults,' he raps. '*Yo me quedo con todas esas cosas.*' Harold is always paying homage to his culture in his songs, always defending his *manera de ser.* His chest swells with patriotism. It's not jingoism but something he feels inside, an almost spiritual belief. He reminds me of that great Cuban heavyweight Teófilo Stevenson who once said, 'What do I need five million dollars for when I have the love of eleven million Cubans?' to explain why he had declined a lucrative offer to fight Muhammad Ali. I envy it.

Perhaps this cultural self-sufficiency is the fallout of being America's enemy: in their self-defence and solitude, the

 Cubans have built an identity. I wonder why Lázaro is not comforted by this cultural pride, torturing himself with impossible aspirations of American material glory, like the Venezuelans.

The cameraman tries to vocalize a bass, and I guess I am the rapper's ho', picnicking in the Caribbean sunset with the little Russians – more Madness surrealism than Puff Daddy glam. At the end of the day everyone is delighted with the rehearsal.

■

When I get back to the González home, Lázaro is in a mood with me. I ask Maria what the matter is and she tells me she doesn't know but to take no notice of him. I confront him and he snaps that I took his scooter away from him. He goes on about my keeping bad company and how I shouldn't trust any Cuban, that all they want to do is rip me off. He is obviously referring to my new 'black' company. He resents the Afro-Cubans and their culture – music, dance, sport – that earns Cuba fame and foreign currency, the source of Cuban pride, the stuff of Harold's optimism.

The other members of the family give me the warmth and generosity of before. 'This is *my* house,' says Maria, when I suggest that maybe I should move. '*I* decide who stays in my house. You are not going anywhere.' So Lázaro and I live like enemies for the next few days, and I begin to feel bad. This isle of timelessness is also an isle of wasted talent, a swamp of impotence, whose reeds strangle the life within. Even Harold, who has a little more hope – what chances does he have of fulfilling his dreams? Hope is the fine thread that divides them, but still nothing happens. They just wait.

From the bedroom I watch Lázaro pour buckets of water down the toilet to get rid of three days' shit.

■

I go to Harold's uncle's, a record producer who has agreed to let me hire his computer, to get these wretched reports done. His name is Teo, a daddy cool dressed in white from cap to shoes, his teeth beaming out of his violet face. His music collection goes from Monk (after whom he is named) to Tchaikovsky. His current choice, however, is Michael Bolton for the artful ticks, licks and slurps of his production technology.

I have sketched out most of the Venezuela report on a notepad. Perhaps my choice of inconvenience living was a last desperate attempt to convince myself that this is 'just a job', an adventure. In the end it does not matter where I work from, Miami, Cuba, a rowing boat in the middle of the Atlantic. No amount of space between myself and an office, no amount of rustic illusion, can change my place in the corporate strategy. Every bullet point is evidence.

From my notebook, drastically thinning thanks to its auxiliary purpose as bog roll in the González household, I manage to make out some random words. The nightmare of jealousy, betrayal, revenge… desperate for sincerity, real communication. THE LIE. Class tension, hate, hate. Want identity, self-definition. Crave solidarity. Obsessions: Boys – must show nothing can hurt you. Girls – physical perfection.

It feels strange listing Venezuela's fragilities, the distrust, the individualism, the *arribismo,* the dog-eat-dog competition, the preoccupation with defeating your rival before he or she defeats you. Here in Cuba, while the lack of opportunity keeps the Lázaros frustrated, the Harolds have at least the strength of their culture, the identity that Venezuelans crave. There are no billboards of whiter people with perfect teeth gleaming, 'Hey, you're worth it!' There are no expectations of perfection, of being whiter, stronger, no billboards rubbing salt into the wound of poverty.

And, though life is not without its complexities, I cannot find the insecurities, the neuroses, the paranoias that torture youth everywhere else. They love without demands, without the tireless needs of 'self'. When they want something they say it, and they give without fear. There are no games. Everything seems so much simpler. Maybe this private freedom compensates for public censorship and restriction.

I sit punching nine hundred Venezuelan vulnerabilities into the Levi's archive, so that Levi's can comfort anxieties with blue jean empathy.

Now I am working at Harold's uncle's house, I am spending more time in the centre where a solitary woman is a favourite target; perhaps she is looking for lurve, Cuban style. One day, when I am drinking an early evening Mojito, I am saved by three women, two Italians and an English girl, Ruth, who are here for their seventh time. They've got the Cuban bug badly.

They invite me to go to a concert with them in the evening, given by Los Van-Van, Cuba's most famous salsa orchestra. I remember when they came to Miami, all the old *anti-Castristas* in combat gear came out to demonstrate, but the new generation just wanted to dance and reclaim their roots.

Before the concert, the girls invite me to the flat they've rented just a block away from the Malecón. There are ten young men sitting in the living room and two more boys in the kitchen cooking dinner. With a teenage entourage like this they must think they are the female Rolling Stones. No wonder they keep coming back.

I feel very self-conscious. Is this why they have brought me here, to set me up with one of the *jineteros*? What do they think I am after? Do I look rich and lacking in love?

I tentatively begin talking to one of them, the one with floppy dreads hanging in his face so that I cannot see his eyes. He is quick to tell me he has already been to Europe and does not need to go again. Then he adds that he doesn't like English women anyway. 'Too difficult, too much character; they are always contradicting you.'

He tells me his trip to Europe was paid for by the Cuban government, as a reward for being an exemplary leader of the Communist Youth, which surprises me for he does not look the political type. 'I'm not,' he says, angrily. 'Fidel is an arsehole. I only pretended so that I could go abroad. That is the only way you can get anything in this country.'

Behind the façade of the loyal activist, upholder of the cause, his hatred for the system was growing all the time, and now he has jumped ship to become Fidel's nightmare: the hustler, the saboteur. We also have to toe the line to get on in the capitalist system, I tell him. Corporations don't like dissenters; they call them snobs, cynics, weirdos, selfish, not 'one of us'. They encourage individual desires (because I'm worth it!) to sell us their products, but in the office they'd rather people share the same values, be 'part of the team'. Like Fidel's internal propaganda, corporate internal marketing systems brainwash wavering employees with as much determination as their external marketing campaigns target consumers.

There are bad vibes flowing in the apartment, a psychological standoff between desperation and pride. I am relieved when it is time to leave for the concert. On the way out there is some muttered discussion among the girls concerning money. They tell me we will at some point have to announce that we can only pay for one boy each. Ruth decides to break this news in the car. Two of the boys get offended and say that they have their own money and don't need anyone to pay for them. They tell us to stop the car so they can go and get their money. They never return.

Our tickets cost twenty dollars each, although they are also selling in pesos to Cubans, at the equivalent of ten cents. Once inside, I realize that the dollar tickets are VIP, an area inhabited almost totally by tourists and their Cuban sidekicks, and that the real party is going on down below. 'Why the hell are we up here?' I ask.

'It's dangerous down there,' one of the boys says. I think he likes the hierarchy – for a day at least.

I look down: people are smiling, excited, dancing already. The concert is incredible. This is Cuba at its best: European orchestral structure energized with African rhythm and without the frowning concentration. Here the flutes perch on lips like twittering birds, violins and double basses flow with the players' bodies as if extensions of them.

I find a good partner to dance with who tells me that I smell much better than Russian women – the only other blondes he knows who dance like the Cubans. 'Poooof,' he says, scrunching his face and waving his hand over his nose at the memory. 'Sour milk and onions.'

The next day after work I pop in to see the girls. They are alone this time and the Italians are gathered around Ruth, who is in a state because she has just seen her Cuban boy with a German woman. When she confronted her lover with it he confessed that although it was her he really loved, the German was already doing the paperwork to get him out of Cuba. He said he was sorry but blamed her for not having done enough for him, which made him doubt her commitment to him.

Ruth is devastated, having been convinced that they would live happily ever after in Skegness. Now her dream of an exotic youthful injection into suburban middle-aged ennui is disappearing. I ask her what she likes about him, given the fact that he's hardly Don Juan and has the energy of a snail. She replies that he makes her feel like a woman. 'Yeah, intimacy is their speciality,' I say.

But Ruth is determined to wrest Roberto from this wicked German adversary and have him all to herself. He's got her hooked. The Cuban emotional clarity is to the rich world's hearts what the rich world's brand manipulation is to the poor world's pockets. Fidel should put up a sign. Beware: highly intoxicating substances at loose.

Only Ruth's absurd romantic aspirations stop her being a sex tourist. How can they believe in love, when there is so much inequality? Maybe their respective inadequacies, one emotional, one material, complement each other.

■

'You *gringas* are easy prey,' laughs Teo, when I tell him about the day's traumas with the girls, 'because you are emotionally obvious. You lose your dignity in the challenge.'

Yes, I suppose our way is to think nature exists to be defied, conquered, not absorbed or shared. And yet this is to live on life's surface. So we become obvious. The fierce independence that we think makes us strong can be cracked like a shell.

I go round to tell the girls that I am leaving Havana for Santiago, right on the other end of the island. We spend the evening on the Malecón with a bottle of rum, watching the sunset and the children jump into the water. Lovers, families, friends gather to bask in the last light of the day and sigh, their problems setting with the sun on still waters.

Later we go to the centre to see if we can find a jam session, but everything is fast becoming exclusive to tourists. The boys complain that they are being excluded from their own culture. They send me in to one to see if it is worth mustering up the dollars. The room is virtually empty but for the band and five portly middle-aged Italian men, each with a Lolita bouncing in his arms as they sing and laugh on the dance floor.

Fidel's revolution may have transformed what had become

known as 'the whorehouse of the Caribbean' under the military regime of Fulgencio Batista. But while Fidel's billboards still read: '22,000,000 children sleep in parks, and none of them is Cuban!', all the revolution's advances in education and health now lie prostrate before economic desperation.

■

I have been driving for six hours, the map beside me glaring up as it erodes my hope of shooting to Santiago and back in a matter of days.

As the light fades, I decide to turn off at Santa Clara, about halfway along the island, and head for Trinidad, a cobbled colonial town on the south side of the island. Both the road and visibility are bad and I still have thirty miles to go. Having no guidebook, I stop to give a girl a lift and enquire about a place to stay for the night. She tells me there is a big hotel up in the *sierra*.

I drop the girl off at a little village and she tells me to follow the road until I get to a big sanatorium. Up I wind, deep into the forest. Another half an hour and no sign of life. Does this place exist? Have I missed it? Then, just as I am getting desperate, something concrete, white and cruise-ship size peers out over the treetops. It looks eerily Stalinist, a rehab centre for lapsed communists perhaps.

I imagine unshaven loonies, their hair static from years of electric treatments, emerging from the foliage in blood-splattered hospital gowns, with their drip machines. There are several fenced-off tarmacked areas. Outside one stands a man in a boiler suit. His bemused eyes peer into my car window. I ask him where the reception is and he points to the path that leads to the other side of the building.

The entrance boasts an oval driveway and a white veranda with pillars, like Miami's Delano Hotel, preserved rather than restored. I expect a butler in white tie to appear, but the marble foyer is empty and my call echoes back to me. The only live thing I see is a very big fluffy black thing, the size of a flattened tennis ball, moving across the polished marble. It stops and is about to scuttle away when a shadow falls over it, followed by a big polished boot, slowly, very slowly lowering itself. Crunch.

'Tarantula,' says a deep voice. The man in a bellboy's uniform asks me what I want. I ask him if the place has rooms. Yes, he booms, but not for you. Not even one night? I plead, putting on my most helpless voice. No, he says, you cannot stay here. This is not a normal hotel, it is a special hotel. But as he sees I am on the verge of tears, the man helps me to park the car and leads me back down the driveway to a building of dirty pink cement where an old woman gives me a room. I do not ask any questions. I am just grateful that my liver hasn't been cut out.

I wake up to squawks, screeches, purrs and coos. The place looks friendlier by day. Youngsters, oldies, families walk about, all of them Cubans, no hustlers. In fact, no one takes any notice of me at all. Here it is the Cubans who are on holiday, having a break from the trauma of tourists, and here I am invading again, even when I don't mean to. It is my accidental curse.

I still do not know what the difference is between the pink dump and the mysterious palace up above. I don't bother asking at reception because the official tourist answer in Cuba is rarely enlightening. As I have already been told that I cannot stay another night here, I ask if someone would take me for a walk through the forest before I leave. They call a boy, the official jungle guide. We set off alone because I am not allowed to join any of the Cuban groups in case I give them my capitalist disease.

We go on a long walk, through breathtaking waterfalls, lagoons and caves. I imagine the asthmatic Argentine wheezing through the jungle forty years ago, leading a revolutionary brigade who in the end had to carry him when breathlessness clung to his throat. Yes, Che, too, was a foreign interferer, poking his nose in where it didn't belong. But surely what matters is who you interfere on behalf of the powerful or the powerless, the bully or the bullied. As Che said himself during battle, 'No country until now has denounced the American interference in Cuban affairs, nor has a single daily newspaper accused the Yankees of helping Batista massacre his people. But many are concerned about me (being) the meddling foreigner.'

■

My guide, Yedi, is unlike anyone I have met in Havana. He does not offer me marriage, nor is he on the defensive because he thinks I might be expecting him to. He is not a little Fidel who wants to tell me the way things should be. He is curious, hungry for knowledge. He wants to know where I come from, to exchange ideas, to piece together a better understanding of his surroundings in relation to the world outside. Above all, he does not have the hungry eyes of a predator, wanting to take you dancing to let the feeling flow through your bones and weaken your resolve. In fact, he hates salsa.

'How can you dislike this wonderful gift your country has given the world?' I ask and think of Linzaro. 'Is it because it is black people's music?'

'No,' he says laughing, 'not because of that.'

'Then why?'

Yedi pauses for a moment. 'I would like to speak my mind to you,' he says. 'But you know it is dangerous. I work for the government. I could lose my job.' I assure him I will not rag on him and insist: so why is it you don't like salsa?

'Have you ever read Karl Marx?' he asks.

'Sort of.'

'You know what he refers to as the opium of the masses?'

'Religion... I suppose as the distraction of downtrodden people from their condition.'

'Well, that is what salsa is here. It is the only form of expression permitted here because it makes life bearable. Salsa, *santería* and sex are our distractions, they placate our frustrations. All the tourists come here, and they love the music and learn to jigaboo, and rub themselves up against another body and feel all sexy. It is their liberation. And it is our oppression.'

'Since we are being frank,' I say, 'what is that Soviet-looking building?'

It seems to me such a weird cultural combination. Fidel has kept African roots so alive, proudly and uncompromisingly, and yet on top of it lies this Russo-Germanic model of discipline, so antithetical to the natural expression of his people.

'The sanatorium? Well, that's what it is. A de-stress camp. For people who have problems of stress, the state invites them to come here and stay for a few weeks.'

'That's funny, since it is probably the state that causes the stress,' I reply. But it's no different in my world, where pharmaceutical corporations lobby doctors to dish out Prozac to those too sensitive to stomach corporate-controlled life.

'Yes…' Yedi says. 'People are breaking here. There is too much pressure. The system is pushing people too far. They cannot cope. We cannot breathe.'

Back home people are crushed by the pressure to produce results; here they get depressed because they cannot produce anything. In Cuba, nobody is allowed to voice a different opinion, but neither is our media free to be truly independent. It's tied to whichever conglomerate owns it, or advertises in it. What happens to the people who cannot conform? In Cuba, they don't have ghettos that feed them crack; they have only the shark-infested ocean to jump into in the hope that beyond the horizon lies freedom. 'Everybody has lost a loved one because they can't stand it any more,' says Yedi.

When we return there is an unspoken understanding that our encounter has not run its course. There is more to be said. Yedi happens to be starting a short break from work and, since I am getting chucked out of the pink building, he invites me to visit his home near Santa Clara, Cuba's fourth biggest city, in the middle of the island, where Che marched in victorious as the dictator Batista fled Havana like a coward. The only condition is that I don't open my mouth and lose him his job. I am sworn to secrecy. Maybe, since Cuba is not on Levi's hit list, for once I can keep my promise.

Yedi holds his head in the crash position as we drive down the steep winding road and screams like a woman when we lose control and almost leap over the side.

At the bottom, *guajiros* on horseback and go-carts made of ironing boards pass by, as does a truck carrying a huge birthday cake on its rear. The bearded face appears whenever possible over the pledge '*Seremos como El Che*'. He is Fidel's Coca-Cola. Yedi's house is a large windowless straw-roofed shed. Yedi's mother is very skinny and never stops moving, working in her open kitchen in the garden surrounded by mango and coconut trees while her husband wanders around silently. He is in mourning because his brother, a chemist who left Cuba for a conference in Europe, has just written saying that he has appealed for asylum and won't be coming back.

They show me my room in the shed. On top of the bed a swan made out of a towel is floating, and pink flowers have been scattered over the pristine white sheets. For dinner, they insist on sacrificing a pig, which is very embarrassing as they have been fattening it for a year waiting for a special occasion, and I am not sure I want something killed on my behalf. I get very drunk on rum to bear the sight of the pig's throat being slit. Yedi's mother doesn't drink; she says alcohol reacts badly with the pills she must take. 'My nerves,' she explains, 'my nerves.'

I wake up to the sound of a cockerel. I find myself drenched in the vapours of chicken fat. Yedi's mum is preparing the day's food at six in the morning and there is only a thin curtain dividing me and the kitchen.

The feeling is different here; there is no pressure, no expectations. I offer Yedi's mum payment for the room, she accepts and that is that. On top of everything else I enjoy Yedi's company. We go for walks, we talk about Russian literature, about our cultures, and the people and ideas that move us. He is not hustling for something, nor does he vent his frustration. He is poor, but he has patience and hope. One day he will travel the world, but until then he can do nothing else but enjoy the natural blessings of Cuba.

It is sad he cannot come to visit me in London. But would he be any more able to visit me if he were Peruvian or Colombian? The only difference for Cubans is that it is their own government that restricts them; for the others, it is our immigration policies that keep them out.

In the end I never get to Santiago, or Trinidad. The goal of my journey has been absorbed by the process, Cuban-style. As I head back to Havana I sense my stay in Cuba is ending, even though I have totally lost track of how long I have been here. I know that my report-writing time must be about up. I have heard nothing from Levi's, but they must be expecting me in Colombia very soon. I will send my report to San Francisco first thing when I arrive there.

I sometimes wonder why I have never been invited to San Francisco. Perhaps they know deep down that I am not 'one of them' and want to keep me at arm's length so that I do not contaminate the team spirit. Or they think that the spell of their power, the Atahualpa factor, is enough to ensure loyalty.

But I wonder why they *did* choose me to do this job. Maybe

 they were intrigued by the 'other' and wanted to bring me in from the cold, like Carlos Cisneros, or perhaps they thought my waywardness had its uses. They thought I was open and authentic enough 'to seduce the groups most difficult and averse to giving over information', as Levi's puts it. Someone tinged with corporate office life would never be convincing; the kids would smell it a mile off. Yet they needed someone who was fundamentally on their side, who understood what they meant by 'development'. Did my contradictions make me the perfect candidate?

If I really think about it, part of me, the English part, is bred for this. Oxford, after all, was always the breeding ground for imperialist mercenaries. We are specialists in objective analysis, in the true British tradition of self-interest. It is no coincidence we are famous for our spies. We are natural investigators; we never get involved. Everything happens around us, never to us. White-gloved pirates; the aura of civility, naivety and integrity being the perfect disguise. What happens if you do get involved, 'go native', as Reuters feared my dad had? What happens if you do take sides? Perhaps my father found his side too late; he already had responsibilities, his framework was set. But part of me already belongs here. I cannot be detached. And I am still free to choose my destiny.

Whatever the reason for me landing the Levi's job, the timing for them was good – before the bud of reflection flowered, before confusion blossomed, before I swung to the other side. Or maybe not. Is it not a spy's nature to betray?

8

PAIN AND CONSOLATION

'Love demands, but real love surrenders.'

LILIANA, 19, MEDELLIN

Glittery threads balance on silicone breasts, stiletto heels push buttocks up to pert perfection, and low-cut elastic jeans (mostly white) streamline the Amazon curves. Wow. I gaze in wonder at the Latin beauty around me. Somehow their scanty glad rags don't look shoddy and cheap like your equivalent Top Shop slapper gear does on white English skin under the orange glare of West End street lamps. White stretchy cotton and perfectly drawn electric blue eyeshadow glares brilliantly against soft coffee skin. Their hair is luscious and full and golden teardrops fall into their breasts.

We loiter on the edge of the discotheque car park; our dual

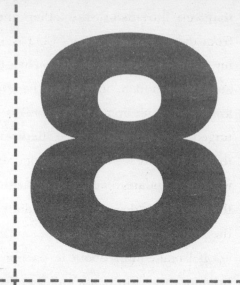

 mission to look ravishing and note which men get out of the nicest cars.

I was briefed in a harsh-lit living room above a *licorero*, where I too had got the Colombian beauty treatment. Naomi, Isabel and Liliana plucked my eyebrows and packed my eyelids down with a gram of gold eyeshadow. Then they made me try on some trousers that were so tight my one-time experience with hair-removing wax and the ensuing fortnight rash came back in a flash. I protested on the grounds of the delicacy of English skin, its allergy to leg-long plasters, but they paid no heed. Time ran too thin for either liposuction or a breast implant so I was limited to the lifting effect of the finest Colombian brassiere and curve-defining G-string. Then we practised for the car park sequence:

1. Parade up and down, with upright posture, tossing back head (with hair flick).
2. Laugh and seem absorbed in girly giggles.
3. Pucker lips.
4. Subtly dart eyes to make necessary observations and attract desired attention.
5. Give demure look should attention be thrown your way.
6. On eye contact, turn round swiftly to friends (hair flick, chest out, giggle).

Now in live performance, this intricate weaving of body languages is beyond my coordination, and I watch the choreography of my nineteen-year-old experts. Their art is rewarded with screams, whistles and gunshots in the air from Mercedes and BMWs speeding past at a hundred and twenty.

Those are the guys we want: Medellín's wannabe power players. Flaunters of the Escobarian-style omnipotence, they are the legacy of the late drug-lord who scrambled to his death over the roof of his own mansion, chased by US-trained anti-drugs squads. His 'reign of terror' earned him a place in Forbes 100, a seat in Congress and enough wealth to offer settling the national debt. A reign of terror maybe, but my girls loved him. He gave their family jobs, and they believe he is still alive, drinking Mojitos in Miami with Perón and Che. With him disappeared the jobs of the narco-economy, leaving only the taste for glamour and the alluring idea that if you have money, you can break the rules.

The girls hurl coquettish abuse after the Merc. It answers by backing up with a screech.

'Love is easy, but not everyone has a car like that.' Isabel smiles, taking a look in her pocket mirror to check all is in order.

'Yeah, life may end tomorrow, you gotta enjoy every minute you're still alive,' Liliana confirms. 'And get someone to pay for the clothes, the beauty parlour and the operations...' Noticing my alarm, she stops, then adds reassuringly, 'Don't think I want to add anything, uh-oh, I just want to take things off, do me a lipo...' She pats her plump thighs.

'But we need someone to PAY!!!' they shout in unison, giggling.

The men come strutting across the car park, their chests bursting with puissance. The girls are giggling. I consider tottering off into the car park maze but fear I'll trip over my ridiculous heels if I make a sharp move. I try not to look at one of the men, short and robust, who wants to catch my eye. He wears a pair of pleated black trousers, black cowboy boots, a chunky Rolex and a yellow Polo Ralph Lauren shirt, the sleeves rolled up to his elbows.

He tells me he used to live in London and begins searching his wallet for evidence. I assure him this isn't necessary but already he is reciting the exact location of all the phone boxes in Soho. He was in the flyer business.

That shirt. It's blinding me. Together with the fluorescent Florida orange variation, Ralph Lauren's luminous sunflower line seems to constitute the Medellín 'power look'. Is the atomic brilliance some sort of gang trademark? A power symbol? A choice favoured by the great legend himself?

I have the urge to tell him he looks like a walking light bulb and, being English and partial to an insult when nerves take over, I do. He pauses, then lets out the most bizarre cackle, which ends in a paralysed smile. Drawing his face to my ear, he whispers, 'Watch the things you say,' and lifts his shirt to show me a pistol tucked in his trousers. Seeing my alarm, he chuckles again and places his hand on my arm affectionately. 'This is a dangerous town. You don't want to be offending people around here.'

Inside Templo Antonia, Latin America's largest discotheque, three thousand gold-bangled arms cling to chequered chests. Together they swing to the romantically mournful words of the *vallenatos,* the music adopted by the gunmen and gangsters of the cartel era and subsequently popular among Medellín's new generation (salsa is dismissed as music for *negros cochinos*). With eyes shut, they savour each other's flesh as if it were the last they will ever touch, as if they must make this moment eternal. It is a rave of consolation, producing an emotional intensity that no drug could manufacture.

I stay on the sidelines, because if I enter the crowd I will get lost and have to cling to a chequered shirt for safety. But the explosion of emotion overwhelms me, caressing me with its intoxicating comfort. It is more than romance they cling for, it is loss, absence: a mother, victim of her husband's unleashed jealousy; a boyfriend, unlucky in his game of Russian roulette; a neighbour who was shot in a garden-fence dispute that flared up a little too much; a cousin accused by paramilitaries of being an insurgent. The underlying sorrow penetrates my bones, making my skin frisky. Suddenly the wave that has run over me turns from pleasure to panic. I feel sick.

When dawn arrives the girls want to go off with the atomic shirt brigade, but my sensible side persuades them to get a taxi and go to Isabel's house. The taxi driver gives us a free ride because of a gunshot we heard while coming over the bridge – he says you must never let a murder steal a moment from humanity.

■

They call Medellín the City of Eternal Spring. All year the sun shines, cooled by a light breeze that gently rocks the flower baskets hanging from street lamps like a summer fête in the English countryside. Winding through the pine-carpeted hills from the airport towards the city, with its myths and legends, was like twisting through the intestines of a beast. Every time I return south I sink down further into new corners and pockets, the north I once inhabited a blip on the far corner of my memory. Here, deprived of Anglo oxygen, my rational resolve has weakened; another reality confuses. Can I really ever go back north, put my blinkers on, resign myself to a life in an office and toe the line, like my father did? What would I do if I stayed? Even here I would have to choose which reality I wanted: ex-pat luxury or the majority world with its constant struggle for justice. There is no in-between.

In the car, Clarita, my Levi's chaperone, tells me that this region, Antioquia, of which Medellín is the capital, is the Switzerland of Colombia. They called Costa Rica the same, for its relative order in war-torn Central America. Others called it the traitor.

'A lot of Germans here, you know,' she said. 'That is why we are so disciplined and organized. That is why we are the country's industrial capital and the envy of Colombia. Everybody wants to come here. And you'll see how clean it is. Because that is what *we* are like.'

Yes, I wouldn't expect Levi's to plant itself in Colombia's shambolic majority world. For Levi's must also be perceived as the envy of Colombia. Levi's latest addition to the Latin America licensee club is run by the Rodríguez family, whose textiles plant has been producing jeans for Levi's for years. Only now are the conditions right to market jeans themselves in Colombia. I have been commissioned to do three reports, one on each major city where they are going to launch the brand.

Clarita had booked me into the Medellín Country Club, a luxurious labyrinth of palm-tree gardens, tennis courts, swimming pool and golf course, which had once dared to refuse entry to Escobar himself, being of a lower social order. So he built his own.

The next day I went to the office to meet tall, slim Juan David Rodríguez, with beautiful eyes and soft smiling voice. He's very nice. They call him Don Juan. I sat under his spell until his two younger sisters (the marketing department) marched in and snapped me out of it.

They invited me to an audition they were holding for the Levi's catwalk launch. Drama students from the Antioquia University filed in to perform slithery movements on the floor and other drama-school things like pushing the air with their hands while the sisters sat painting their nails demanding a 'different effect', without making any suggestions as to what this might be. There was something of the Cinderella siblings about them. I pretended I was colouring my map.

Then they took me to lunch and showed me a comic strip from their advertising agency named, 'The Levi's Kid'. Between 7.05 a.m., when he wakes up and enters his day with its bus-stop ads, billboards, bus posters, radio, TV, magazines, logos, tags on people's clothes and product placements, and 11.30 p.m. when he sleeps, it is possible, the cartoon claims, that the sixty-seven Levi's messages will have subliminally penetrated their Medellín target teen. That's excluding Friday nightlife sponsorship. Thus I am presented with Levi's Colombian goal.

The Rodríguez family are taking a big risk with this venture in a country caught up in civil war. Don Juan says at least the days of Escobar are over.

'It was a living nightmare before. Nobody could go about their business without a visit from Escobar's thugs. They had our hands tied,' he told me. 'You couldn't do anything without negotiating it with the Cartel. Everything you did put you in danger if it happened to annoy the Cartel. At least now we can get some business done.'

Today's violence mostly affects the countryside, where villagers are caught up in the government's war against the Armed Revolutionary Forces of Colombia (FARC) and other insurgent groups. Peasant leaders, trade unionists and human-rights workers are routinely murdered by paramilitary groups, who accuse them of collaborating with the FARC.

In Antioquia, Juan David tells me, the hard-line governor Álvaro Uribe Vélez restored order to the region before he left office in 1997. He set up cooperation communities called *Convivir* in which peasants who collaborated with the army against FARC insurgents received protection and many other benefits. Uribe, Juan David says, made Antioquia safe for foreign investors again. Perhaps he means that while Escobar's control had been total, now in normal civil war the propertied can at least count on one side: the army, or the paramilitaries, which were formed to protect them when the army failed. The investor's brochure sitting on his desk boasts that Colombia is

'South America's longest-lasting democracy, in a continent rife with dictatorship'.

Don Juan's main concern is the counterfeit business, because, like Perú, Colombia has a strong textiles tradition. Now that Levi's is launching the brand officially in Colombia, it wants a more concerted clampdown, through raids on illicit factories and warehouses.

I walked round the offices and found at the back a balcony that overlooked the Rodríguez production plant. On the other side of the glass stretched the immense floor. Blue-overalled men, swamped by stacks of denim, zigzagged round units of young women hunched over sewing machines. The industry was impressive, everyone involved in their chore, nobody chatting. I watched their repetitive, robotic movements. Nine hours every day spent in this mindless alienating function and grateful for the job to boot. But this is order. The workforce under control. Everybody knows their place. Nationwide fifteen hundred trade unionists have been assassinated in the last decade, the worst record in the world, their murderers almost never brought to justice. To think of work conditions, of wage negotiation, makes you a terrorist suspect in the eyes of paramilitaries. Maybe people still silently dream those things. But this is the reality: 51 cents an hour to hunch over a machine (another 'democractic' attraction for investors).

I felt the urge to talk to them, hear their story. What would I have said to them? 'Oh, is this how you make a pair of jeans?' Like royalty, who might even shake a working hand without gloves. They'd never tell me how they felt. They might think they'd lose their job if they did. And what would the Rodríguez family think if I started asking questions? No, now is not the time to ruffle feathers.

■

The morning after Templo Antonia I wake up early in Isabel's house. The girls are still asleep in the big double bed we shared under a large wooden cross. Isabel's mother has gone to see her sister in the little town they come from, a hundred miles outside Medellín in the Antioquia province. Her brother, Raúl, has stayed to protect us and sleeps in the other room.

The Castillos migrated here during the height of the narco-economy, when construction enterprises, from luxury apartment blocks to shopping malls, drew people from all over the country. Raúl got a small mechanics business going, mending and recycling things for cartel leaders: the Mr Fixit of the Mr Fixits. Since the cartel got busted he's been at a loose end. A job here, a job there, but nothing stable. Drugs money, he says, used to give him employment; now it funds a war, and has created armies of monsters.

'When the cartel was in control there were lots of dollars around, so there were lots of jobs,' he told me. 'People bought more things, there were always things to fix. There were always clients.'

He has this picture of himself with Pablo Escobar in the neighbourhood, which he likes to bring out. 'He did more for us than any politician or businessman,' he says. 'He built the school, the sports stadium, the hospital and a zoo with the most exotic selection of animals in the world. Yeah, he was violent. You think the big industrialists, the cattle ranchers, the politicians, the estate owners aren't the same? You think that in the US nobody killed to get to the top? They *still* kill to stay at the top, only they don't do it in their own backyard any more – they come and kill here in Latin America, all over the world. We are their backyard.'

In the early 1970s, the poor had a real chance to be incorporated into Colombia's political and economic life. In the footsteps of Jorge Eliécer Gaitán, the 1930s Liberal leader who first criticized the oligarchy and was assassinated as a consequence, the government of President Carlos Restrepo of the late 1960s mobilized thousands of peasants to halt the expansion of cattle ranchers and commercial farmers. Restrepo had opposed the World Bank's Operation 'Colombia' (another proposed Latin surgery), which sought to intensify agriculture and force peasants to migrate to urban employment. He wanted to keep the peasants on the land, increase their means of production and build the country's infrastructure.

In 1971, fifteen thousand families occupied estates and retrieved land. Raúl tells me his father was one of the leaders who organized semi-cooperatives, education programmes to increase literacy and technical capacity. They demanded a more responsible rural government, and indigenous communities met to create their first manifesto in defence of their land and culture. The US, who were not about to let another Cuba happen, funded the first Latin American counter-insurgency school in Colombia to help the rich repress peasant mobilization.

Meanwhile, the two-party political elite swamped rural towns with party bosses. By 1974 they had squashed all political alternatives, Restrepo's land reform was replaced with subsidies to commercial farmers, and the neo-liberal plan was put into action. Economic marginalization forced many small peasants into marijuana farming to avoid starvation, political exclusion led intellectuals to seek alternatives outside the bipartisan state, and repression radicalized the peasant movement. By the late 1970s the FARC was perceived as the only force to offer protection to peasants from militia-backed ranchers, and in some areas it became a virtual rural civil guard. FARC recruitment exploded from nine fronts in 1979 to twenty-seven in 1983.

As I travel from one country to another, the pieces of history seem to fall into place. I think of the early 1970s I was born into, when there was a vision of a different future. It was not just in Argentina where people thought change was really possible. So many saw the chance for a continent more equal, stronger, independent, self-sufficient. Most countries had leaders who defied US hegemony and pursued policies to defend national interests and, where not, popular movements were growing so strong that their governments couldn't ignore them. Velasco Alvarado in Perú, Torrijos in Panamá, Allende in Chile, J.J. Torres in Bolivia, Rodríguez Lara in Ecuador. In Venezuela, new wealth came with new visions. In Colombia the peasant movement was stronger than ever before, pressuring its government for representation and reform. Fate hinged on those years, and looked like edging towards a brighter future.

I walk out onto the streets of the *barrio*, alive with Sunday bustle: children dipping in and out of alleys between cramped houses, running round the legs of old men and pull-out domino tables, climbing onto the flat roofs to fly their kites among television aerials. Clarita was right, everything is very orderly (although the residents don't look German, only *mestizo*), but on closer inspection one can see how the shabbiness is quickly eroding the pride and hope with which every brick had been laid. Nostalgia hangs in the air. Escobar was the hope they had been reduced to when every other legitimate route to representation had been thwarted.

So here I am, thirty years later, searching for the hopes and dreams of the time into which I was born. And yet, in my labyrinth of solitude, of present voices and ghosts of the past, I am the product of their defeat. This job that I threw myself into with blind gratitude, the best job in the world, is part of something bigger that I am helping shape and express but have no power over. I thought I was the one who was winning, with a job that gave me the freedom to travel the world, free of corporate shackles. But I realize it is not the invisible hand of market forces that brought me here but an iron fist that has squashed real progress. It has slowly come to control everything; it has the power to shape destinies and freedoms, to choose winners and losers.

I find Raúl sitting on the pavement at one of the bars, with his friends, one of them a policeman who hangs out at the house. He points to a group of youths, loitering on the other corner like a solid block. Even from here, I can feel the weight of their thickset bodies, their beady eyes watching. *Sicarios*, Raúl says, assassins, the only ones still in employment: the paramilitaries hire them to keep the neighbourhood in order, collect their taxes, kill anyone who doesn't toe the line.

Since Uribe's governorship, Raúl's policeman friend says, the paramilitaries have been slowly creeping into Medellín's neighbourhoods. The army and paramilitaries began to mount a special vendetta against the FARC, who killed his father, a cattle rancher who allegedly allowed paramilitaries to operate from his ranch. Uribe's close personal links with the paramilitaries, the policeman says, enabled the army and paramilitaries to mount joint operations to get the FARC out of the *barrios* and leave the paramilitaries in control, and the police are not doing anything.

Why is he telling me this? I think.

'I am ashamed of what is happening. I am scared. I just have to shut up, but I can see what's going on here.'

'How do you know who is a paramilitary? Do they wear uniforms?' I ask.

'We know who they are. They are our new mafia. But they are worse than Escobar. Escobar loved the poor, but the paramilitaries have always worked for the rich. They say assassinations have gone down. I can show you where the *fosas comunes* are; I can show you where they put the bodies of the disappeared. The disappeared don't count as dead, you see.'

Is this the order that is making Medellín so attractive for investment?

■

The girls have to go to church so I get the tube back to the hotel. Clarita was right about the litterless tube – not so much as a crumpled chewing-gum wrapper – but more alarming is the official Medellín politeness, the hands-behind-back kind one only sees between a ball boy and royalty. Almost anxiety-ridden in their reverence. The receptionist at the hotel, for example, bombards me with niceties with an urgency as if terrified that I might be offended by her silence and report her. Then I'll step into the street and '*gringa* slut' will shoot out from some car.

Hotel subservience has never seemed so at odds with my context, a context that is rudely encroaching on my mission.

Bill offered me a twenty-four-hour bodyguard. Kidnapping is the *gringo* obsession. Insurance companies make a killing out of corporate paranoia. Employees get huge bonuses for even setting foot on Colombian soil. But I have been standing on street corners, in many poses, in many cities thought dangerous for over a year now, and despite my glaring blonde hair and smart foreign looks not one kidnapping offer has come my way, not even a mugging.

Mr Yellow had told me: 'We are more reliable than you think. There is always a reason for vengeance. Be sure not to betray, and you'll be OK.' A simple piece of advice to follow. Only under the circumstances it might be harder than he thinks.

I am back in my room now having spent the last five days with the girls in the *barrio*. I have so much fun with them. Their feelings are intense, their senses are alive, alert, vital. If it was up to me I'd stay there all the time. They are so full of life, perhaps to ward off the death that hangs round them like a veil. Besides, I have no inclination to explore any more. I don't want to go back to my world of idea-snatching and bullet-point emotions. But I must pay the price of this adventure. While the Escobar wannabes purge the week's sins with the Catholic ritual, I continue to snatch souls. I head for the grey cement centre where the girls told me I'd find the dark side of Medellín: little satans, devil worshippers and 'Dracula-types who make our beautiful city look dirty and sinister'. As I approach the steps of an official-looking building, I see them. There is one chubby boy with long black hair, in a black sweat-shirt and sweat pants, who looks cross-eyed. A beautiful blonde girl sits beside him, with black eyeliner, a black choker, a short black skirt and tights.

'I don't go to church because it makes money out of selling promises that it never has to keep,' says Valentín, the cross-eyed boy. 'Nobody can come back and sue after they die.'

The girl strokes Valentín's shoulder gently while he speaks, but he looks always up to the skies and I realize he is blind. He had his eyes shot out when he tried to prevent his motorbike from being stolen. He tells me he sees more clearly now.

Slowly other black-eyed, drainpiped, long-haired youth gather round in curiosity. They don't look like devil worshippers, only in need of some sun. They bombard me with questions about where I'm from, what I'm doing alone in Medellín, which places I've been to in the city, and just from a few names they quickly deduce who I've been hanging out with. They turn to each other knowingly and say, 'Los *vallenateros*.' They

hate the music, the false romance and groomed respectability
that goes with it. It harbours the city's real violence.

'They spend the whole day plotting and threatening to kill each other and then dance *vallenato* and feel they are the most sensitive, romantic people in the world,' says Martín. He has shaved one side of his head, but the hair on the other side falls down to his back, a half-skinhead, half-metal schizophrenic punk. 'They reckon if they get into the lovey-dovey and smoochy-moochy embrace, it will cleanse their aggression.'

'Yeah, and their *gallina* girlfriends,' says the beautiful blonde, 'who paint themselves so they look like clowns, they encourage the aggression.'

Almost offended, as if I too had become one, I feel the urge to defend my *gallina* sisters. How can they escape the violence if it is institutionalized in their increasingly militarized *barrios* and sanctioned from above? I want to say. It is a world away from middle-class neighbourhoods. A concert is about to begin, the beautiful blonde says, and leads Valentín into a long seedy corridor that spills out into a hall filled with long-hairs. This is their church. Through the darkness a single spotlight shines on a small stage on which several spotty grim-reapers appear and dive into a guitar-screeching and drum-banging contest.

In front of the stage, heads flop, hair flies and death-dressed bodies fling themselves around. Several fans are standing with one foot against the stage, playing invisible guitars and screwing up their faces in ecstasy. The girls take a more measured approach, standing on the fringes with arms folded, frowning in concentration. There is no embracing.

The way they shout and scream during the concert you would think a hundred murders had taken place. But when the lights come on, the audience looks refreshed and glowing from the therapy. Shouting, they tell me, is what it's all about.

'They bring you up to hide your feelings, because they are scared for you,' says Martín, in the Rocky Horror interval. 'They are scared that if you are too outspoken it will get you into trouble.'

'They should teach us to show our anger when we are young, to liberate our hate,' adds the beautiful blonde. 'Then there would be less violence in Colombia.'

Martín's hair may be schizophrenic, but the real schizophrenia, he says, lies in the narco-mainstream. 'We are the only ones who confront reality. They just want to cover up the violence with false romance, and let people continue getting their heads blown off for saying the wrong thing. The *vallenatos* sing about love; they hold no respect for life.' I think, surely they wouldn't be so harsh if they knew the nature of this new paramilitary mafia. How can you speak the truth when a gun is pointed at you?

As if hearing his cue, the lead grim-reaper takes the stage and begins slurring the mournful moan of a metal ballad. It is a rendition, Valentín tells me, of a Norwegian hardcore-punk composition. His face has turned to misery, a defeated adolescent standing on the edge of death, not in the gasping-heartache way of the *vallenateros,* but in a droning melancholic Nordic way. In heavily Spanish-accented Norwegian English he agonizes earnestly over the pain and pointlessness of life.

After the concert, the devil worshippers (as Liliana calls them) pull out the tables and chairs to begin a candlelit deliberation on moral issues. It is like an underground meeting of the St Petersburg opposition. Not that they are planning rebellion. There is far too much of that already in Colombia. No, they announce, they will discuss the art of living through reflection and moderation.

'Here you are considered violent if you tell the truth,' Lucas begins, 'but if you pay someone to kill your enemy in secret, that is normal. Reflection is a crime, vengeance is king.'

'It is up to us to lead the way,' answers a sunken-cheeked boy with charcoal-smudged eyes. 'We must rise above the others and exercise self-control and consideration.'

'Yeah, we have to be strong in our convictions. I don't care if nobody listens to my shout,' says Martín. 'I know that it is the truth and I did it for me.'

I search for demonic activity. Difficult to find. I see adolescence burdened with a responsibility to change a violent world they've inherited, struggling through a minefield of injustice, made incomprehensible by hidden agendas and foreign interests. My youth was free of these things. Between Oxford's jaded walls, nobody ever talked of the need for change, for a fairer world. Only career, opportunity and success mattered. The smell of success froze the seeds of ideals. Yet, ironically, we seemed more fearful, anxious, wrapped up in our little all-important worlds. Here, their young cries and their hope infects me. With each day rebellion is growing in me, just when it should be a fading phase.

On Monday I go back to the Antioquia University, having decided to start telling the truth. When I introduce myself to a group of kids as a Levi's scout wanting information about their feelings, they tell me to bugger off. It happens four times. It is incomparably more comfortable to lie, maintain the illusion of freedom, the fantasy that this is *my* journey. Besides, I'll have nothing to put in the reports if I carry on like this.

■

It is three thirty in the afternoon. In Prado, about fifteen minutes' walk from the campus, Jaime, director of a well-known Colombian human rights organization, receives a phone call. A boy from the university wants to come and interview him about the *desplazados.* Jaime tells him he is about to leave the office and suggests they meet another day. 'No, now,' the boy insists. 'It has to be now.' Jaime refuses and the boy slams down the phone.

Twenty minutes later, four masked men with Kalashnikovs charge in and round the twenty or so screaming staff members up into the corner. Jaime is in his office on an upper floor, packing up to go home. He has his back to the sheet of glass that separates his office from the rest of the floor and is talking to a colleague, who is signalling to a woman behind him, hunching his shoulders and cocking his head in a 'what is it?' gesture. Then he goes pale. Jaime turns around, and the masked men who have run in behind the woman grab him.

The gunmen take them downstairs to where the other staff members are being held. They begin to read out a list of names. Jaime Gutiérrez, they call. 'That's me,' Jaime says.

The man with the list throws him onto a chair and points a gun to his head as he carries on reading. Jaime tries to listen to the other names being called out, but the hand holding the gun is shaking so much he is scared the young boy will pull the trigger by mistake.

'Look, just calm down,' he tells the boy. 'We will do what you say. But just calm down, for God's sake. Tell me what this is all about. Who are you and what it is you want?'

'We come on behalf of a... very important man who wants to talk to you,' the boy says.

'Well, OK, he needn't make such a scene. He only has to ask,' jokes Jaime, seeing his gunmen are more nervous than he is. Only the gun woman is not shaking. She is still, slightly dozy, as if drugged. She holds her gun through folded arms and is pointing it at Jaime's colleague, Carla, who has also been called.

When the intruders finish rounding up the four they came for, two men and two women, they tie their hands, blindfold them and lead them out of the building. Jaime gets into the boot of the car because, of the two men, he is the slighter, and he soon feels the car twisting up into the winding roads around Medellín. It is night when they reach their destination. It is cold and the coos and rustles tell Jaime they are far from the city. The guards take off their blindfolds so they can eat. They say nothing, answer no questions, but the captives guess they are paramilitaries.

Laura, the only one in the group who is not a director, has been in charge of investigating paramilitary murders. Three years ago, for example, in the Antioquia village of El Aro, soldiers encircled the community while paramilitaries executed four people in the square. The next day they tied a store-owner to a tree, gouged out his eyes and severed his tongue and testicles before killing him. In the following days, with soldiers standing guard, paramilitaries executed eleven people, including three children, and virtually destroyed the village before leaving. Laura had also found that Uribe's civilian-military networks of peasant soldiers and hooded informants was not as welcome as the media made out. Many communities in Antioquia did not want the 'protection'. The military, who often worked with paramilitaries, was the *cause* of their insecurity, they begged. Many wanted to ban arms altogether, so that none of the paramilitaries, the army or the guerrillas could accuse them of collaborating with their enemy, but these peace communities were increasingly unable to resist militarization.

Despite the investigations, Jaime had always had good relations with the authorities. He had been working alongside the Medellín police in a special project for community policing. It had all been going well, the police had been actively cooperating, until the Medellín chief of police was replaced. After that the project was cancelled. Things were changing in Medellín.

'Look at it this way,' Jaime consoles Laura, laughing, 'at least we will provide material to keep our successors busy.' There is no doubt in their minds that they are being taken to their deaths.

■

Liliana, Naomi and Isabel expect me to spend my last day before leaving for Bogotá with them. It is a question of duty. They have embraced me, showered me with affection, and in return they expect a certain loyalty. In Cuba, I couldn't engage in this commitment. But I am learning to accept their *entrega,* the gut desire to give passionately and spontaneously that has no English translation. And I have somehow to give back more of myself to match this compulsive generosity. Even if I didn't invite it, I accepted it. Yet the biggest part of myself I cannot give. The nature of my job is to snatch their offering and give nothing in return. Levi's would probably say it's not our fault that they are so generous with their emotions. I want to say to them: 'Don't tell me your secrets. Don't tell me because I will betray you.'

I cannot stop the girls from taking me to the parade. Today is the opening of Medellín's annual flower fair, when cowboys from all over the region ride into town to display their horses to the city. 'It's the biggest horse show in the world,' they say, begging me to come.

We transport the entire living room to the roadside, along with the rest of the city, to watch the thousands of fine horses pass by. It is the city's show of gratitude to those who supply the food they eat.

On the way, the cowboys scoop up the city's finest women onto their horses. Their red silicone lips and coconut-cup breasts defy the gravity of the horses' trot, and the make-up starts to stream down their faces. The poor animals don't react well to being stabbed in the side with stilettos, but the cowboys love the city's plastic glamour.

'The fine ladies of Medellín are the finest in Colombia!' they shout as they swig down *aguardiente.*

We sit on the sidelines swigging it down too. The politeness dissolves, the groping begins and we dance to the *vallenatos* until the sun goes down. At night the crowds drift away. A few dead horses are left on the road.

We head for a bar nearby to catch the preliminary World Cup match between Argentina and Colombia. Nobody seems to be bothered that you can hardly distinguish the players from the fuzz on the tiny TV screen. We order rum and *aguardiente* and cheer and jeer blindly at the pin-size players scrambling on the distant screen. By half-time the game has disappeared into insignificance. The audience orders the *vallenatos* to be turned up, people climb over tables and couples begin to dance, blocking what little view we had of the game.

Not even the projectile vomit of one woman, which travels over several people, spoils the proceedings. When the final whistle blows, the national pride which had been so heartily sung has evaporated into general drunkenness. Miniskirts are being tugged, breasts and buttocks grabbed (neither are under much protection) to the delight of all parties, and nobody cares whether Colombia won the match. They are living.

Eventually we find ourselves climbing up the hill, singing our way home. Through the night we can hear the drunken shouts of horsemen flogging their horses up the hill. Cars come speeding down and swerve to avoid them. The drivers hurl abuse at them, and tell them if they don't move they'll get themselves killed. They don't care. 'No better way to go!' they scream back, laughing, as they gallop off into the night.

9

KNOWING 'THE MARKET'

'This may be chaos but, in its entrails some of us look to the stars.'

ANDRES, 17, LA CANDELARIA

'Higher, higher!' cries the child to his kite, urging it to reach beyond the others. He turns to his father. 'If it kisses God, then my wishes will come true, won't they?' Father smiles and nods.

When the wind gets up in Bogotá, kites cover the skies, fluttering butterflies tickling the grey clouds. Street vendors sell them between the cars that crawl along the edge of the Simón Bolívar park. Parents watch their excited kids untangle the threads, set off their mascots and follow them with wondrous attention, as if the Liberator himself were setting their flying dreams free.

 Bogotá weather reminds me of Britain, cloudy, grey, windy, teased by sunny spells. Only the sun burns more here. Everything burns more.

I arrived yesterday and am escaping from the hotel manager whose politeness is even more sycophantic than in Medellín. Every time I pass reception he traps me. I know he is only trying to help, but it's that subservience again that makes me feel uncomfortable: Basil Fawlty gone Colombian. I find myself crawling under the counter to avoid him as I spin out of the revolving doors rather than seek help for my map.

■

The Levi's Bogotá contact arrives in his BMW with the obligatory side parting, classic Spanish features, business-school English and the usual bag of contempt. He says that the problem with Colombia is *la malicia indigena* (indigenous malice), whose 'greed' is what has kept this country in civil war.

I'm scared the world I'm representing might rub off on me. I never want that sour expression of omnipotence, the cold laughing of take, take, take written in my eyes, the crinkle of intolerance on my brow. There is a cold and overt aggression about him that clashes with the soft, sweet Colombian manner that can melt even the most bitter reality.

I wonder if this is the version of 'local' that Levi's means to 'empathize' with. An instinct tells me this power-steering man beside me knows no solidarity for his own people. His love is money; his loyalty to the multinationals who make him rich.

I'm doing another kind of research now, and I think maybe it is the business elite's seeming contempt of their people that allowed eight union leaders at a Coca-Cola bottling plant to be killed by paramilitaries because they were organizing strikes. Communities protesting against an oil pipeline, in which British Petroleum is a major investor, complain of constant harassment, their lawyers threatened, one investigator murdered, by paramilitaries linked to security services contracted by the consortium that owns the pipeline. To protect the pipeline, the consortium, Ocensa, approved the sending of sixty pairs of restricted night-vision goggles to the 14th Brigade, notorious for its paramilitary links and involvement in massacres.

Is this the order that multinationals find so favourable for global brands? Coca-Cola says they do not own the Colombia plants and even tried to sue the union for libel. BP also said they 'had no evidence of the intelligence network' linking their security contractors to paramilitaries. But if I, by talking to people, know that paramilitaries are in the business of protecting private property, how can they not at least strongly suspect? Brands like Levi's go to so much trouble and expense to send the likes of me to 'know their market intimately'. But do Colombians only matter when they are consumers?

I think of Juan David, owner of Levi's Colombian subsidiary, his soft brown eyes and warm gentle manner, telling me he could never do what I did. He admired me for it. In the moment, flattered by his charm, I did not think to reply: No, how could you go into the bowels of your own market? You would have to face the other reality. You are today's *latifundistas* relying on military power to keep the workforce in order.

 You send me, your Medusa, to do your seduction, while you rule from behind your bulletproof screens. Well, I will research the country situation. After all, it doesn't take long to read a few Amnesty International reports off the web.

I ask Mr Levi's Bogotá to drop me in the centre, on Avenida Libertador, where carthorses and children court death as they swerve through the traffic in a double slalom. I walk through the chaos, and someone is hissing in my ear. I turn round. A girl's face, with the lines of an old woman and eyes wired with the electric agitation of basuco, is almost touching my cheek. She begs me for money. I walk faster, my stomach contracting. Then she gives up and crosses the road between the traffic. I find myself turning back and following her. She disappears into a narrow street filled with what looks like brown smog.

I nudge through the crowd, intending to go down the street, but I realize the brown is a mass of humans in rags stained by dirt, squeezed between the buildings. Carrying wheelbarrows full of junk, they spill out onto the avenue and disappear into the grey, becoming the *indigentes* that everyone tries to avoid. I stand on the edge of this inferno and, for the first time, my insatiable curiosity evaporates.

I take a bus in the direction of the hotel. For days I haven't interviewed. It is the wider picture I now hanker after. The framework that the interviews illustrate. On the way home I stop off at a bookshop to find a map, and anything else that might illuminate. A good-looking chap with dark Italian features peers at me over a book and as I walk out of the shop I hear footsteps behind me.

'Hey,' he calls in English, 'where are you from? Are you studying here?'

Felipe tells me he teaches English in a school. I tell him the lie about my research for a book and he invites me to his house to join him and his girlfriend for dinner. 'We live with a whole load of students. If there is anything you need, you just call us. We can show you how this city works.'

It is funny how, sometimes, when you stop looking, the answer seeks you out. When you shed the agenda, the veil of deception lifts itself, and the world offers itself freely.

As I enter my hotel I collide with a family hurling itself at the security guard. The father, mother and daughter, with a poodle in her arms, look like they have just seen Hannibal Lecter. Between grasps of breath the father manages to describe some kind of menace lurking round the corner from which they have escaped.

'Who was it? Did they hurt you?' I ask. 'What did they do?'

The man shakes his head. 'No, no, nothing happened,' he says, 'but they looked very suspicious. They were *indigentes.*' It is the fear that sits in wealth, seeing in every dispossessed human a desire to take away what you have.

■

The next day I get a phone call from Felipe who tells me to meet his gang at a Thai-Japanese restaurant near my hotel in La Zona Rosa, the trendy zone of Bogotá. He brings his girlfriend, Magda, a tough nut with short hair and perfect features. There is a very beautiful young man called Pato, who is a video-jockey star on a music channel, and his friend, a

 Venezuelan Irvine Welsh, who boasts about his life of decadence. He is here to set up the Colombian branch of Lo Que Sea, the US-Venezuelan youth internet site I'd seen in Miami and Caracas that exports the new Miami-Latino role models to South American youth. They are the young Pan-American, brand-sponsored media jet set, the world I would appear to belong to. I keep my new loyalties to myself.

The television presenter is immaculately turned out (the channel pays for his gym, his clothes are sponsored by Diesel) and draws the interest of all the Bogotá beauties, who stroll past on the arms of young *gomelos* sporting expensive Italian suits.

It would be an enchanting evening were it not for the kids scampering round the table legs and popping their dirty heads up under the soft pink light. Next to us, a woman fidgets in her seat and snatches her soft brown arms away from their hands. Her date viciously waves a boy away, but he comes back, like the petulant fly. The waiters flap their towels but the kids run rings around the tables.

Once diners feigned sympathy, then came indifference, and now they cannot be bothered to hide their contempt. The kids, having long lost the hope of any voluntary donation, and with nothing left to lose, swear back louder rather than wince and crawl away. If they are destined for a life as untouchables they can at least show they are equal in anger, scorn and disrespect. Their relentless defiance is impressive, forcing gentlemen to smile apologetically at their dates, and those entertaining foreign businessmen to wince. Only the police get the kids moving, but they even shout back at them. The game of loathing has become a way of life.

The kids come from the refuge the Red Cross has set up in the middle of the Zona Rosa, as if a provocation to those trying to pretend this is Miami. 'These refuges only encourage people to come to the city,' growls Pato.

'Where are they supposed to go?' I ask. 'There is a civil war.'

Yeah, he says, the war. But no one wants to talk about that. The violence has gone on so long it has just become background music. For them, being Colombian and the 'complicated situation' of Colombia are two different things, the latter a parasite that has seized them but is not part of them. It could be another continent altogether, war-torn Africa, unrecognizable to them in their enclosure of order and luxury, where classic European styles fuse with American consumer ideals.

The news is like a bad soap opera of speculation and devastation. When a church is blown up with its congregation inside or a millionaire is kidnapped, nobody knows who to blame any more. It is just a blur of hatred, but the insurgents are mainly portrayed as the root cause, while the paramilitaries are a symptom.

'I don't think even the guerrillas know what they are fighting for now,' says Magda. 'Once they may have had ideals, but now it is just a cycle of vengeance.' She does not mention the paramilitaries, who also live off taxing coca farmers. The Amnesty International website says 80 per cent of the massacres are committed by them as they scour the country for FARC sympathizers. The US adminstration has also got impatient.

 It reckons the Colombian government has gone soft on terrorists and has asked Congress for another eight hundred million dollars to help rid Colombia of *all* obstacles to 'friendly democracy': political enemies, narco-kings, and whoever it is that keeps blowing up the new oil pipelines being built. Experts believe Colombia's oil reserve could be as large as Venezuela's, which is currently the world's fifth largest producer. My trendy friends think the hard line is right.

'President Pastrana is sitting on the fence letting the guerrillas acquire more and more power. He hasn't got the guts to take the bull by the horns,' says Pato.

We talk about Carlos Castaño's debut interview that was televised yesterday, and the kids say how surprised they were. They never expected the paramilitary commander-in-chief to sound so convincing.

'I am not saying he is a nice man,' says Felipe. 'Obviously he is a killer, but at least he has the guts to take on the guerrillas.'

Yes, they have also lost patience. They are tired of understanding, tired of this discussion. They also talk of *malicia indigena.* I want to say: I suppose it is the fault of indigenous unionists that they get killed for demanding more pay and better conditions, that it's the fault of peasant leaders for getting killed because they don't want to 'cooperate'. I suppose it is the fault of peasants and workers also that 230 elected officials, including two presidential candidates of the Patriotic Union Party (UP) – formed to represent them as part of a 1985 peace agreement with the guerrillas – have been assassinated. Paramilitaries killed three thousand UP party members in all – a political genocide.

More than malicious, you'd have to be a martyr to even mention the rights of the poor, let alone advocate them.

■

A week has passed since the kidnapping in Medellín. Jaime guesses they've been taken north-west of Antioquia, in the jungle of Urabá, near the Panamanian border, an area which the FARC once controlled but is fast losing to the paramilitaries. He overhears the guards saying that they were supposed to meet the helicopter to take them to Carlos Castaño, but that the place had been surrounded by guerrilla forces and instead they are going to a Colombian army base which has agreed to let Castaño's helicopter land. This means another three days' walking.

Jaime tells the others: 1) Don't look at the guards' faces. If they think you could recognize them, it will make your death more certain. 2) Never cry in front of them. If they think you are weak, you are willing them to pity you, and this will only irritate them and make your death more certain. 3) Sleep well. You must keep strong. 4) Eat well. Do not resign yourself to death.

Laura has broken all the rules already. She cannot be bothered to tell the guards to turn the other way when she bathes in the river. The certainty of death has made her lose her fear and her shyness. She becomes more brazen by the day.

'Doesn't your chef even have the imagination to put a little onion or tomato in the rice?' she scolds the guard. 'Aren't you ashamed of giving us this rice, so bland like this?'

At night Laura tells jokes and Carla sings. Even the guards are astonished.

'I admire you, close to your deaths and you can still be in a good mood,' says one of the guards, meaning to be friendly.

'What are you doing mixed up in all this mess?' Laura asks the boy.

'My father was killed by the guerrillas,' he says. 'I've killed seventeen of them and I still don't feel satisfied.'

Castaño's father was also killed by the FARC. He took his first victim at sixteen, before building a whole army of revenge.

'Don't think I don't understand the FARC,' urges the other guard, mistaking his prisoners for *guerrilleros*. 'I know what it's like; I fought with them. But the paramilitaries pay us, and the FARC never did. They let us go home and see our girlfriends once a month, and also, if we want to leave they won't kill us like the FARC would.'

Laura is the only one who talks to the boys. Too much, thinks Jaime; at any minute she might say something that will be taken the wrong way. It is almost as if she forgets what little her life means to them. But the guards have taken a liking to her. Perhaps she reminds them of the maternal tenderness they have sacrificed for this life of war. One asks her to help him write a letter to his girlfriend. And she does so, teasing him with sisterly affection.

The next evening this same soldier comes in. He tells the group that he had overheard that the company they work for is going to pay the ransom and so they would be released. The hostages burst into laughter. 'We do not work for a company. NGOs don't have any money. Nobody is going to pay the ransom,' Laura says in a tender giggle. 'Sweetie, you have no idea what you are involved in.' The boy blushes with embarrassment. He had wanted to console them.

Finally the helicopter arrives. Jaime is told he will be going alone. Laura, Carla and John are taken elsewhere. The helicopter ride takes about an hour. When they land, a car is waiting and they begin a long drive uphill. Jaime thinks they are heading towards Nudo de Paramillo, another *sierra* towards the east, where it is said the paramilitary headquarters are. The mountain has three faces bordering three provinces and is a known strategic point. It had previously been occupied by the FARC, until the paramilitaries cut off their food supply from the bottom and drove them out.

When the road gets too bad they continue on horseback, through the night, along a narrow ridge steeper than the last one. Jaime's handcuffs are bridged by a short metal wedge rather than a chain, and do not let his hands get round to clasp the saddle pommel. With the rain pouring down he is slipping off and he tells the guards he will fall over the precipice if they don't change his cuffs, but his guards take no notice. Perhaps it is better to throw myself off the cliff now, he thinks, and put myself out of my misery. He lets himself doze, hoping he may just slip into death, but the falling jolts him awake. And then morning comes. The sunlight slips under his blindfold and he can see the ground on which his horse stands. As he looks down, a hand offers itself to his handcuffed fists.

'How do you do, Mr Gutíerrez,' a voice says. 'My name is Carlos Castaño.'

■

 Magda has agreed to take me to El Cartucho, the brown street. 'You may not come out alive,' Felipe teases. The mystery ignites their fantasies of ghetto glam. They have been brought up in high-security hamlets, patches of paradise, but they cannot buy their way into El Cartucho.

The Venezuelan Irvine Welsh boasts he would take me but he tempted fate last week and a gang held him hostage in a crack house and spent six hours stubbing out cigarettes on his arm. Magda says she knows it well. She used to buy her basuco there when she was a teenage addict.

It was a long bus ride from where she lived, the northern suburb of Las Delicias del Carmen with its country clubs, shopping malls and posh universities, but when she turned sixteen her father bought her a jeep and she would venture down. They were her rebellious days, she says, when she found everything boring and stifling: the tradition and convention imposed by high society, the fear of not becoming the perfect daughter with the perfect career and the perfect husband. She wanted freedom and individuality, and she found it in the exciting, anonymous labyrinth of vice. First she'd go there to buy cocaine. Sometimes she'd consume there. Then she tried basuco and got swallowed by the big brown hole, before her dad sent her to the rehab centre in Miami.

'Your shoes are not scuffed enough,' Magda warns me when I enter her living room. 'And you can't wear a brand name – they'll have them off you in no time.'

We spend a good half-hour arranging our Cartucho costumes. I hide my blonde hair under a black woollen cap, and we go into the garden to rub mud into our jeans and faces.

The bus drops us off on Avenida Libertador and, as we walk towards it, the hashish-coloured blur becomes the heaving mass of filthy people. Inside, the shuffling rags carry sacks of junk over their shoulders and drop them off at the decrepit dens on the side. The stench of rotten food, urine and faeces fused with the fumes of smoked crack and basuco makes me retch. I have to hold my breath to avoid vomiting. Crouched on the pavement, kids smoke or are slumped in semi-consciousness. Along the street, women display brick-sized lumps of marijuana wrapped in newspaper on folded tables and shout 'Two pesos!' – the equivalent of a dollar. The police dare not enter, although it's said they get a cut of the profits.

Everyone goes about their business, some scurrying like rats scrambling for food, others zigzagging along in a stoned daze. When I dare to look into eyes, they stare right through me as if I were invisible. It's like being in a dream that makes no sense. So much activity, yet none of it improving the squalor in which they live. The only objective is to get money for the next fix, to exist another day in this hellhole.

For some reason I think of London and a packed Habitat on Tottenham Court Road on a Saturday afternoon. I remember standing there once with my about-to-be-filled basket, staring at everyone as they grabbed at objects on the shelves, eyes wide with gluttony, darting as they spotted something better to snatch off the shelf and into their basket. That 1970s pimp-style Afghan rug, this Barbarella ashtray. They had to have them.

Young couples, domestic yet fashionable in feigned hippy carelessness (precision rips and colour clashes). Oddly wealthy and yet so uncoolly driven by desire, as if desperate not to stray from this new-found meaning of life. Love, loss and heartache may have lingered in their subconscious somewhere, but this alluring, enticing, hypnotic moment of lifestyle-quenching numbed all other feelings and experiences. I left my basket on the shop floor and walked out engulfed by anguish. Yes, the same Cartucho desperation harboured in Habitat, only packaged better.

Magda is scratching herself, sniffling and looking very nervous. She's pretending to be a basuco addict but she looks so ridiculous it makes me laugh. We turn into a road that is deserted but for the collapsed corpses slumped against the houses. We walk past several heaps of rubble where houses have been knocked down. Rag-clad skeletons creep out of the debris and begin to follow us with bloodshot eyes, like the half-dead of a Michael Jackson video. I notice that Magda is no longer pretending. She is nervous. 'We've got to get out, please, let's get out,' she snaps.

We run down the road as fast as we can until we reach Avenida Libertador. When we are out, Magdalena crouches down, hangs her head to the floor, holds her wobbling knees and begins to vomit. 'What's wrong?' I ask her. She's shaking and wheezing and I must say I'm surprised, considering she was once a regular. As it turns out, Magdalena has never been into the entrails of the Cartucho. She always bought her drugs on the borders. We head back home, with our one-dollar brick of marijuana.

■

I can't believe I haven't done an interview yet. Two weeks have passed; I cannot avoid them for ever. I head for a church, El Niño Jesus, only blocks away from El Cartucho, where I have seen schoolgirls in little blue tartan skirts and white short-sleeved blouses playing, while their *barrio* above fights for its grip on the hillside. When I arrive a group of four is discussing the dilemma of a family stereo that had been kidnapped. Two days after it had gone missing, a boy relates, the thieves called asking if they'd like to buy it back. It struck me as slightly strange but logical. Why hunt for a buyer when you know just the person? Thieves are not high on police priority lists.

The kids are polite, their neat uniforms, combed partings and braided hair betray a mother's desperation to maintain respectability. Here, they could not recover status so easily after a teenage rebellion such as Magda's. But the kids say they like coming down here amid the traffic chaos and the stinky residue of food stalls, watching the prostitutes and hustlers. It is the city proper, holding all the forbidden fruits that their parents dread. 'If they don't let us see the dangers out there, how can we know to protect ourselves from them?' they protest. A boy comes scuffling along in a daze of basuco. He wears a dirty tracksuit, his laces are undone and his hair is long and greasy. He grins, lost in the cheap and lethal high, and he walks in a zigzag. The kids tease him, for he is well known, a neighbour who was once like the rest of them.

'He went to the US to be a *rapero* [a rapper],' laughs Liliana.

'Yeah, but he went in a fishing boat, that's why he smells so bad,' laughs Matias.

'He used to be a *rapero,* but now he's a *ratero.*'

The boy just smiles dreamily. They let him hang around the group, with his stench and his strange grimace. They do not banish him as their parents would, fearing he might drag their children into his inferno.

We talk for several hours, about life in the *barrio,* about loyalty, friendship, sticking together, solidarity and the *real rateros,* as Matias describes the group of policemen loitering on the other side of the square, watching with their beady eyes, hands on guns, who drag them off for a beating now and again. The girls talk about how their parents want to overprotect them, are always worried about them getting pregnant. Yet they are thirsty for life, their excitable innocence bubbling with curiosity, mindless of parental anxiety. Only one girl, Lucrecia, a little older, darker, with slightly Afro braids, as if from the coast, and a serious expression, is conspicuous for her silence. But she looks at me intently as if wanting to express something.

It's getting dark. I tell them they should be getting home; their parents will be worrying. But they don't want to stop. Loads of kids have come round to join in and observe the strange goings-on. There is an older man too, who keeps interrupting and answering on their behalf. He hovers like a rival spy. I tell him to stop butting in and let them speak for themselves. When the man leaves, the kids tell me he is an evangelist who is always trying to preach to them, but they thought that he had come with me so they didn't want to say anything.

I want to tell them: Your parents are right, stay at home, where they can protect you from the manipulators and bullies of the world. We are everywhere. If it is not the police it is an evangelist, if it is not an evangelist it is a market spy. Only Lucrecia stays behind. She asks me if I am a journalist and if I will tell her story to an international newspaper.

She was raised in Urabá, north of Antioquia, where her father was a local UP party activist. Then one day in 1996 the army came to the house, smacked him up and warned him to stop his political activities. As the paramilitaries began to take over villages and towns in the area, killing anyone they accused of being a *guerrillero*, people began to flee.

They went to Aguas Frias, where again the army followed them. Eight of Lucrecia's relatives had by now been murdered, all members of the UP. She had seen some decapitated before her eyes, others just disappeared, their bodies found later. Again, Lucrecia's family managed to escape and had moved to another village, when the paramilitaries came looking for her father again. This time he escaped by a freak chance, loosening himself from a tree they had tied him to while they were rounding up others.

After days, he rang telling Lucrecia, her mother and brothers that he was safe and had arrived in Medellín, so the family went to meet him there. They began to tell of the terror of the joint army and paramilitary operations that were sweeping the region. But they were safe in Medellín. Until one night, when her father took a reckless stroll unprotected, from which he never returned.

'One day everything that is happening will come out. It may not be tomorrow, or the next day. But one day the people in government who are letting this happen will be revealed and be tried for war crimes. I will never be silent. My father is my inspiration. He wanted a better world. And I will continue on his path in search of that place, because it is a way of him being present.'

■

I had a nasty incident at the hotel today. Basil Fawlty accused me of being a conwoman because it turns out I booked the room thinking the rate was in pesos when it is in fact in dollars, making it substantially more expensive. 'Huh, you think we are fools enough to buy your little trick do you?' he shouted down the phone. I was so stunned by his radical volte-face (or a *volte arepa* – a flipping corncake – as they say here) that only a stammer of an explanation came out, to which he quacked: 'Don't try and make out you don't understand me!' Then he ordered me out of the hotel. I was packing when the bellboy appeared. He said that the staff had been 'very, very ashamed' by the manager's outburst and confessed that the manager 'sometimes gets a little nervous'. Then he added, 'And, well… the receptionist asked me to come up and beg you not to leave.'

I can't imagine receptionists of a five-star London hotel

revolting against management in the cause of justice. I am awestruck by the guerrilla spirit of the staff, who decided to act against their boss. A true mutiny! Perhaps when you live in a state that does not deliver justice, your own sense of it intensifies.

Bogotá is full of distrust. The kids say they cannot make a mistake 'because people always assume that your intentions are bad'.

'We are unable to look into each other's eyes,' Matias had said. 'For fear that we might see the hate; for fear that we might sympathize. And most of all for fear that we might see in the other our own pain.'

How can I put that in a bullet point? I hardly even recognize myself in our conversations. And the humanity and affection that the Spanish language awakens in me, its hidden messages and meanings – all to get lost in a coloured circle on a grid?

In Medellín they said love is easy, but here in the chaotic immensity of Bogotá everyone feels unloved and excluded. The poor feel excluded from being given a fair chance. The rich are ghettoized in their luxury, and they don't always want it to be this way. I don't see the hate of the other side that I saw in Caracas, just a terrible confusion, a cloudiness, like the sky that hangs over the city. Felipe told me he thought everyone should be made to see a place in Bogotá they haven't been to before, once a month. There is a need to see things more clearly, break the barrier, touch and feel what is on the other side.

Magda and Felipe are taking me to an 'after' party tomorrow, before I leave for Cali. These sprung up about a year ago, when the 'Carrot Law' was imposed making normal discotheques close at 2 a.m. for security reasons.

So at 2 o'clock on a Sunday morning we join the mass exodus of cars and buses charging towards the edge of town. We arrive at a big field near a plantation of roses. Under the laser lights, amid the blips of trance music and stomping in the muddy earth, I feel like I'm back in the Hackney Marshes. People are hugging each other, telling strangers that they love them. Just like they escaped from Thatcher's loveless inner cities, young people of all backgrounds and races come together to get lost in the music, let down their defences and free themselves from the misery of indifference and exclusion.

'At the afters, nobody judges you or discriminates,' says Magda. 'There are no barriers. The doors are shut to nobody. Everybody is made to feel they belong. If you are acting in a crazy way, people don't think you have bad intentions. They just think you are high.'

Nobody checks for guns because here we are outside city legislation and, as yet, nobody has expressed the desire to kill anyone. Also, they have discovered ecstasy. 'When I take ecstasy, I feel I can be who I am, I am not scared to show my true self,' Magda confesses, 'and you can do it because everyone else is acting the same. It's like there are no problems between us.'

She tells me that cocaine is passé, 'that bullshit belongs to the cartel generation', the era of narco-sleaze and money-grabbing scavengers. Cocaine is arrogance, pumped-up testosterone, the cold barrier of false superiority that separates people; ecstasy is harmony and hope.

Some guy offers me some pills. He doesn't have cocaine, he says. 'I only get that for the *gringos*' – those strapping blond boys who arrive on their year off to lap up the white stuff so they can go back and tell their friends they have had the Colombian experience, toilet-bonding with the natives in true local style. He spreads his hand out to show me pills of several colours.

'These ones are from Holland,' he says proudly, 'but I also get them from a contact I have in Ibiza.'

There are those who have come just for the good vibes. 'We have to treat each other better and give an example to the next generation,' says a girl who has a giant strawberry on her T-shirt and a pair of fluorescent eyeballs bouncing on a hairband.

'This may be a crazy country. But in its entrails there are trapped those of us who look to the stars.'

I squeeze into the corner of a jeep heading back to Bogotá with about seventeen happy people crushed inside with me. And then, as I wander into memories of raving in wellies in England's green and pleasant, I hear a voice muttering something. What? I say, thinking it sounded slightly strange.

'I said, I must pray extra tomorrow at church, so that God will forgive me for taking ecstasy.' No, I am not in England.

10

FEELING THE PRICE

'The heart has reasons that reason will never understand.'

MAGALI, 17, AGUAS BLANCAS

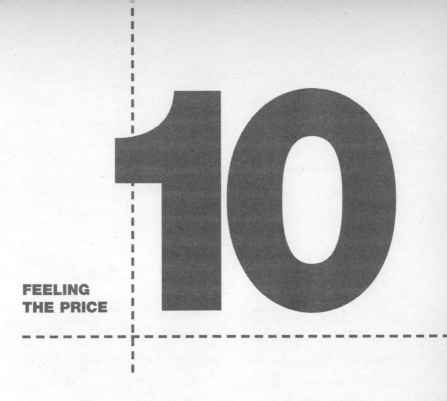

Whenever I talk to other purveyors of brands, while drinking Martinis under the flattering lights of hotel bars, they always reassure me that the production of consumer desires is perfectly legitimate. 'People don't want reality, they want to escape,' said the Venezuelan Irvine Welsh, as if this were the most obvious truth that ever existed. I protested: 'Listen, I hear their troubles, my instinct is to help them. But instead of helping them overcome, we just use the confessions to manipulate them, to make them better consumers.' He answered that it was patronizing to assume *we* should tell them what's best for them. Maybe by helping to deliver fantasies, I *am* giving people what they want. I am *their* servant, as Levi's website proclaimed. It is, after all, torture to think about the opportunities one will never have. Why can't one just dream, believe the world is better than it really is? Nobody wants to think about what you can't have. You want to believe things are possible.

That Apple advertisement, for example. 'Think different,' it says. John Lennon, Martin Luther King, Gandhi. How inspiring. Yet in Lucrecia's reality, the majority of Colombians' reality, thinking different can mean a death squad gouging someone's eyes out.

I think about the realities I've dug out of the collective subconscious: dignity in Perú, independence in Panamá, courage in Costa Rica, sincerity in Venezuela, tolerance in Medellín, inclusion in Bogotá. We collect words so that the reality can be taken out and replaced by fantasy. No, branding is not advertising. It is transforming truths, substituting meanings. Turning negative into positive for a world of cool things, devoid of meaning. Ideals = desire. Identity = aspiration. Principles = status. Consciousness = greed.

I have heard what young people want, what would make them happy. It is what any normal kid wants: opportunities to fulfil their dreams, to be recognized, represented, to have some control over their destiny, to live in dignity. If you offer a prisoner heroin to quell the depression and boredom of his life in prison, he's likely to take it, isn't he? He might even crave more. But if you offered the prisoner freedom, would he still take the heroin? The brander's argument in Latin America is the argument of the jail's drug pusher.

■

From Bogotá I have flown south, further into the veins of this beast, closer to the equator, but not close enough to the Pacific. There is no breeze in the Cauca valley, only heat rippling in a blurry haze over the flat sugar-cane pastures, slowing everything, even the wheels of the car. Along the roadside red eyes set in violet-black faces follow me. They wait, chewing tobacco, and yet I can feel the pounding of collective passions as we crawl into the city as if they were of my own heart. Ba boom, ba boom, ba boom.

They say the Cali cartel was less power-hungry, less ostentatious and more laid-back than Escobar's. But the thought that death is less conspicuous is not a consoling one.

This is the heart of plantation Colombia, where Africans slaved for the Spanish. And now it is Colombia's capital of salsa, the music of black Colombia. 'There's a joke that's going around, and the joke is on me,' go the words of Cali's most famous group, Grupo Niche.

I've got a big nose and big lips,
And they can't find anything good in that,
I'm black, it's true, I'm from Mother Africa,
And I feel proud of it.

In the image of their song, Cali *must* be a city full of African pride. Felipe has given me the address of some friends of his. He says they share a house and will probably have a room to rent. I book myself into the Intercontinental and make my way down there as the sun is setting. I find Franz, Antonio and

 Mariana sitting on the porch of an old colonial house in the neighbourhood of Granada. It's five minutes away from the fine arts school where they study.

A gentle breeze is doing its best to lift the heat of the day. 'Thank God he's turned the oven down,' says Mariana, throwing her eyeballs to the sky. She is slumped in a wicker chair in worn-out, saggy-bottomed corduroys, breasts hanging freely in a baggy khaki vest, and with one leg over the arm – an unusually laddish pose for a Colombian woman. I was starting to think that anything other than vacuum-packed fashion was prohibited.

Mariana wipes the beads of sweat from her brow, and pulls back her fine mousy hair. The moist shine on her pale forehead glows in the dark. Without getting up, she tells me to look round the house. Nothing of the Medellín formality here. It's just too hot.

Inside, everything is painted white as if to protect the interior from the urban jungle. There is a particular affinity for all things German: literature, philosophy, music, installations more suited to a Munich museum than the muggy tropics. The exception is a bedroom, which is plastered with Johnny Rotten posters.

When I come back out, Franz is roaming about looking pensive in a thermal boiler suit. Antonio, who wears black drainpipes and T-shirt, is still flopped in the same position as when I arrived, his mouth hanging open like a heroin addict's. His cheeks are sucked in and he's so pale you'd have thought he'd never seen the sun in his life. Something is not quite right, affected, out of place. And why are they always complaining about the heat? Have they just arrived from Alaska?

'I would have thought you'd be used to it by now,' I say.

'We come from the countryside,' says Antonio. 'It's different in the country...' and he waxes lyrical about the rivers and cane fields of his plantation childhood, jungle adventures and river swims, flora of colours brighter than in any rainbow glowing luminous at night, and the noises of copulating iguanas.

He came to the city when the anonymous letters began arriving almost daily at his family home. The guerrillas threatened his family with kidnapping and the estate with plunder if his family didn't pay up. He doesn't go back to visit very often because travelling back there by road has got so dangerous. Now and again his parents fly in to visit him, trapped under the steaming blanket of the city.

'The problem with Cali,' Franz says, 'is the lack of culture.'

'What?' I cry, astounded. 'But your salsa groups play in concert halls all over the world.'

'Huh. If I could I would ban people from dancing salsa,' says Franz, crumpling his face in disapproval. 'I can't bear the sound of it. Salsa is not culture, salsa is a lifestyle void of sense and scruples. Pure lust.'

'Everything here is about bodies,' Mariana explains. 'People here are animals.'

'They are so lazy,' Antonio adds. 'They are too lazy to think, too lazy even to be lazy.'

'But you are all from here. You too are part of this culture.'

'But we are different. We are the only progressives in this city,' says Franz. 'We are a minority. Nobody listens to us. The government should force people to think, but it is run by monkeys for monkeys.'

'How can you force people to think?' I ask.

'For a start I would prohibit them from having more than one child,' offers Mariana. 'I would give poor women an injection to stop them having children, because they cannot look after them.'

Antonio laughs, he has thought of something funny: 'I would put a chip in the brains of people who steal so that every time they go and steal their fingers would start getting jittery and they would suddenly get chronic arthritis.'

'And you call yourselves progressives?' I say.

'If you lived in a place like this you'd understand,' says Franz. 'Barbarism requires barbaric measures. People don't understand anything else. Something has to be done to curtail the mayhem. We need order and authority.'

I can't wait to see what their artwork is like.

■

However good friends they are of Felipe, I can't accept their room offer. I can just see the smirks as I click down the stairs in my high heels and J-Lo sparkliness ready for a salsa spin. And can you imagine if I brought back any of the loathsome specimens of Cali barbarism? Turn my back and I'd probably find them lynched in the garden. All that talk of monkeys. 'What does a monkey call a black man?' was Franz's favourite joke. 'A monkey with his tail the wrong way round.' I wonder how Levi's would convert *that* bullet point into a marketing campaign. Suddenly the businessmen in the hotel seem refreshing.

I take a taxi round the city and begin to mark places on my map. I like the city. It has a Caribbean feel, even without the sea breeze. People are on the streets, laughing, flirting. There are banners hanging across the streets urging people to be more 'SOCIABLE'. How much more sociable do they want people to get?

When we get to the east, I can see on my map that the taxi driver has cut across and missed an immense district called Aguas Blancas. I repeat that I want to cover *the entire* city and, shaking his head, he turns back. Aguas Blancas is a putrid swamp with wooden shacks built precariously along the edges. There is no refuse collection, no clean water supply and no proper sewage. Everyone is black.

The taxi driver tells me, as if to explain, that Cali has fallen on hard times. Like Medellín, the city attracted narco-migrants and is now suffering unemployment after the cartel break-up. But here the quiet desperation is exacerbated by a sense of enclosure. The paramilitaries are sweeping down this side of the country from Antioquia, he says; imminent occupation hangs around the city. Teenagers are already being recruited, the money on offer a tempting alternative to unemployment. 'They want to privatize the services here, and they need the paramilitaries to keep opposition quiet.' Add the heat and racial apartheid to the boiling pot, and it's on the point of explosion.

'It explodes every night,' the driver says.

Hostile eyes watch me get out of the taxi, my clean clothes conspicuously brilliant against the dusty brownness. All intentions are suspect when you step in from a privileged life you cannot share. I am surrounded by a group of girls in tatty hot pants, bikini tops and flip-flops. They are laughing at me. They call me 'mi leidy', and curtsy, pretending that their grubby lime-green Lycra shorts have taffeta skirts attached. They ask me if someone is playing a joke on me by leaving me here alone.

Within minutes of our encounter we are distracted by a drama. It happens so quick I can't make out what is happening. But Magali, the eldest of them (seventeen), darts across the road shouting, 'There she is, there she is, that bitch!' She proceeds to batter a girl who, as far as I can see, was just strolling along. The other girls beside me laugh and jeer.

'What happened?' I ask.

'Love is blind. But the neighbours aren't,' laughs Julie.

Men gather round to separate the girls and Magalí struggles, screaming and writhing, until the other girl escapes out of our sight and they let her go. Then Magalí returns still fuming: 'Slag, slag, the fucking slag.' All these girls are already married with children, and they are barely old enough to enter the Levi's target range. I wonder how Levi's would make their lives look 'cool'. Pregnant by fifteen, married by sixteen, cheating husbands, no future, no stake in society. Just like in Venezuela, the black majority are too 'irrelevant' to be reflected in commercial advertising. On billboards only cinnamon skin and long soft hair appear to count, not black skin and Afro curls.

The girls know this and don't care. '*La suerte de la fea… la bonita la desea* [the luck of the ugly one the pretty one desires],' says Julie. They all have mottos of self-defence. 'Cruel words, deaf ears!' is Magalí's. 'Black by nature, proud by choice!' Shilley shouts. Perhaps I should encourage Levi's to *make* them relevant, as producers of 'cool' things, music, movement, humour, because they have to improvise to live. Survival makes them authentic. Brands thrive on others' authenticity. Isn't that why I'm here?

The girls say they are on their way to a party. They begin to walk off and I remain sitting. When they see I have not followed they call back down the street. 'You coming?'

The midday Saturday disco is in a shack a little bigger than the others. In their rags and sandals they come from all over the neighbourhood. The DJ puts on old salsa tunes and new reggae, the expression of young Cali. Freshly scrubbed bodies melt into each other like plasticine, as if man and woman were made only for this embrace. Like shapes of energy, a move from one provokes a magnetic reaction in the other, so instinctive, so immediate, not a thought, not the slightest cerebral activity breaks the flow.

This is their consumerism: the one commodity they can afford. As Shilley put it: 'Man is very materialist, because he likes to touch a lot!' The girls exude the sexuality of grown women. They say 'vanity', a euphemism for sexiness, is a virtue, because all other happiness is beyond their control. And yet in this prison, they believe themselves to be free.

'We know how to be happy at least,' says Julie. 'Despite all our problems they cannot deprive us of our feelings.'

Perhaps this is a kind of freedom. If they were wealthier, their feelings would be subject to commercial interest and appropriation. For now, it leaves them alone. As they dance, every possible emotion seems to be compressed into the tiniest corporal synthesis, connecting bodies in a sublime exchange of unspoken, unthinking understanding. Here there is no image calculation, there are no conflicts of expectation and frustration to interrupt harmony.

They have surrendered control.

I remember the controlled socializing on the manicured lawns of Oxford: rugby shirts, floral dresses, champagne and smirks of smug indifference. All decorum but for the muffled chuckling of naughty boys' club jokes that tutors whispered into favoured pupils' ears and a suicide that our tutors advised us to not let distract us. Exams must prevail. No time to question. The world is waiting to be conquered! But then at night, after ten pints of lager, the rugby-shirted society would become rampaging gangs scouring the streets looking for 'townies' to thump, and be found at dawn slumped in a pool of vomit and gasping in existential panic.

But here there is no panic. They are familiar with life's instability, the unexplainable. They relish the flawed moment, for in it also lies the beauty of life's intensity.

The girls ask me how we dance in England. I do my raver impression: cutting the air with tight finger-pressed hands to the imaginary techno blips, hopping from one foot to the other as if on cinders. This has them in hysterics. How can you dance together while hopping like that? they howl. I try to explain: 'Where I come from, we don't embrace. You go to classes if you want to dance in a pair, like ballroom, you know?'

'Ah you see,' says Magalí, and taps her temples. '*You* feel through your head. Here it's the other way round, we reach reason through feeling. Feeling *all* the possibilities of good and bad is the only real way to know right from wrong, to feel it through instinct, not through the mind.'

Maybe she's right. I ought to be making my way back. The sun is low and I have to get out of the swamp to see where I can get a taxi. I walk back the way I entered, ignoring the calls that follow me everywhere. I reach a road that is tarmacked and then some shops where people go about in more respectable clothing – a sign, I suppose, of civilization.

On the outskirts of the slum I spot a very alluring swimming pool behind some iron bars and a sign that says Youth Recreation Centre. The chlorine blue water looks good and I pay my way in. I have this little oasis, with palm trees and a view of the hills beyond the valley, virtually all to myself. I roll my trousers up and dangle my feet in the pool. There is only one girl here, who has an enormous smile on her face. In fact, she is positively ecstatic. I make no attempt to approach, but she is determined to talk to me, to share her happiness. She comes towards me and announces that her name is Luz. She tells me she has just found out she has won a scholarship to go to the Universidad del Valle.

'I've survived!' she gloats. 'I am nineteen and I have not got pregnant. I have not fallen into the holes. I can see a future now.'

■

'In a way I envy black people,' says Mariana. 'I walk round the streets in fear that I'll be mistaken for a *gringa* and get kidnapped. The blacks don't have to deal with that. They just live for sensual stimulation. They don't care about the state our country is in. They live in the blissful stupor of ignorance.'

I think about the Afro-Colombian community on the Cacarica river further up north in Urabá who, for refusing to leave their land for the timber and palm oil companies, were visited by the 17th Brigade and paramilitaries 'looking for guerrilla'. Go find the guerrilla, said its community's leaders, we'll stay put until then. They ordered a young man called Marino Mena to climb a tree to fetch coconuts and when he came down they slashed off his hands. As he ran screaming, they caught him and cut his head off. Laughing, a soldier picked the head up and kicked it to his mates, who proceeded to play a game of football with it. 'Just a taste of what we're capable of,' they warned.

Since then, the whole community had been camped in a football stadium in the nearby paramilitary-controlled town, waiting to return. How can they not worry for their country? For it is a question of their own survival. Only they have another vision, one where they can plant and reap the fruits of their land in peace, and not just be plantation employees for the fruit, palm oil and timber corporations who want the land they are sitting on. That is the vision of the government, the army and the paramilitaries, and is probably more understandable to Mariana. After all, the Africans were brought to work on the plantation she grew up on.

I have come to the Bohemia house, the cultural refuge

fuelled by cable TV, looking for Antonio, who is now my photographer. Mariana is fixated by MTV, a bubble she wished she could live in. I try to explain it is not the symbol of freedom and alternative expression she thinks. But I shouldn't be exposing my opinions. This is the Levi's target, people who are ashamed of their culture and want to be something else, who see their freedom in another way of life. If I were a diligent spy I would be living with the bohemians, infiltrating their world. They'd probably volunteer to contribute to Levi's mission, be the chosen disciples for a common cause. But I don't want to be encouraging their prejudice. This is becoming a habit; the minds I should be infiltrating are the ones that depress me. Their jaded power and contempt depress me.

'Where is Antonio?' I ask.

'I don't know, haven't seen him for days,' Mariana replies. 'He might be upstairs in bed, making himself pale.'

I pop my head round the door and there is no Antonio. Instead, Franz is taking pictures of his eleven-month-old son crawling among some carefully placed spilled bottles of a *guardiente* and kilos of white powder. He is so engrossed in what he is doing that he doesn't even hear me say hello. After seeing him shove cardboard-corners of the white stuff his child is playing with up his nostrils for the sake of art, I leave the room.

■

I want to go to Juanchito, the heart of Cali, which lies 'across the bridge' as sung by Grupo Niche. Juanchito was born in the late 1980s, when a curfew was imposed in Cali proper to curtail cartel violence. If you went across the bridge, you were outside the boundary of municipal legislation, so here, under the disco lights and the Black Label blur, the cartel and salsa began their accidental association: two sub-cultures, criminalized and marginalized by society, united in the rhythmic *pena*-shedding ritual.

Grupo Niche's founder Jairo Varela was thrown in jail because he owned a disco in Juanchito that was found to be a money-laundering operation. In Aguas Blancas they say Varela was stitched up by the white establishment looking to punish an uppity nigger who was earning money and foregrounding black culture.

'There is no one in Cali who has not touched drugs money,' Luz told me. 'Drugs money is everywhere. It was our economy, our currency. The police chiefs picked on Varela because he was earning money and was an inspiration to black people.'

In Aguas Blancas Jairo is a hero. 'Jairo Varela has never forgotten where he came from,' they say in Aguas Blancas. His songs talk about his race and his roots. 'He is *our* Cali.' His distinct, breathless, gasping salsa that so captures this gentle spirit of human co-dependency, as opposed to the aggressive horns of New York salsa, is loved everywhere, from Miami to Milan. Niche's music (Niche means black) tells the world that Africa is the soul of Cali, and Cali is the soul of Colombia. But it reminds the whites of Cali that they are the minority – albeit a wealthy, powerful minority.

I can't find Antonio, so I have to go alone. I ask the taxi diver to drop me at a place called Palo de Mango, which has palm trees wrapped in pretty little electric lights arching over the door just like the Mermaid. To blend in as much as possible, I have got myself up in my finest Medellín slapper gear, just like Liliana and Isabel showed me.

There is no bar. There goes my refuge. Just tables of men in power suits and dagger-eyed women who follow my every move. And the waiters are all too busy serving tables to pay me any attention. If only their clients could busy themselves with something and ignore me too. The mirrored walls multiply lascivious glances. I am trapped in a labyrinth of a million beady eyes and moralizing smirks. After feigning a relaxed pose that lasts about five minutes, I abandon my flailing composure and scramble out, trying to make my escape look as purposeful as possible until I burst out of the doors. The bouncers stare at me and ask me if they can get me a taxi. No, I thank them, determined to look like I am in control.

I walk along the road, following the cha-ca-ta, cha-ca-ta, cha-ca-ta sound of the salsa beat. On the other side I spot the word 'Baracoa' in neon lights, a much bigger disco with a long queue of younger people. This will be easier, I think, once I am lost in the haystack of clammy, clinching bodies inside. I get in the queue and watch the men and women be searched in front of me. Then I hear the bouncer raise his voice at somebody.

'Who are you with?' he asks gruffly. I look behind me. He is pointing at me. The whole queue turns and stares at me.

'By myself,' I answer meekly.

'You can't come in,' he booms.

'Why?'

'No women alone.'

I want to shout that where I come from nightclubs beg women to come to their discos. They even let you in for free! I insist on seeing the manager, who comes out, takes one look and says, 'No way. I don't want another dead *gringo* on my hands.'

I ask him to explain what threat I could possibly pose and he takes me to one side and whispers, 'Look, I am not saying you are a troublemaker. But I cannot take the risk. I have had wives come in finding their husbands with their lovers. I have had women looking for their lovers and finding them with their wives. And I have had pretty girls starting a fight between men. It all ends in death.'

He offers to pay for my taxi and sends me home. Like a heretic, I am banished from the kingdom of Juanchito. My British ticket to acceptance didn't work here.

■

The only bar I am allowed to go into alone is the one owned by Antonio, Franz and Mariana. They have clubbed together to open their own place away from the world of booty worshipping, where they play Portishead and Green Day, invite their friends and put their own art on the walls.

I am still on the hunt for Antonio, and I know that tonight, Thursday night, it is his turn to manage the place. The latest art project they have on the walls consists of snaps of Cali's luxury homes and people going in and out of them. Antonio and Franz have been working on the project for several weeks. It entailed secretly obtaining the addresses of their classmates, taking photographs of their houses and then sending the photos anonymously to them, one by one. The idea was to track the encroaching paranoia on their classmates. 'A chronicle of fear,' Franz puts it, and, as if to quell my alarm, explains: 'The world of ideas is the only freedom we have.'

Antonio is not around. I ask Franz what is going on with him and he says he doesn't know why he's disappeared, only that he was offended when I teased him about his ambition to become Colombia's Sid Vicious. Perhaps I was too vocal about the Glasgow heroin chic he sports being the equivalent of an Essex tan against green meadows. 'You are right,' he replied in shattered resignation. 'I can see it now, the entire London punk scene laughing at me.'

Then I envisaged Antonio announcing his separation from the group, resigned to a life of despicable lust. Yes, I have made a mistake. Franz says I should be more careful with the things I say.

'You have a power,' he says. 'You know that what you say is influential to anyone here and you should not abuse that power.'

'I don't have power,' I protest. 'Why should you care what I think about anything?'

In Aguas Blancas the kids did not care about what I thought. They are too worried about their own lives, too engrossed in their own culture to care about what I thought of them. For all the squalor of Aguas Blancas, they value their culture. They own their identity.

Even so, what right have I to tell Antonio that his passion, his expression of discontent is not authentic? Why have I become so judgemental? Is this what my job has made me?

 The brash foreigner, spouting naive opinions with such certainty they even convince me. Antonio's frustrations at Cali conformism are probably very similar to what punks felt about middle England. What is the difference between my attraction to salsa and his to punk?

The difference is I can come here, choose what I like of 'otherness', dip my hand in the cultural pick-and-mix, bring it back to England and let it enrich my life, protected by the fortress of economic self-sufficiency. Here, there is no protection. Foreign brands persuade local business leaders to help them bedazzle the market with special effects and a glossy, wealthy lifestyle, and make it seem a magical and mystical experience that renders the indigenous opaque and poverty-stricken. How can mere self-belief, even truth, compete against the giants whose money can buy enough air space to swamp all other realities?

The Cisneros Group, 'the joint venture king', bringer of all things American – AOL, Coca-Cola, Pizza Hut, Playboy – would provide their American partners with useful advice such as not to rubbish local culture, for people are emotionally attached to their cultural symbols. Better to convert it quietly into a museum relic, quaintly nostalgic, a dash of colour but useless in the modern world. The Cali bohemians think they are prisoners of their own society, but are they not enslaved to foreign culture by embarrassment of their own?

Why does this attitude repel me so – not Antonio's, whose adoration of 'the other' stops at Sid Vicious, but Mariana's and Franz's, who long for the foreign hand to bring order? Is it so repugnant to want something else if their own situation seems lacking? Is choice not the essence of life? But I see in their request for adoption by a foreign, more powerful being the support for a military solution that accompanies it. I see in their resignation to a foreign solution a refusal to see the price that others, the majority, have had to pay for their inherited privilege, a refusal to see in themselves the reasons for the violence they blame others for and thus the solution. Yes, I have taken sides.

■

Carlos Castaño, a boyish-looking thirty-seven-year-old with a rough, stubbled face, orders his soldiers to uncuff Jaime and take off his blindfold. Jaime sees scores of soldiers running around this military outpost hidden in the jungle hilltop.

'Come, we have things to talk about,' Castaño says, and leads Jaime to his office in a large wooden shed. Jaime is soaking. Castaño sees him shivering, takes off his jacket and offers it to him. Then he sits, puts his legs on his desk and digs into a packet of crisps. There is a copy of Henry Kissinger's *Diplomacy* on his desk. He picks up a wad of paper, which he says is the public declaration he has had to make to justify the capture of Jaime Gutiérrez, FARC terrorist. He reads out the seventeen-page document, which declares Jaime a prisoner of war, to be released when the war is over. Then he throws it down on the table and says, 'So, what do you think of that?'

Jaime pauses. 'Well, first I'd like to know if you are sure you have the right Jaime Gutiérrez.'

Castaño stares at him, irritated, and repeats, 'I asked you what you think of the document.'

'We are a small NGO. We are of no significance to anyone. If you think we are connected to the FARC, or that they even care about us, you are wrong. You will get no money for us. We are of so little importance to anyone.'

'You shouldn't be so modest,' says Castaño. 'As a matter of fact, you seem to have many friends all over the world. Even the EU has called for your release. They do not know you are a terrorist, as we do. This has really become a very complicated business.'

'I have nothing to hide,' Jaime says.

'We have a witness.'

'Show me the witness.'

Castaño sighs, impatient and rattled. He wants to change the subject. 'I can see you are a cultured man, Mr Gutiérrez. Perhaps you can teach me a thing or two.'

He tells Jaime he wants to debate with him. Jaime knows what the right circumstances are for debating, and it is not when your opponent has a gun at arm's reach. He is stunned by Castaño's loquacity. He talks and talks, confident of his dubious arguments. Jaime tries to avoid responding. He notes how quickly the man becomes nervous when he senses he is being contradicted. Every time Jaime refers to the 'paramilitaries' he flies into a rage.

'How many times do I have to tell you?' Castaño shouts, thumping his hand on the table and jumping to his feet. 'We are not paramilitaries, we are self-defence units.' Then he takes a deep breath and sits down. 'I'm thinking of studying sociology. What do you think of that?' he asks.

'Why sociology?' Jaime replies, answering everything with a question to avoid confrontation.

'Perhaps it will make me more understanding. But then again one cannot change one's nature.' Castaño pauses, then sits up. 'I will tell you a story. The story of the frog and the scorpion, who are sitting together on the side of the river. The scorpion asks the frog for a ride over to the other side. And the frog protests. "You will sting me and I'll die if I give you a ride." The scorpion replies. "No, I won't. If I sting you I will die too, so what would be the point of that?" The frog reflects. This sounds sensible enough, he concludes, and agrees to carry the scorpion. Halfway over the river, the frog feels the scorpion's tail in his side and he begins to sink. "Why did you sting me when you promised you wouldn't?" he cries as he dies. The scorpion replies: "I cannot help it. It is my nature. That is what I do."'

Castaño leaves the room, patting Jaime on the shoulder as he walks past.

■

I am meeting Luz, my swimming-pool friend, to buy my last batch of Colombian lingerie, a pleasure introduced to me by my Medellín sisters. Having viewed three cities' worth of seduction masterpieces, I could deliver any lecture on the superiority of Colombian lingerie over its French and Italian rivals. In appreciation, Luz ventures up to the Chipechape shopping mall, the world of Cali's Southern Belles.

The Chipechape is also the courting ground for the upper class, where Cali's most beautiful women come to find their princes. Their posture is tight with the pretence of unavailability, demure indifference and feline delicacy, like plastic dolls in a crystal vase. *Chicas plásticas*, Mariana calls them. Everything about them is designed to provoke envy: their golden skin, moisturized daily by the latest Parisian products, the delicate gold angel hair balancing a single pearl against their bosom, deeply conditioned sunlit locks, perfectly sculptured nails and every garment impeccably stylish. Cali's handsome princes, a luxurious childhood glowing in their complexions, almost choke on their hot dogs as these perfumed angels pass. Their polite murmurs belie wild excitement. Cali Belles look for boys who can provide the life they are accustomed to: shopping trips to Miami and New York, apartments on the Venezuelan coast.

I am a bit nervous. Perhaps Luz will feel uncomfortable here. The Cali snobs will sneer at her. Luz is not particularly blessed with beauty; her legs and arms are dry, her hair is matted. But what she lacks in beauty she makes up for in attitude. Now she has got into university she feels nothing can touch her. She does not believe in the false morality the Cali elite preaches. 'They say poor people are irresponsible. But it is the rich who are irresponsible. They have the tools to change things – the money, the education and the power – but they just want to keep it all for themselves so that no one can compete with them. At least we share what we have, however little it is. The rich don't care about the country. They put all their money in the New York stock exchange, or in buying property in Miami, rather than investing it here. The oligarchy knows no nationality.'

We are in the shop now, surrounded by snakeskin silk, dainty floral chiffon, sporty stripes in fine cotton, heavy silver embroidery all in the most perfectly shaped cups and exquisitely cut vaginal triangles. I am in heaven. When I get back to England I'm going to get myself a boyfriend and show it all off. I notice the shop attendants keep their eye on Luz. With no discretion at all, they watch her fingers to see how nimble they are. Not a movement escapes them. She walks around the shop with her head up ignoring them, then she calls out to me lifting a turquoise and gold-embroidered set piece and says loudly so the whole shop can hear that she wants to buy it for me. I just smile. A little Muhammad Ali in the making. It'll get her into trouble.

■

I am leaving Colombia tomorrow. I lie in bed thinking of the leap I have to make, this time a leap across continents back to England: a leap of faith, a leap of mind, body and spirit, from guts to brain. It seems tremendous. Even though sometimes I gasp for air here in the entrails of this beast, in my breathlessness, my vanished bearings, I see, hear and feel new clarities. Here it is all mixed, the love, the loathing, the fear and hope; a magical cocktail of unpredictability. In the cracks of the impenetrable walls of history and fear reinforced by vengeance and rage, lie sweet tender voices enamouring you of the most mundane details of life – a glance, a gift, an invitation, a greeting, a goodbye – as though they were the most precious things in the world. Every second one has to choose, right from wrong, good from bad, which side to be on. The truth is an hourglass, curved like a Colombian woman, sifting through to the other side as soon as you seem to have it. Nothing is tangible or solid. Everything is alive and moving. But I have to do it. I have to return home, or at least I think it's home.

The phone rings. It's two in the morning. It's reception. Antonio is downstairs. He apologizes for having disappeared. He has been on some peace workshop down in the FARC territory for the last five days. He got back earlier in the evening to find that his wife has packed his bags and left them by the door. He asks me if he can sleep on the sofa in my suite. Of course, I say, relieved; I suppose he's not that angry with me after all.

'The Americans are coming in,' he says as we lie in the dark. He tells me an American company called Dyncorp has got the contract to destroy the coca plants, but that they are spraying all the other crops and leaving land infertile. I envisage a generation of kids called Deencor. 'And it won't work. It will only make the price of cocaine go up. But people will find somewhere else to grow it as long as poverty exists and people in Europe and the USA are willing to pay.'

There is a knock on the door. '*Señorita Amaranta, señorita, usted no puede tener ese señor en su habitación,*' says the voice the other side. I look at Antonio and cover my gasp with my hand. The man keeps knocking and his voice gets louder. 'Señorita, this will not be tolerated.' They can't very well break the door down. We carry on talking in a whisper, hoping the man will go away.

Antonio continues. 'Maybe Bush will kill everyone, leave us with a country full of dead people and then go back to his people saying he liberated us.'

The knocking won't go away. The man is furious. 'I know you're in there,' he shouts. I can't stop laughing and we have to hide in the bathroom to carry on our conversation.

After half an hour the knocking stops and we go back into the bedroom. I am exhausted. I get into bed and I am falling asleep but Antonio is so awake and buzzing that I can almost hear his thoughts rising up from the floor. Just as I fall into unconsciousness I hear him say: 'I composed a song about it all, about a town waiting for the war to happen, Amaranta. It's a punk song with a salsa riff.'

11

POWERPOINT AND BROKEN DREAMS

I had forgotten that you can tell an English boy likes you if he is rude, and that nobody talks to anyone they don't know until the party is nearly over. Just when you give up hope of any meaningful engagement, you notice that caution has been soaked up by alcohol and the cross-eyed goofs who previously noticed nothing beyond the end of their noses are up close, spluttering booze in your face as they dribble pornographic wishes. Stiff bodies that looked like they were fixed in braces start to jerk to a music they never noticed was playing. Solitary spasms form a small cluster that sways in unison until its uncontrolled weight is about to keel over and form a bundle on the floor, when by a miracle they all spring back up like jack-in-the-boxes. Just like the Cubans achieved harmonic miracles as if by accident, it is a freak of nature that this unsightly and hazardous mass of energy keeps standing.

This is my rebirth into London Life, a party in Notting Hill, being given by an old Oxford acquaintance, who, friends keep telling me, has become outrageously rich.

I had felt nervous. It's been seven years and I am a foreigner in my own home. I feared I'd forgotten how to speak English, and I realize I might as well have done since the references of the new dialect – revolving around property agents, interior designers, style gurus – are lost on me. I don't remember royals, celebrities and property ever being the pivotal points of conversation, or that lifestyle consultants filled such an important social role. The English were always good at self-parody and it helps make the trivia bearable, though only just; at Oxford I had thought it clever, now it just seems weird. Is this where I should be at now I'm twenty-nine? Loft conversions, terrace extensions, returns on investment?

A barrister with droopy eyes and a loud slurring voice, who wants to be the youngest QC in history, is telling me: 'Let's face it, no more than three per cent of people who walk this planet are worth having a conversation with.' Oh, and which percentage are you in? I want to ask. I laugh as I wonder what Marcel or Alfredo would have thought. I find myself seeing and hearing through their eyes and ears.

Upstairs in the 'chill-out' lounge, other old Oxford acquaintances who have gone into media, marketing and PR yap in queues to snort lines of coke. They have shed their upper-class accents for semi-cockney, mid-Atlantic fusions, their rugby shirts for shapeless techno gear, and their foppy hooray hair for designer shaggy-crops. It is strange that only now I detect, through the layers of acquired coolness, the stain of empire management that I had never seen coming while we were in those ivory towers that bred us for it. Perhaps my escape to the other side of the world, and their disguise, is the same attempt at negation. All in vain, though; if you've been bred for empire management, they'll drag you out wherever you are.

'Oh, you mean you're one of those cool hunters!' exclaims one guy in shin-length cargo pants and yellow-tinted goggles. 'Like, you go round and see what kind of jeans kids are wearing and all that, right? Fuckin' 'ell, I heard about that, that's *soooo* cooool, man.'

'No, I don't ask them about jeans,' I say. 'We just talk about things... life, beliefs, values.'

'Ah, right,' he says, knowingly. 'Get into their minds, the psychological stuff? You travel the world doing that? Fucking genius!' he says. 'That's the fucking job of the century!'

He thinks brands are 'fascinating' and talks admiringly of the power of Virgin in our lives. Richard Branson: 'fucking genius'. But he informs me that tribes no longer exist in Britain. Punks? Goths? Trendies? Brands have successfully assimilated them into a youth culture defined only by consumption. This must be the ultimate development stage Levi's refer to. Everyone says how lucky I am, but nobody asks me about the places I've been to, how the people live, about real things. Apparently, brand identity is much more interesting than people's.

Outside on the balcony I watch the wet streets of west London. There is something lovely about the pulp of damp leaves, the slushing of feet, the splashing of kerbs as taxis turn corners and the clinking of bottles as a lone drunk stumbles. This is the London I missed. The predictably tranquil clutter. I walk down Portobello, a wonderland of boutiques and neon-lit bars, a far cry from the run-down neighbourhood that welcomed the Brazilians, Argies and Chileans fleeing here from their dictatorships around the time I was born. Spain and Portugal, the more obvious destinations, were run by Generals Franco and Salazar; Stockholm and London became the unexpected refuges.

Enrique, my mother's jesting sociology professor friend, went from lecture podium in Córdoba to pizza kitchen in Stockholm. Others came here, famous Brazilian singers, artists, writers. My mother's Argy friends told me they were astounded at being treated so gently by the state. Immigration laws were friendlier then. And yet nobody cared what they'd been through, what they had to offer – merely assuming that they were from one of those wretched foreign places that has never known joy or laughter. What must they have thought of the famous Swinging London?

Just then, as I walk down Ladbroke Grove, the gentle voice of Caetano Veloso, circa 1970, fills my head:

Sunday, Monday, autumn pass me by,
and people hurry on so peacefully,
A group approaches a policeman,

He seems so pleased to please them,
It's good to live, at least, and I agree
While my eyes go looking for flying saucers in the sky
I choose no face to look at, choose no way,
I just happen to be here, and it's OK
Green grass, blue eyes, grey sky, God bless,
Silent pain and happiness
I came around to say, yes, and I say…
While my eyes go looking for flying saucers in the sky

■

It was inevitable that I find Bar Salsa, a replica Latin cantina on the Charing Cross Road that plays non-stop salsa on Monday nights. I can feel quite at home in my-all-in-one Lycra-denim catsuit, purchased on the streets of Caracas. It is about the least ridiculous garment amid the collective emulation of an imagined Latino glamour: yellow-tassled glitter mini-dresses – fruity Carmen Miranda meets *Come Dancing* – and black silk chest-revealing shirts – David Hasselhoff meets Jim Davidson.

On the dance floor, born-again predators flaunt their new-found testosterone in strange pelvic movements while after-office accidentals who have wandered in fancy themselves as John Travolta.

I am expected to react spectacularly to the jerk of a hairy arm, whipping faces with my flying hair as I spin through the crowd, like the others do. Before I can think, I find myself upside down with my hair dragging on the floor, sliding through my partner's feet and being thrown into the air. By the fifth dance I am so dizzy I have to sit down. Where is the soft tender embrace?

Virtuosity rather than intimacy is the byword among the London dance extraordinaires, like the spinning top in a floppy African shirt down to his knees, or the one who does quick little scurrying-mouse-like moves on tiptoes, or the balding ogre from Barnet who looks like he wants to eat his partner and walks his fingers down her back in an imagined Latin lover gesture.

Sprinkled amid the English salsa lovers are the Latin lovers for export: sweating beasts in leopardskin T-shirts and see-through stocking vests with spiky sideburns and biceps of which a *pavo* would be proud, or the open-shirted medallion and ponytail brigade. 'No, really, this is how it's done, like this,' they whisper as they rub their hairy chests and pelvises up against skinny blonde girls.

Grupo Niche fills the room with its tenderness, finding vindication in the urban solitude of first-world singledom, far away from the Cali prejudices. I spot the Colombians nestled in the corner: too much upheaval in their lives already to be aggravating it with dizzy spells on the dance floor. I swear I didn't seek them out. I am not infiltrating here. Please, spare me that. It was as if Héctor smelt Colombia on me. Long-haired, no older than fifteen, wearing a heavy metal T-shirt, he could only be a Medellín *metalero*. He grabs me to dance and then invites me over to his corner to meet Sammy and Charlie, whose Escobarian atomic-polo style makes them odd company for a *metalero*. Héctor shrugs his shoulders. 'Nostalgia forces forgiveness.'

Their snug corner provides refuge from what they call 'sleazy women' who appear out of nowhere to demonstrate their little moves in front of them. They have a name for everyone: the spinning machine is El Maykal Ja'son, and the scurrying mouse they call El Fas'forward.

I give Héctor and Charlie a lift to Wood Green, stopping by the Kurdish greengrocer's on Green Lanes, alive with midnight hustle and bustle. It has that *barrio* feel, the spirit of co-dependency. Over the counter, the moustached man passes Héctor the late-night bottle of *Etiqueta Negra* with a nod of immigrant fraternity. They understand that these illegal concessions are what keep them sane in this cut-throat city where nobody cares.

■

Crouch End also went posh sometime during my time away. Apparently, it all started when Bob Dylan nearly bought a house here. The event is recorded in a mural outside a trendy world music café, where you can get rice and peas and other third-world food at £30 a head, and lavish development decoration: revolutionary posters and souvenirs of identities that we are fast bulldozing. On a Saturday morning it is packed with ex-trendies in Che T-shirts reading the lifestyle sections of the *Guardian*. Colombian kids who have fled poverty serve in Starbucks, a company that pays coffee farmers back home the lowest prices for a century. Fairtrade coffee is proudly available (for group drinkers), valuable for its boost to Starbucks' caring image, but not valued enough to be offered as regular brew.

London bombards me with visions, sensations I never

noticed before. Sunday morning calls offering prizes that will change your life. Brands seem to occupy every public space, from a patch of green now sponsored by a chain restaurant to transport and maintenance services now privately run. Diehards of the old Crouch End are protesting against the town hall, where I once saw pantomimes, being converted into a shopping mall. Just like in Latin America, where it is up to individuals to watch out for the sale of the next community service – or is it just that corporations are encroaching on people's lives everywhere? Even on the walls where fly posters and graffiti once vented frustrations and expressed silent voices, brands have crept in, ever on the hunt for authentic space in their quest to seduce the more rebellious into their sphere of influence. Will there remain any space in our lives that cannot be bought, reproduced and emptied of meaning?

I feel differently about things that I once accepted, even valued. Like the charity telethons where celebrities have sacrificed their luxury cruises to present (with well-practised doe-eyed looks of sympathy) pre-recorded images of themselves scurrying through rubbish heaps hand in hand with children, brandishing the plight of some South American poor. The night is a glorious show of great British philanthropy, full of self-congratulation for our generosity towards these wretched peoples who somehow can't manage to get it right and be like us. There is no mention that if perhaps our own governments did not arm and support other countries' quasi-dictators – who control the media, who massacre and displace those who are fighting for a fairer society... no mention that if we practised the free trade we impose on others and made our corporations accountable for their behaviour in their countries – that then they would not need our charity.

■

Everywhere I go in London I see and hear the Colombians. There are over two hundred thousand in London, the largest Colombian community in Europe after Spain. They came as economic migrants in the late 1970s, when the cartels were busted in the late 1980s, and are now seeking asylum from the civil war. Héctor came in 1990 when he was ten. Bred in language and mannerisms in his Wood Green Comp, he speaks a Medellín-accented Spanish cockney: 'Es una mierda, innit?' 'Si, se me acerque, le reviento la cara. Na'mean?'

His vision of England was built on British Council propaganda: *Monty Python* and *Brideshead.* A nation of shopkeepers? 'The only shopkeepers I've met are Pakistanis and Turks,' Héctor says. English Roses? 'More like triffids!' Civilized? 'How can a society in which people eat on the tube call itself civilized? In Colombia only *indigentes* eat in the street.'

I notice sudden movements that never caught my eye before, like a guy getting out of his car in mid-traffic, storming between the cars to smash someone's face in through the window of another car. Since when did hooliganism go mainstream? Too much cocaine around, says Héctor. English teenagers walk and talk like the kids in American films. They say 'like *so* cool', curl the ends of their sentences as if everything were a question and hang out at the shopping mall.

 I even hear the children next door chant jingles from Waitrose adverts, as if they were nursery rhymes.

All those I know who embodied the best British characteristics – principled, original, fair, balanced, unwilling to get carried away in tides of hysterical sorrow for the loss of the Queen Mother – have sought refuge abroad, as far away from Cool Britannia as you can get.

But Héctor takes his hat off to this island. It has been good to him and he says he'll never go on the dole because it would be a sign of disrespect. He loves London, Newcastle and Edinburgh, where he often goes to play his congas at salsa festivals. But when it comes to international football he always supports Ireland.

'Why Ireland?' I ask.

'They are our brothers,' he says, gently thumping his heart with his fist. 'Remember? No dogs, no blacks, no Irish.'

■

They've started calling, the voices from the other world. Maria phones twice a week from Cuba reverse charge with bankrupting gossip. '*Malagradecida* [ungrateful cow],' the Medellín girls scream down the phone when I don't return their calls, 'you've abandoned us!' One of them, Liliana, has got a job in the new Levi's store, which pays her two hundred dollars a month, only slightly more than the factory workers. She delivers the gossip on prince charming Don Juan and his wife.

As I finish my Colombia reports and prepare my next trip to Chile, I receive a circular email from the Levi's Corporation, informing the delegates of next month's annual Americas' licensee meeting that 'Amaranta Wright will be giving a comparative presentation on the Youth Tribes of Latin America'. Was it not enough to cram children into bullet points? Do I really have to parade them in slideshow form to fifty Levi's executives? They'll be wanting blood samples next. I don't know how much longer I can keep up the façade.

The letter of invitation, the bank statement and documents I sent to the British Embassy in Lima were finally accepted and Marcel appears on the doorstep direct from darkest Perú, looking like a cross between Paddington Bear and an Islamic terrorist. He is penniless. I commission a painting off him and get a friend to do the same so he can live off the advance.

Poor Marcel, who was expecting the high art he has dreamed of seeing, is instead dragged into London's Latino low life, first by the Peruvian who married the English backpacker. Watching his friend prove he can get a snog on account of his terracotta skin and Inca features was embarrassing, Marcel says: 'I didn't know where to put myself while he was flaunting himself all over Covent Garden. He was never like that in Perú.' Then I convince him to come with me to the Colombian underworld in Peckham, where *gorditas* totter in high heels under the disco globe of Baracoa (named after the famous Cali club), their plump buttocks peering out under sequinned dresses. Across a room of Black Label, men in wide-lapelled cream suits, black shirts and medallions flash death smirks just like in Cali. But it is a woman who, finding her boyfriend snogging her best friend, starts tearing the girl's hair out. Their catfight spills out onto Peckham High Street, with knickers in full view, bra straps hanging and stilettos in hand. Tonight it's only a catfight; a week later the owner gets murdered.

No more salsa clubs, Marcel begs, and only wants to go to a Joy Division concert; 'The greatest band that ever existed.' We cannot find any comeback concerts so he makes do with posh west London parties. He is fascinated by Englishness, the way they drink unsatisfied until it turns them into a blubbering mess; the way they snort coke in neat little lines, precise and individual. In Perú nobody has a line all to themselves. They just dig into the bag with the edge of a credit card then pass the bag round – a more social ritual.

I want to die when I hear a plummy voice talk to Marcel about high London house prices. 'Oh,' the woman declares, 'I consider it a premium for living in the most exciting city in the world.'

■

There is an entire programme about Levi's 'cool hunters' on the television. I watch it, looking for myself. The protagonist is a Danish designer girl, purveyor of freaky androgynous fashion. They send her to China to get ideas for new products, where she scours street markets, takes pictures and then reports to headquarters in Brussels. No engaging. No lying. She must work for the artillery department of Levi's secret service, and I for the winning-hearts-and-minds department.

You see her marching around Beijing, a style tourist snapping away at the locals and rewarding them with a thumbs-up. 'Look at that guy over there selling the vegetables.' she

whispers excitedly in her Danish-American accent, pointing to
a vegetable seller in a shabby ski jacket so old the colour has faded out of it. 'Isn't that *soooo* cute, the way he has his sleeves rolled up like that and how the sun has bleached where those folds are and left the cracks dark.' Snap snap. 'And the contrast between the faded colour and his bright cords, he's *sooo* cool, and he don't even realize it!' She relished this rare patch of authenticity.

And yet her comments about how drab the place is show that she is not without sympathy for her impoverished hosts. Poor people, who have no access to the sacraments of brand salvation. I must put my superhero Levi's suit on immediately, hear their confessions and convert them into Levi's desires right away!

The excitement the Danish cool hunter feels about all the new ideas she has collected rapidly dispels her anxiety about the state of the world and she is soon back at the office protesting for the right to put the fading, creasing, bleaching idea into practice. She takes on this mission with quixotic fervour, although she has a hard time convincing her bosses of her crease ideology, not least because the shade contrast on the first jean samples look like someone has pissed their pants. But she is not one to give up easily, and protests until they concede her the right to offer the world the gift of ready-made sun-faded jeans as seen on the Chinese vegetable seller.

As I walk around London I see billboards, tube ads, fly posters, TV ads exuding moments of ecstatic laughter and orgasmic joy, as if only through the associated brand could they be achieved. Emotion converted into propaganda. One image projects angry youngsters with banners under the Diesel slogan *Protest!*. I can see the bullet points behind it proclaiming worries that kids have about the environment, about the food-related cancer epidemic we are living, about our world being poisoned by toxic waste, about global injustice and poverty. And I can see the marketing manager react in orgasmic excitement. We must capitalize on this feeling! Show them that we are with them! Just change the banner to: 'I love my mother!' Tap the emotion, scrap the meaning.

■

En route to Chile I have to stop off in Miami to give the slideshow. Another plane back west, but South America still seems a world away. I turn to my screen in business class, which kindly offers useful business news items, specially designed for the likes of me, as if having probed into my own professional mind. One is about tapping the pre-teen market. Having proved so successful in channelling teenage vulnerability into consumer desire, market research companies are now apparently exploring the possibilities in the 'nag factor' of what they call 'tweens'. In a primary-school setting a woman with a kind bubbly voice engages little boys and girls in friendly, exciting conversation about how and when they feel angry with their parents. Her caring eyes emulate those of a doctor or child psychiatrist attempting to cure the confused patient. But she is not there to help parents cope with nagging or the child to cope with peer pressure always to have the latest gadget. Her purpose is not to encourage the child to build a strong inner confidence, rather it is to help them feel less secure, to need more and to nag more effectively. She is so matter-of-fact, the report so upbeat, I feel it must be me who is crazy for thinking the world is really screwed when brands encourage kids to harass their parents. Why not just sponsor a nervous breakdown?

Miami's warm mugginess injects soothing liquid memory into my skin. I look out from my room at the Richmond Hotel. Wispy grass tickles the blinding bright sand as they frame the electric turquoise sea. I had forgotten how stunning the Miami backdrop was. The most heavenly of Babylons. By the pool, I wait for Bill for a pre-conference meeting. Two forty-something PR women from New York lie beside me ogling a fine-featured *mulato* pool boy from behind their Gucci glasses. As he mops the floor and collects and delivers towels, they purse their lips and rub their long white legs together in an attempt to excite him. Smiling wickedly, they make lewd suggestions and then, quite unashamedly, offer to take him up to their room. The boy smiles uncomfortably and thanks them for their generosity but says he has a girlfriend in Cuba, and bringing her over is the inspiration for his long hours of labour. Indignant, the women sulk.

I've never done a presentation before. Bill says he wants me to use PowerPoint 'to draw similarities and differences between the tribes that appear in each country, to help us form a regional marketing plan'. Coldly, in my room, I begin to collect from my reports the kids from each country who most typify certain groups: The *Patas, Panas, Parseros, Pelados, Socios, Chabones* who made up the continent's mainstream; the angry young things –

 Radicals, Hardcores, Metaleros, Rockeros – who everywhere defied convention; the children of neo-liberalism – *Plasticos, Nuevos Pitucos, Ricky Pelados, Neuvos Ricos, Pavos, Gallinas, Carangas* – who aspired to the new Miami-manufactured Latin glamour; their neo-alternative counterparts – *Ravers, Modernitos, Yes-yesitos Locos, Nuevos Hippies, Tranzeroes* – who looked to Europe for a more sophisticated influence; and the *Reggaeseros, Salseros, Raperos, los Guapero, Romanticos, Vallenateros* who, by being themselves, barely made it onto the grids.

I spread all the photos of the kids over the bed, trying not to look too long or hard at them for fear they might stir something inside, make me remember what they meant to me. For now, they must be just faces, blank and meaningless, existing only to be organized and compartmentalized. Did the meaning in words spoken between us matter? Today, I must not ask questions. I am the corporate person – strategy rules.

I can feel myself becoming detached from the cause and effect of my labour, becoming a game player, a pilot in a video game, a modern-day shepherd, steering sheep into that gate. It is easy to forget you are dealing with people. Companies are always going on about giving their products a human face. Personalizing, customizing: 'Because we care!' 'Because local knowledge counts.' In reality, people matter less and less. In the process of selling the personal, the seller becomes less personal, less human. People exist only to fulfil a purpose in a mission. And even the mission one avoids defining. To say profit would be too crude.

Empathetic marketing is more appropriate.

I look at my reports and begin to compare the most similar groups in each country. There *are* comparisons to be drawn, common emotions underlying idiosyncrasies and subtleties: The neo-alternatives' need to be different and unique; the traditional elite's need for security and status quo; the new rich's obsession with success, money and status; the street tribes' yearning for opportunities and recognition behind the hard-faced bravado. Enough to draw parallels between each country's particular expression of a tribe, enough to create a brand identity that taps into pan-regional common denominators. Where foreign policies have divided and devastated, Levi's will convey emotional solidarity, unite the peoples of Latin America, a kind of Blue Jean Bolivarianism.

But will branding *reflect* their needs or invent new ones through them? When they are rebranded in Levi's image, do they become Levi's inventions? Real emotions and identities are a pain. Unreliable, unpredictable, disloyal, the corporate nightmare. They must be controlled. In an ideal corporate world, the only emotional loyalty would be with the product. Nike and Levi's would be like countries, entities that draw automatic allegiance. If feelings and ideas that define people's loyalty can become manipulated, then what is to stop brands appropriating them altogether?

Like that company RiceTec, which has patented strains of basmati rice and sought to collect royalties from Indian farmers who develop the strains. Like Carefree Wonder, who patented a strain of rose bushes and warned that any untrimmed branches sprouting new bushes would constitute unlicensed reproduction and thus be chargeable. Patents protect invention, not life itself, but now biotechnology is blurring the boundary between life and invention. Patents for cloning life have already been granted to bio-tech corporations who argue that they need to protect their costly investments in scientific research. If they are already patenting life in the 'invented' form, what will stop brands – who, with media partners, have proved as effective in manipulating perceptions as science has proved in manipulating genes – patenting thoughts and feelings they have 'invented'? They too will argue that their investment in market research justifies their claim to control the result.

Do my catergorized tribes now belong to the categorizer? Will Levi's claim to own the tribes I have documented just because they have paid me to convert them into bullet points? Perhaps one day there will be no authentic thoughts and feelings left, only branded ones, formulated to inspire needs before the needs exist. Then my job might no longer be to hunt out thoughts and feelings but to catch those who are violating patented ones.

I shudder.

■

The next day, we all move up to another place in Miami's hinterland where the Levi's Latin American headquarters are. The place is called Weston, if you can call Weston a place. There is no telling where it begins or ends: a cluster of chain stores – Dunkin' Donuts, Taco Bell, PC World – on a highway running through the Florida swamp, only distinct from the previous cluster because its business park houses different corporations.

The delegates begin to arrive at the monster-size Sheraton Hotel with mall attached: Latin American licensees with their top managers and the big cheeses from San Francisco. Oscar from Venezuela is here, Juan David and Clarita from Colombia, the Chilean owners of the Perú licence, delegates from Costa Rica, Panamá, Argentina, Uruguay and Mexico. We have drinks at an Italian bar that Bill has hired in one of the commercial centres and nibble at fried plastic bits, which they claim is mozzarella.

I drink too much. I am nervous about my presentation tomorrow. I am nervous about being here. I don't belong. Ramón from Chile reassures me: 'In a presentation, the key thing is to know your subject. I am sure you won't have any problems.' They are all so friendly.

I find myself flirting with Juan David who bats his long eyelashes seductively and tells me he has split up with his wife. After the drinks, everyone bids me farewell and tells me they are looking forward to my speech, which kicks off the conference at nine. I should be getting an early night too, but Juan David and I decide to try to find a salsa bar. We drive around for ever trying to find a flicker of life in this nightmare of indistinguishable concrete containers. We give up and head back to the hotel.

At night I can't sleep. I try in vain to open the suicide-proof windows, then lie suffocating in the big shhhhh of air-conditioning and ice machines, the white noise of convenience living. Outside, the moist Florida night caresses the lush flora. Crickets tickle the grass, frogs croak, alligators soak, and here I am freezing to death in the midst of an air-conditioned blizzard, drowning in fake floral scent. A friend once warned of men with acclimatized homes, whom she put in the same category as those with short moustaches, as if the two were indicators of psychopathic tendencies. I wonder what that says about the guests these hotels are built for. In the morning I wake up so tired. My only consolation is that in a few hours it will all be over.

I wait in the conference room alone while the interpreters install themselves in their boxes, the conference engineers test headsets and my audience trickles in. Bill introduces me as the 'intrepid investigator', the source of product strategy, and I am still shaking as I begin to talk.

I go through the tribes explaining their physical characteristics and mental conditions, what possibility Levi's has of reaching them and the strategies they should pursue. The slideshow works perfectly and the executives are captivated, looking at pictures of schoolchildren with their jaws hanging open. You'd have thought they'd never seen people standing in the street before. They laugh, they sigh, they are engaged by descriptions of teenagers striving for personality, fighting off vulnerability as they struggle to grasp the world. They are touched by the emotion in the young faces telling of their hopes and dreams, but still seem detached, as would a sheep farmer who adores lambs but also owns the abattoir.

While I have their undivided attention, I fantasize slipping in some extra tribes: racist marketing managers, greedy licence owners, democratic dictators who have opened up the markets while their army and media control dissent, governments who sell them weapons, murdered union leaders. In my dream, they walk out shaking their heads in disappointment and disgust at my sudden aggression. The hour flies by. I'm not quite sure what I've filled it with. I never even looked at my notes. I get a round of applause. Everyone says it was a marvellous presentation. I guess I do know my subject after all. How skilfully I have subverted humanity to a neat little consumer ideology!

One of the licensees even stands up and tells everyone how useful my report has already been in his country, how it helped them identify the target, reach the kids, increase brand loyalty. A debate begins about whether my description of the lower class, the darker street kids, as youth's most authentic expression, counts. It is concluded that the argument for their dark faces to be recognized in adverts is irrelevant since they have no consumer significance. I had been angry at the exclusion of black faces from advertising, but now I am relieved that their lives will not be meddled with. Their feelings, their identity, that Magali said 'they can't take away', will still belong to them a little more, a little longer; the only compensation for being forgotten. One licensee confesses that his people don't know what to do with this weird, abstract market information, and Bill reassures him that San Francisco will help them put it to good use.

The head of Levi's for all the Americas congratulates me personally. For a second I feel pleased. All thoughts of the broader picture dissolve in the praise. My little ego is pulsating with joy. The Atahualpa complex is taking hold of me, for the sheer belief in manifest destiny around me, the self-righteous conviction of civilization, is quite stunning. I feel powerless and alone. If I had the courage, I would tell them that they are mistaken, that their mission is fatally flawed, but who am I to say this?

Besides, everyone is so nice to each other, so polite and diplomatic. They talk in sentimental ways about the 'kids', recognizing their needs and feelings, involving the consumer, offering a platform, just like on the website. They don't know what it's like on the other side, being a poor teenager facing the most powerful and deviously crafted tide of commercial manipulation in history before they are old enough to make sense of it. And they *are* nice people, individually. It is just this organized pursuit that drives the collective, the pursuit whose real nature is not even contemplated in the strategy of every day, its cause and effect so far away.

But now is not the time or place for expressing these concerns. I don't want to blow my cover. There are still dots to join. I still have one country left. I have finished my presentation and can relax at last. I feel that I've been through a battle that is about to come to its climax. It was a battle I was not prepared for. I poured all my emotional energy and productive forces into something I did not understand. Levi's saw in my thirst for discovery, my passion for reality, my ability to engage, an opportunity, but it did not anticipate that these talents would make me a liability.

I need a release. I have to shed this other skin I have been wearing, this other being I have stepped into. I tune in to Sol 98 and find that tonight they are broadcasting from the Bermuda Bar, a place I used to go with Yoel in North Miami. My old escape from the Cisneros. It only means a thirty-minute trip down the highway. I convince Juan David to come with me.

Clarita, Juan David's redheaded protectress, insists on chaperoning us. All the salsa dudes are out, looking sharp. The buzz flows through me again as I walk in under the pink lights and percussive sounds shower harmony over us. We cherish the escape, the breathing space to feel rather than think. 'Who doesn't tell a lie, to avoid another's pain?' Grupo Niche sings, caressing my troubles. The salsa lie is a different league of lying: small and personal, to make life bearable, not big and institutional, a never-ending quest for profit.

Clarita takes one look around the place and says it is full of *negros cochinos* and she doesn't want to stay. She says she'll take the car and come back for us in a couple of hours. Juan David grabs my hand, takes me to the dance floor and holds me in his embrace. We don't let go for two hours. The music flows through me and I can feel a new liberation. Tonight, in the arms of the enemy, I will set myself free. I have chosen my side. Everything is becoming clear, and soon I will shed this skin like a snake in metamorphosis. Just one more dot and the picture will be complete.

12

9/11: THE PREQUEL

'Our minds aren't vacuums to be filled but fires to be lit.'
Gustavo, 17, Santiago de Chile

Down, down into the entrails of the beast, with its jungles of shrouding poisons and cures, mountains of wisdom, folly-tempting deserts, rivers with currents of vitality and estuaries of blood, down to 'the dagger pointing to the Antarctic', as US Secretary of State Henry Kissinger once called Chile. It is my last Levi's country. What questions are there left to ask? I have searched out the truth. But I must bear the worst of it: perform a function despicable to me, in full consciousness, with my senses raw, stripped of the protective layers of ignorance. Mine is no longer a search for discovery. Negation or reinforcement are my options. To complete or destroy the picture, proclaim the verdict. Then what?

The thought of going out onto the streets again makes me feel so tired. I feel numb, indifferent, heavy. A broken illusion makes you despise people, as if it is *their* fault that you spied on them, like a husband who cheats on his wife and then blames her for neglecting him. The bully enraged by his victim's weakness. You begin to hate decent qualities in others like generosity and trust; they are intolerable because you cannot offer the same.

The Sheraton San Cristóbal is a palace of polished brass and marble. Flower arrangements and bouffants tremble in the air-conditioning and white horses run through paintings of misty lavender. I have a vision of my father, who brought me here as a toddler, in a white linen suit looking out through the foyer's glass sheets onto the garden. He also wandered across borders, in his solitude, searching, questioning the power invested in him. A character out of a Graham Greene novel. As a child, I wanted to think he was a spy. Now perhaps I wish the rebel on him. I want to ask him what happened when he got back to England. What allowed him to slot back into a system he knew was unfair?

Since then a tower of luxurious suites has been added to cater for the increasing numbers of foreign business visitors. Levi's have put me in the tower, where I sit in a white bathrobe as white-gloved butlers bring me dinner. Later I go downstairs to get my free welcome *pisco* sour. Wired security guards are scanning the lobby, poised for lunatic invasion. This is the first day of the conference for the Inter-American Development Bank (BID) and there have been anti-global capitalism protests outside the conference centre some miles away.

In the garden there is a party. 'Citibank' is projected by laser onto the hillside, and Santiago's business elite and their larger US visitors hover around the pool. The acclimatized Brazilian band plays 'The Girl From Ipanema', lightly Latin, watered down for foreign comfort. Travel, sports and industry gossip are the favourite topics, false modesty and flattery are in abundance, and the visitors take this chance to express how much they like doing business in Chile. Near by I hear the protest being mentioned. One executive is boasting how he practically had his head knocked off by a flying egg. At least he can tell his children back home how he braved terrorists, he laughs.

'It ees really very embarrassing,' says a Chilean in a stiff suit, shaking his head apologetically. 'Yoo wood ha' thought heere people would know better. We are the leaders een Lateen America and we should set a good example. Ees jus' a few ceenical people determined to be nuisance. We call these kin' o people *pesado. Son muy pesados.*'

'Yeah, my gaad, why are they picking on us? It's not our fault they lost that soccer match yesterday against Perú,' says a pinstriped woman, trying to lighten the topic with a touch of humour. 'I mean, for chrissakes, can't they come up with anything more original than "Yankees go home"? It's like a scratched record.'

'They don't represent real Chileans,' one Chilean says. 'The real working people of Chile are very proud of our achievements. We have proven that you don't *have* to be a third world nation; it just takes a little discipline and hard work. You know why the Argentines are in such a mess? Because they never had a Pinochet to put things in order. It is thanks to him that we are what we are.'

'I gotta take my hat off to you boys,' roars a portly New Yorker. 'You people are totally focused, very proud people.' He turns to his colleague. 'Even their shanty towns are the cleanest you've ever seen. That shows their spirit.'

A dance show begins that climaxes with a great firework and laser display and a booming American voice like the ones in movie trailers says, 'Thank you for your business!' Everyone claps and turns to congratulate each other. A sense of triumph is evident in the air, and indeed it should be, for together these local and foreign partners share a special achievement. They are the players in Chile's transformation from Kissinger's Latin American 'dagger' into the jewel in America's crown, all thanks to General Augusto Pinochet.

■

Early next morning, as I breakfast and listen to the muzak playing over the tannoy (the *Star Wars* theme and 'I Just Called To Say I Love You'), I spot bodyguards shrouding the US Secretary of State and the businessmen with Escobarian puissance (save the atomic colours). I make my way down to The Jeans Company, Levi's Chilean licensee, and meet the smiling eyes of Ramón, the owner, as I walk in. He is also part of the 'special achievement' that began thirty years ago when Pinochet's coup, backed by the US State Department, ousted the elected socialist president, Salvador Allende, on 11 September 1973.

Pinochet became the first Latin American leader to impose IMF prescriptions, slashing trade tariffs, increasing interest rates, deregulating prices and privatizing state-run industries to encourage foreign investment and make local industry competitive. Hundreds of local medium-sized firms disappeared, unable to compete with new foreign rivals. A smaller select breed of holding companies swept up their bankrupt firms along with former state-run companies. Ramón was in on this. As well as running the Levi's licensee company, he is on the boards of a huge salmon farm and Lan Chile, the national airline. He is a curious and likeable man; his shy and gentle manner disguising Darwinian convictions. 'A natural historical process' is how he describes Pinochet's transformation, 'and nature is sometimes cruel'.

I find myself in an office with a young pretty girl, who begins to twitter on about the Chilean market at a rate I can't keep up with. Andrea is her name, and though she is full of enthusiasm, there is something sad in her eyes. This time, I am to investigate 25- to 35-year-olds for Dockers, Levi's mature brand, as well as the young guns – this added report a tribute to Chile's consumer 'development'. A tall, thin, handsome boy in his late twenties walks in to greet me. He is Lucas, the marketing manager, and Andrea's boss. Something about him makes me feel instantly nauseous. Three years of engagement has made my instincts animal.

We get a map of Santiago and with his marker Lucas slashes a red line down through the middle, dividing the city's east side, at the foot of the Andes, from the west, towards the coast. Then he draws a circle on the east side of the city.

'This is the middle/upper-class sector,' he explains, tracing the circle with his finger like an officer showing a military target. 'You'll stay in this area. There'll be nothing of interest to you outside it.'

■

The next day I do as I'm told and head east, up Avenida Las Condes towards the new suburbs – Vitacura, Las Condes and Barnechea – with their mansions peeping out over Andean shrubbery. The area has an eerie resemblance to Weston, with its clusters of McDonald's, Burger King, Blockbuster, Dunkin' Donuts and TGI Fridays off the main avenue. Only the terra-cotta earth gives away the unique Andean context. Red dust is everywhere because of construction work. I choose one of the new private universities called the Development University. Inside, I do my little introduction to a group of students: my name is… I am from… and before I finish I am being hounded by a young man with golden stubble, hair almost to his waist and a face contorted in anger.

'I'll do your interview if you give me a thousand pounds,' he says. I laugh. The boy is serious. 'That would buy me a plane ticket to England so I can visit your prime minister and kill him. Before I killed him I would ask him why he wanted to harm my country.'

It is less than a year since Pinochet was arrested in London and detained by the British government.

'Why have you done this to us?' shouts Vanessa. 'Is this the thanks we get for helping you in the Falklands war?'

I ask them what they think of the tortures, the 'disappearances' that went on under Pinochet's regime. This sends the young man into a fit. 'What do you know about the way we live, the choices we've made? You don't understand. Pinochet is the MAN! He has character in a world of wimps and fairies. He is a man who knows what he wants and gets it. He inspires awe. Nobody has nurtured the love and admiration of a nation as he has. How did he pull off that coup? It was a work of genius... it all worked to perfection.'

He goes on to say he has watched Pinochet's bombing of the government palace so many times on video he knows every move off by heart, from the initial blasting of the building to the landing of the helicopter on top, from the storming of the soldiers on the ground to the lining up of the president's men face down on the ground outside (most of whom were never seen again), and finally the announcement of the overthrown President Allende's suicide. The most impressive image of all, he says, is the strongman himself, triumphant yet elegant in shades and military uniform, addressing the press afterwards. He has that image on a poster in his bedroom.

'There is nobody else to look up to,' says Vanessa in a calmer tone. 'Chileans have no personality, you see. We are weak, not like the Argentines. Pinochet is the only real man we have ever produced.'

'Oh come on!'

'OK, give me an example of who we should look up to,' says the young man. 'Marilyn Manson? Ricky Martin? Tom Cruise? They are not *real* men... Give me Jack Nicholson, Anthony Hopkins... now you're talking.' He also adds Nelson

 Madela, who 'saw the error of his ways' in prison. But Brad Pitt, Leonardo DiCaprio? Gay fuckwits, all of them. They make me sick. I would kill them all.'

Why does he want to kill everyone? Perhaps it's the Pinochet syndrome. You can't just dislike people, you have to wipe them off the face of the earth. He says he would like to give me his list of the people he would most like to kill. Go ahead, I say.

'OK, top five people I'd most like to kill: in fifth place, Saddam Hussein. He is an evil dictator. Number four, that guy Milošević. Number three, Tony Blair—'

'You already said you wanted to kill him.'

'OK, that Spanish judge who sent the arrest warrant. Judge Baltasar Garzón. He is always poking his nose in where it's not wanted. Number two, Salvador Allende.'

'He's already dead.'

'Well, I'd kill him again, just for the pleasure of doing it myself.'

'OK, OK,' I concede. 'And number one?'

He takes a long pause, taking the matter very seriously; he doesn't want to waste his last death wish. 'I got it, I got it. You know who I hate most?' he says after a while, jumping up and down in excitement. 'I hate him so much, if he ever came to Chile, I would shoot him before he even stepped on our turf so he doesn't leave his stain on our beautiful country.'

Let me see: Stalin, Hitler…

'MICHAEL JACKSON!' he screams.

There is silence. Then I explode into laughter.

'What on earth has *he* done?' I say. Could it be the allegations of child molestation?

'He makes me want to vomit. He doesn't know what he is. He is neither white nor black, he is just grey,' says the young man. 'He is trying to be something he is not and ends up just, just... unidentifiable.'

I go back to the hotel a little bemused. What was all *that* about? What is it that makes them hold Pinochet to their bosom as if he were the very core of their existence, like Maradona to Argentines? The coup, like the Hand of God, admirable in its craft, his 'disappearances' an understandable caprice of greatness, like a drug habit.

■

'THE LIE, I hate THE LIE.' The words spit out of gritted teeth. I have crossed Levi's forbidden Red Line marked on my map. In fact, I am far beyond the Red Line, way across the west side of the city of drab grey concrete poverty. Chile's economic miracle also produced the continent's second most unequal income distribution. Yet, in these forgotten entrails, the human warmth does not emerge to fill my senses as usual. Instead a chilly distress seeps into the core of my bones, making them shudder. I feel scared, threatened, not physically, but my head winces as if restless ghosts lingered searching for peace. No, my sense of mission has dissolved; eerie signals hang around my path, whispering things.

José and Luis were in solemn conversation when I approached them. Around our patch of grass the frenetic traffic circulates like sharks around a desert island. 'Welcome to *Santiasco*,' they say. 'Asco' means repulsive.

The Andes' majestic peaks stand in the distance behind an orange film of pollution, a memory, an idea of a Chile that was, that might still exist. The poetic Chile of Pablo Neruda, the idealistic Chile of Allende, the Chile without Pinochet.

'Usually we would be on the other side of the park where our friends are,' Luis said when I arrived, 'but we're leaving *la caina.*' He tapped his finger on the side of his nose to indicate the substance, not a place.

'Luis has been off it a month. He is helping me,' José says. 'You see these scars?' He points to the side of his face and his arms covered in scabs. 'I was on a *caina* binge all day. I was so out of it that I fell off a chair and crashed onto my desk. I made a real mess of myself, blood everywhere. I didn't want my family to see me so I stayed in my room paranoid until everyone had gone to bed. Then I went and stayed at Luis's for a few days.'

They laughed together. José and Luis are seventeen. Neither of their parents knows about their four-year addiction. Practically everybody I've interviewed since I arrived seems to have some kind of drug habit, prescribed or illegal. Even the Pinochet kids. Especially the Pinochet kids. In all my Latin encounters, Chile, the Latin American tiger, was the last place I expected to find everyone strung out on cocaine. Colombia perhaps, I had thought, but as the Colombians say: 'We flog it to the world. We don't eat where we shit.'

'Everyone goes on about what a success we are, but it's a lie. We don't have anything here. We have no identity, no personality,' says Luis. 'We are not a nation. We are just a country defined by geographical borders. A nation is made up of shared experiences. The only shared experience people have are religion, consumerism and football.'

'We *did* have a personality once. You cannot create great poets without a sense of being,' insists José. 'But now this is the only country in Latin America without a ministry of culture. You cannot have a personality if you have no culture, no communication.' He takes a coin out of his pocket and shows it to me. 'See this?' he says, pointing to the side of the 100-peso coin. I read the words 'By reason or by force'. 'That is the ethos we have inherited. We have become a nation of robots forced to obey orders. Everybody talks about Chile's progress, but it's a lie because we let foreign companies destroy our environment. The tax system is worked out to subsidize the big corporations. Poor people work their asses off, pay more and more tax, and we don't even get free education and health for it. The rich people here supported the coup to bring capitalism to benefit themselves. Everyone else scrambles for little crumbs.'

'Pinochet took away our ability to think,' says Luis. 'Under Pinochet, if you thought differently you could be killed. People are still scared to think for themselves. Everyone lies here.'

The word 'lie' is beginning to give me the creeps. Here they say the Chile that Pinochet produced is a lie. Up in Vitacura they say that Pinochet critics are lying to spoil their success. One country, two histories, nobody sure of the truth.

José and Luis are not sure whether the lie of history is a figment of their imagination, adolescent angst or paranoid confusion. They guess at it, but I know, because I am lying for the 'winners' who have stolen their destiny.

The boys invite me to their house. Like many of the kids I've interviewed, they sense that my sudden appearance is significant, that I have answers.

'Some other day perhaps,' I say.

■

There is a video waiting for me at reception when I get back to the hotel. The writing on the envelope is messy, impatient. Perhaps it is from one of the kids I have been interviewing; probably a joke, porn or something.

There are shots of the bombing of the presidential palace, and then footage of Pinochet saluting, untouched by the dust of the deed. Must be the Jesus look a like Pinochet fan, I think – the General's Greatest Hits or something.

But then it changes. The film cuts to women talking. I fast-forward: there is one called Nelly, another called Gabriela, Cecilia, Gladys. Most of them are in their fifties and sixties. They look like ordinary housewives. I stop at Nelly who talks softly, smiling.

'They came into my bedroom and they took him away. I never heard anything and I never saw him again. I kept a suitcase in which I packed all the things I would take to my husband when I found him. When I had found the concentration camp, I would take him these things. Clothes, his favourite chocolates, almonds, magazines he liked… then as time passed, I would change the things since they were no longer any good. My hopes were also dying. While I had the suitcase,

I was also passing on to my son the hope that one day his father would come home. When he was four I had my first flash that this wasn't going to happen. I got the first news that it was possible that he was dead. I decided to tell my son the truth: that his father wasn't going to come back. I wanted to explain, in a way he would understand, what had happened. One thing seemed vital: trust. I knew that for my son to trust me I had to tell him the truth.'

■

When I was first at the university I had asked the Pinochet freak if there were any Humanities faculties. I had only seen Economics, Law, Politics, Exact Sciences, Engineering and Business. 'Humanities?' he said, frowning. 'Ah, there *is* a degree called Social Communication, where they do Media, Marketing and Public Relations, all that stuff, but it's full of weirdos, pansies and commies.' Can propaganda really be rebranded as a radical force in society, the balancing factor in a democracy? Maybe it explains why Levi's marketing people talk as though they're doing social work.

I walk through a surrealist landscape of slick upside-down meanings. Even the names of the universities – of Economic Sciences, of Progress, of Development – seem like products out of an IMF brochure. Brochure-fit students in Levi's jeans and polo shirts are leaving campuses for their favourite bar, called Publicity. I enter to the clink of cocktail glasses, a hostile happy hour. The ominous murmur – is it marketing subversion? Or is it just me? There is a group of men a little older than the rest of the clientele who are grabbing all the attention. Two of them ooze New York designer modernity in black outfits, dark glasses and short hair – Matrix style. The other is more conservative, a chequered shirt and cargo pants. Definitely the Dockers tribe.

I am fortunate to have fallen on these opinion-leading entrepreneurs, they tell me, frequently chosen by industry magazines as the top eligible young bachelors. Well, one of them at least. The other two are married and have come along 'to escape from our nagging wives'; mid-life crises at the grand old age of twenty-nine.

'The problem with being successful,' says the Matrix one, 'is that it only makes you more aware of the mediocrity of your environment.'

To avoid this mediocrity, they advise me to stay right here in Las Condes, wherein lie the most advanced fitness centres, the biggest multiplex cinemas, the best luxury apartments and shopping malls. 'You'll see how ignorant people are in this country, the cheap character, how uncouth. They resent us because we won. They hate us because they want to have what we have. But it is not the poor so much, eh?' one says, shaking his finger to indicate this isn't mere snobbery. 'Most of *them* are fine. It is the *communistas chaqueteros* [communist conmen]. They don't want to work and then they take it out on us, because they are not successful. They lie all the time.'

I have to stretch my imagination here to apply the marketing transformation of the negative. Idealist = lazy. Cynical = dynamic. The Pinochet truth.

'You are lucky you have come across us,' says the one in the chequered shirt. 'We are the only cultured people here.' I don't know if they are being ironic, making fun of me. I feel my face tightening, my pretend smile fixing into a grimace.

'You have no idea who you are talking to, do you?' one of them snaps.

'No,' I reply meekly.

'We own one of the most successful advertising company in the country. We turnover ten million dollars a year and have offices in other countries,' he says, and waits for my reaction.

'Oh.'

'You don't get it, do you? You don't get it!' he screams. 'Why the fuck should I be answering your silly questions. There is a waiting list of journalists who want to interview us. Who do you think you are?'

In no time at all this has gone terribly wrong and I don't know how. Why do *these* men feel so insulted when, officially at least, we work for the same side. Perhaps it is becoming too obvious that I am not such a good ambassador for what I do. The mask is slipping. I gather my things and run out. When I get round the corner the tears come flooding out. I don't know where they've come from, but I cannot stop, and I can hardly breathe for sobbing as I go back to the hotel. In my room, I press play on the video. Gabriela has a warm face, slightly indigenous, with soft dark eyes.

'When you've had electric shocks for a long time,' she begins, 'you're left unable to move, like a rag. Then this guy... starts to rape me. In this case, I can say I *did* have the strength to resist. I said, "I'm a political prisoner, I'm not just here for you to abuse me"... Well, since I wasn't, wasn't in the condition to be raped... I don't know... I probably didn't respond in the necessary way... well, he put his penis in my mouth. But I did try to resist. I can only say that... in all this I noticed something strange, that this wasn't part of the interrogation, it was part of something else, like the notion that we weren't people, just toys they could do anything they wanted with. It was an attempt to break you. They would say to you, "It doesn't matter if you don't talk now. I've got all the time in the world. Nobody knows where you are. They won't be able to find you. Here, reporters won't show up, neither will doctors. You are in our power." That was their line: "You are in our power."

'Democracy returned, or the beginnings of democracy, and I was having problems sleeping. I was crying all the time. Fortunately I had a friend at work who worked as a doctor with... with people who had been affected by the repression, and he told me... I mean... even now you don't speak about... about having been a prisoner, except with others who've also been in jail, because in this country... this is a country that still denies its history... and it denies us the right to dignity because... sorry, I didn't want to cry.'

She wipes the tears from her eyes and shakes herself.

'I think this is what hurts the most, that there are so many people who accept it and think it's good, think it's good that people were tortured and killed, that your brother was murdered, that you were tortured. There are people who come and say to your face the only problem with Pinochet is that he didn't kill all the communists, or people who thought differently... this is the hardest thing, because it is the continuation of the dictatorship in those who aren't even military officers...

'I feel able to live with the past. Nevertheless, I think about that question everyone asks. "Why can't you forget it? Wouldn't it just be better to forget? You must forgive." I have heard this many times. I think the only ones who can forgive are the ones who have suffered. Nobody else can do it for them. But how can you forgive when nobody is asking you for forgiveness?'

■

Lucas is awaiting a report of the week's progress. I sit on his desk as he finishes a spreadsheet. Without looking up, he asks me: 'So how is the youth of Santiago?'

'I don't think they are very well,' I tell him, not wanting to say too much. 'Confused, vulnerable...'

He listens attentively, and frowns at the numbers before him. 'Vulnerable...' he repeats, as if thoughtful. Then he turns to me with new enthusiasm. 'But that is good! I mean, it is good for us.' He returns to his spreadsheet.

Lucas shows me the products he has in store for his market and proudly claims that Chile is the only Latin American country to be selling the new 'Twisted' line. I read the strapline. 'Levi's Engineered jeans with their entirely modern shape and twisted seam are always setting the blueprint for things to come.' Perfect for Pinochet youth's conviction of enlightened progress and modernity. Or Twisted jeans for a generation with twisted notions of history.

 I am thinking of making the whole report up. Painting a picture of happiness and joy. Levi's' Chile is not responsible enough to handle the truth. They should be protected from it, like children.

■

Gladys says: 'I was a political leader and a woman: two things that really enraged them. So I had a pretty rough time… the electric grill, the telephone (they clapped your ears hard between both hands), the karate on your back… a lot of drugs, they gave me a lot of drugs because they thought that what I didn't say during torture I would say under the effects of drugs… a lot of psychological torture, I think the psychological tortures have left the deepest scars…

'They didn't let me wash. They made me keep my knees against my body all the time so I couldn't stretch out… elemental things like my menstruation. I remember having a smell, I became used to it, but my cellmates said I stunk to high heaven, with all my blood stuck to my body. The uncertainty of what you are, this mere object you become in their hands, that is the feeling which is most difficult to handle. You get used to the pain, you even build up your own resistance to it… but the hardest thing of all was hearing and seeing other people's pain.

'I have had many nightmares about a scene they made me watch, which was the slow death of a twenty-one-year-old boy called Cedomil Lancic, a Yugoslav boy almost two metres tall with a very strong build who they beat to death with chains because he had tried to escape. Due to his extraordinary physical strength, it lasted many hours. Three of us had to watch and I am the only survivor.

'I remember we held hands and we tried to give him courage, transmit some energy, to give him love, I guess. Then the time came when the greatest act of love we could do for him was to wish that he die quickly. Later they gave him to us… we dragged him away leaving a trail of blood. He was alive for about three more days, conscious until the end.

'I think that of all the things, the hardest thing to heal has been the screams of pain of my companions.'

■

The next morning there is a message to say that my father is coming. He is on a work trip that happens to coincide with mine and will be flying in from Buenos Aires any day now. He says he doesn't enjoy coming to Chile as much as he used to, apart from the chance to see old friends, and that Santiago is unrecognizable as the city he used to visit when I was a little girl. Back then it was buzzing with intellectual activity, ideals, energy. Chileans were romantic, but also blessed with a great sense of irony. You didn't see concentrated wealth as marked as you do now, you didn't see widespread poverty as you do now, and you didn't see the faces, defeated and depressed, of a society whose soul has been ripped out and torn to shreds.

I'm sure I'll feel better when my father comes. He'll be able to make sense of everything. Why I find such hostility in the atmosphere. Why do I feel so sick at the triumph of one side over the other? It's as if the state Santiago is in and my own Levi's function are linked. My own deceit is mirrored in my subjects' obsession with the lie. My desire is no longer for the truth, it is for the exposing of the false victors, the victors the brands want to court and pamper because they have money. My desire is for vindication of losers. The lovely losers, as César in Perú would toast. For the truths to be untwisted.

After watching a Chilean version of Oprah Winfrey, in which a priest castigates the sinners and gives a small sermon to the tearful audience, I decide to go to the centre of town. It's business as usual: outside the Supreme Court a small Pinochet demonstration is going on. Pinochet has just been granted conditional liberty by the court that was following up the charges that led to his arrest in London. The Pinochet-worshipping housewives have come out in full force in 'I Love Pinochet' T-shirts and are throwing chicken bones at the anti-Pinochet protestors.

I look for a place I can get a coffee in the grey functional business district. The Miami disco interior of one looks oddly out of place: the walls are mirrored and there are no seats, only a padded bar to lean on. The woman about to serve me is wearing a leather bikini. I try to avoid staring at her cleavage as she leans over the counter but this is practically impossible due to the fact that the counter seems to have been designed for the precise purpose of allowing her breasts to rest on it at eye level. I look round and realize I am the only fully dressed female in the café. Beside me a man is squeezing a note into the bra of the woman who has just finished serving me. There is no alcohol on offer here; Chileans are very strict about drinking during work hours.

I leave, walk along the pedestrian street and go into the old covered galleries, where I find more 'cafés with legs', as I now notice they are called, tucked away in the cracks of Santiago's grey-suit morality. I follow some men in through a door and find myself in a cramped room shuddering to the sound of techno and brimming with starch-suited execs.

The ladies serving behind the counter here wear small red silky hearts over their vaginas and, prompted by a lick of the lips from a customer, they follow up their coffee delivery with a breast rub in the face. When the clients spot me, the glares of hatred fly. They scan me up and down, but as I pause, wondering what to do, the voluptuous blonde attends to me very politely and does not offer to rub her breasts in my face. I hear whispers. 'Shameful', 'Indiscreet', 'Out of place', they hiss. I'm unsure whether it is because I'm overdressed or underdressed, and decide it is because I am overdressed and notably foreign. 'You've got a fucking cheek coming in here,' whispers one man in my ear.

A red fire burns in my face as the clammy heat of embarrassment creeps over me. Slowly, very slowly I leave my coffee on the counter and make for the door. On my way out something cold and hard hits my neck and then falls to the floor. A coin, I think. Something else cold lands on my hair, but I am running down the gallery before I touch the spot and feel saliva.

■

My father arrives the next morning, in a cream alpaca suit, his ripened Robert Redford looks still glowing through the greying beard. I've never been so pleased to see him. He suggests I take the day off and join him and a friend for lunch. Isabel is a middle-aged woman of Parisian elegance my father has known since his days at Reuters, when she was working for the Allende government's nationalized copper corporation CODELCO. I want to know everything about that time, I beg her, over our Pacific seafood lunch.

'At the end of August 1973,' Isabel begins, 'I was due to go to Europe to counteract a big legal operation mounted by the Americans to stop governments buying our copper. President Allende rang me on the evening before my departure and asked me to come and see him. I told him I had work to do, and asked if it was anything urgent. Nothing special, he said, only that he wanted to say goodbye, adding that he had the feeling this would probably be our last conversation. "Is the situation as bad as that?" I asked. The reply was chillingly simple: "Yes, it is only a question of time. I think we have very little left." I suggested cancelling our trip. "Out of the question," he said. "We are still a government and will remain so till the end."

'Two weeks later, on 10 September, I was on a plane back to Santiago after a successful trip to Scandinavia and the USSR. Just after crossing the Andes, the pilot announced he had orders to fly back to Montevideo, Uruguay. He explained that the airport had been closed for political reasons. It was a terrible moment. The rest of the passengers cried for joy and asked for champagne. On arrival in Montevideo, I heard on the radio that the Moneda had been bombed and the president was dead.

'I knew the military would be waiting for me at Santiago airport. They had arrested all the president's employees. I couldn't stay in Uruguay, because it too was under a right-wing military regime and I would have been picked up by Operation 'Condor' [the Southern Cone's US-funded military intelligence network]. The airline agreed to send me to Buenos Aires, which was still a democracy.

'For the first few days I was in a state of shock. My husband had been arrested and I had no news of him. My children were alone; my mother-in-law was taken to a clinic, out of her mind. Cuba and Mexico offered me asylum, but I decided to stay in Buenos Aires with friends.

'I knew I could make a life in Buenos Aires. I finally got my children sent over, and in the January I was offered work at Aluar, an aluminium company. I received a lot of help from my friends, even Pinochet supporters, who were flabbergasted at our situation. One of them even lent me money to buy a small Fiat to get around in. Little by little life improved. Financially it was tough, but my children were safe, even though the youngest went into a psychological regression from which he was never able to recover. The worst of it was that I finally heard news of my husband; he had been sentenced to death.

'One morning in late March 1976 I was taking the kids to school when my daughter said to me, "There is a coup taking place."

'"How do you know?" I asked, astonished.

'"Because there was nothing on the radio this morning but military music, just like when it happened in Santiago."

'I decided they should stay at home, but that I would go to the office as usual. I didn't think there was anything to worry about, but at about three o'clock a group of men arrived asking to see me. The company refused them entry, but they stormed in and took me, saying I was expected at the military headquarters. For the first time I was really afraid, but I tried to act cool. I refused to be taken in their cars but agreed to follow them in my own. Very soon I realized we were not going to the place they had said but to the Coordinación Federal [something like the Argentine Gestapo]. I was told to leave my car and walk down a street, enter the building and take an elevator. I realized nobody had seen me enter. Was this how they made you "disappear"? I asked myself. Inside, they presented a big dossier to me, with a list of my friends, their addresses, telephone numbers, a typescript of my telephone conversations, photos of myself and my children in all kinds of situations.

'I decided to behave like a high society lady, a little dumb, and wholly ignorant of anything not related to my work and social life. After a couple of hours they let me go under the condition that I work for them. I was shaking from relief when I left. It was very late, a curfew had been imposed and there was not a soul around. As I drove back through the empty streets I felt like I was in a nightmare. I had often feared this *Nineteen Eighty-Four* scenario, persecuted, alone, afraid, but I never thought the moment would come.

'When I got home, my children said that officers had searched and interrogated them. The next day I told the executive of my company what had happened and he advised me to leave the country as soon as possible. It was not going to be easy because I was being followed constantly. Thank God a friend of mine in London understood the situation and let me know through Swiss Air that tickets would be waiting for me at the airport desk on a certain date.'

Isabel pauses. 'I owe my life to this man,' she says and looks at my father.

'On the day of the flight I went to the office as usual and my children went to school. We were all being followed. We came back home for lunch as usual and two Argentine women, great friends of mine, arrived to take us to the airport. I knew since the interrogation that the caretaker of our apartment block was working for the police, but my friends had managed to take our luggage the night before, so he saw nothing strange. We arrived at the airport with plenty of time, too much time, in fact, for the anxiety was unbearable and it felt like days. When we finally got on the plane, I noticed some strange movements up front. Military policemen were trying to get on the plane and they were in discussion with the airline staff. Those moments, which amounted to a delay of two hours, were excruciating. It was like my life was being decided between them. Later I discovered that from the airline's point of view, the fact we were on the plane meant that we were on Swiss territory.'

Isabel was safe in Britain, unlike other colleagues. Former Chilean Ambassador to Washington Orlando Letelier, who had been stirring up a fuss about Pinochet's repression and

 Secretary of State Kissinger's involvement in the coup, was murdered in a joint CIA–Chilean operation.

'But why did Allende's government fail?' I probe, apologizing for intruding so much.

'It is rare that I am asked these questions,' laughs Isabel. 'Nobody wants to know here. It was a very exciting time. We were the first democratically elected socialist government in Latin America. We had the eyes of the whole world upon us. We thought we could make real change for a fairer society. But US intervention was clear even before Allende was inaugurated, when the CIA funded the murder of the army Chief of Staff Schneider because he insisted the army respect the democratic process. His murder only managed to rally support around Allende.

'Meanwhile the US was telling countries like Sweden that if they bought copper from companies we had nationalized it would not buy their steel, even though we were offering very good compensation. All US loans to Chile suddenly stopped, despite our impeccable record on debt repayment. The financial situation became very difficult. What really brought the country to a standstill were the lorry drivers' strikes funded by the CIA and Chilean big business. Food wasn't getting to the capital and housewives took to the streets in protest at food shortages. We had a lot of moral support, but the problem was we did not have a majority in government. It was a coalition and the different left-wing elements of the government began to bicker over strategy. Allende was criticized by the far left for not taking a hard enough line. They wanted Allende to nationalize the haulage companies that were sabotaging the economy, but Allende insisted on not being too radical. He wanted to make reforms gradually through the democratic process.

'Once the conservatives came out onto the streets, so did the revolutionary left, and things began to get out of control. We were getting attacked from the left and from the extreme right. He refused to use force or suspend Congress, which he could have done since he had the backing of the military led by General Prats, who was later murdered by Pinochet. Allende always took the constitutional route, even when it became obvious that many of our opponents in Congress were secretly discussing with their American business partners how to overthrow Allende. In the end, the forces against us were too strong. It was only a question of time, as the president told me himself.'

As we finish our meal and walk out onto the grey streets of Santiago's US-style yuppie district, I feel a great sadness wondering how different Chile would be today if it had been allowed to find its own path. The 'historical process' that Ramón says the coup was part of was about as natural as Michael Jackson's face. But I have a new feeling of warmth. In Isabel's strength I have had a glimpse into the Chilean soul and its dreams.

■

'So what did happen when you got back to England after leaving Argentina?' I ask my father, instead of the question I want to ask, which is: What do I do now? Now that my Levi's mission, the stuff of clever messages, dazzling images, of cool style, has instead unveiled suffering, broken dreams and lives?

'I tried to get things in the press. I was involved with the solidarity movements but I got very disillusioned with all the ideological bickering, and the petty power struggles between left-wing factions,' he says. 'For me it was always a question of human rights, political yes, but not a vehicle for people to impose their ideological agendas on. It was too terrible for that.'

Maybe the same divisions and obstacles exist today. I must find my own way through them. I must make the things this journey has taught me to value – memory, ideals, solidarity, justice, identity, heroism – form my actions. Whatever they may be. There can be no other way.

What will they say? That I've gone 'commie', as Carlos accused? (He'll say he knew it all along.) They branded Allende a communist, and Fidel too: the ultimate anti-brand to demonize nationalist movements. Fear is the motor: in politics to create a perceived threat to our livelihoods so that we give our consent to acts of aggression; in corporations to make us feel that we are never good enough, just a product's reach from perfection. The brander, the frabricator of the truth, becomes our saviour. (The branded become dependent, weak, ever-needy.)

They'll say I've gone political. Today's swear word. But what is political? Is asking questions being political? 'If I give food to the hungry they call me a saint. If I ask why they are hungry, they call me a communist.' Those were the words of Archbishop Romero of El Salvador before he was killed by death squads.

I would also be political if I *didn't* ask the questions.

They'll say I'm a conspiracy theorist. But this is just my report, my interpretation of lives around me. I have used my eyes, listened to my heart. Maybe I should put it in bullet points. Then they'll understand it better.

Dad left this morning and I am running out of time. This map of the continent, the map of history, must be filled, and yet Santiago still echoes with the hollowness of a scraped-out core. I need to find something, a smell, a feeling of the other Chile. I decide to go to Bella Vista, the city's geographical centre, which lies under a skyscraper built in the shape of a mobile phone. About ten years ago artists and remnant idealists began to turn the abandoned nineteenth-century shacks into miraculous works of art and design on the inside, leaving their run-down façades to keep commercial interests at bay.

If the Mapuche river is the negotiator, running from winner east to loser west, Bella Vista is the dividing line, or the meeting point. There is a park on the river and I am looking for it because I remember from a previous visit that youngsters would come together to perform and rehearse, either for school, university or their own workshops. I remember they came with their tricks and juggling things, inventing plays, stories, poems, entertaining each other. Crowds would stand and stare at them on the periphery, gaping. The military police were also there.

When I arrive today, however, I cannot even get near the place where the performers used to be because of the crowd. The leaves on the trees are shaking violently to the booming bass line of commercial techno. On a platform, families in perfect rows are taking part in a mass aerobics session. Pepsi stands and fast-food stalls form a sort of barrier to the arena.

I walk further until I spot the group I'm looking for. I ask them what happened to the place they used to have behind the museum.

'They told us we were a public nuisance,' says Jorgecito, with a glint of irony in his eye.

'That's a shame,' I say.

'Not really,' Victoria says. 'We are very fond of our spot on the periphery... we are timid pamphleteers.' An ironic smile balances on the edge of her lips.

Carolina tells me this is the place where all the poets of the 1950s used to come and meet. Jorge Edwards, Nicanor Parra, Pablo de Roca, Manuel Rojas. 'There are things I will never understand because I did not live at the time and feel what my parents felt. But I know I admire my mother very much for what she believed in, that she fought for what she believed and had the courage to come through what happened to her. She came through it for me and I love her for that. I am not saying what she believed in was right, but she had a dream, a vision beyond just herself and she fought for it regardless of the consequences. I am proud of her.'

'Chile has lost its humanity,' says Jorgecito, 'but we are not naturally weak people. Before, the people had a vision of what we wanted Chile to be, and elected a government radical enough to implement it. Now we have to do it ourselves. Tolerance is the only thing that is going to get us out of this. I will truly take my hat off to the person, no matter if he is a Pinochetista or a socialist, who can say, "I don't agree with the way you think, but I'd give my life for your right to say it."'

'We have to fight to retain what we have left of our own,' says Victoria, 'like our indigenous tribes, the Mapuche. They are the only ones who respect our land. They are the true Chileans, because the Chileans you see on the street are just cheap American clones. We must fight to protect our heritage and our land and resources because these are what will protect us in the future.'

'The Chile our parents wanted was taken away from us. They killed our parents,' says Carolina, 'but they haven't killed us. Our parents' ideas live on in us. That is our victory.'

13

STITCHING THE SHREDS

A year has passed since I left Levi's. I am sitting on a stool at the bar of Ezeiza airport, Buenos Aires, waiting to leave. The clock shows seven twenty-five. No Cosmopolitan, just a coffee. The memories of Argentina no longer twist my insides. I am the memory.

I got the impression that Bill, who first gave me the job, thinks I have become disloyal, ungrateful. He says he gave me the job with the best intentions. 'I never intended for you to be a spy,' he says. 'I never thought you would feel like that.' But nor did I think that selling false identities would be to sabotage a continent's own search for peace and progress. Perhaps he means I have betrayed myself, the values of the ordered, wealthy society to which I belonged, the conviction of cultural hegemony, of cool lifestyle. Was I supposed to call on these to motivate me? Or is the key to believe in nothing? Just do it.

Am I scum for biting the hand that fed me? Only a dog rewards his feeder with loyalty. Humans need different nourishment. I have nothing against Levi's. I feel nothing, neither for nor against them. How can I feel anything? Levi's is not a living thing, even though it lives off others. If it were, I would not befriend a person whom, it seems to me, knows no other motivation than self-interest and profit. Bill thinks I am exaggerating, that I am 'using Levi's as the symbol of western evil' or something. Well, they are his words, not mine.

■

On the way down here, a month ago, I stopped in Miami to change planes. Yoel met me at the airport. 'Miami is full of Argentines!' he said. 'Can you believe it? They are desperate to marry Cubans.' The idea that Argies, the one-time intellectual snobs of Latin America, whose ubiquitous Che decided Cuba's fate, should now be *jineteando* in Cuban-run Miami amuses him. A year has passed since the 'crisis' hit Argentina, just after I finished my Chile report, my last Levi's report. Argentina has declared bankruptcy, defaulted on its nine-billion-dollar debt and devalued its currency. Investors have fled, adding to the unemployment caused by the privatizations that invited them in. The bubble of neo-liberal success has burst. The man who sat next to me on the plane asked me if my trip was for business or leisure. Let's see, I thought. What have I come to get now that there'll be no more hiding behind trees? Money, leisure... leisure, money. Now I have found my answers, perhaps I look for a clue to action. How to spend my stash of answers, the surplus value I've accumulated.

They had told me things were bad in Buenos Aires. A friend of mine who, like thousands of others, thought she had played safe by keeping her dollars in HSBC, is told they are being held hostage until her naughty government (one she never even liked) pays its debts. Now she is slipping away from middle-class life, the product of two generations' labour, and there is nothing to catch you at the bottom of the world. I was scared of seeing the people I cared about – joyful, dignified – reduced to scavengers.

'Oh, you won't be able to believe how cheap everything is. You'll be in shopping heaven!' the man sitting in business class told me, where I used the last of my air miles. He was a sales executive for Pepsi.

'Is there any business left to be done in Argentina?' I asked him.

'Oh, there's always business to be done. But we're hurting, there's no doubt about that. The crisis. Hell, yeah.' He shook his head. It's a tricky task, he explained, having to raise prices to offset devaluation while working out how far you can push the consumer. A question of psychological calculation.

'As long as each consumer buys his one can a day, no matter how much it hurts him, I'll have accomplished my job.'

'Instead of doing that,' I ask, 'why can't Pepsi make just a bit less profit?'

'Oh, they can't do that!' He explains: 'The shares would go down and investors would take their money out. You have to keep your share prices up, at all costs.'

'And *do* they?' I asked. '*Do* they make that extra sacrifice for a Pepsi a day?'

'Oh yeah, sure. The only people who have any loyalty at all are consumers. But man, the Argentines fucked it up big time. What they need is a Pinochet.'

■

'You don't know what it was like!' my friends shrieked, as they picked me up from the airport in a battered Fiat. That fix of hyper-enthusiasm, the contagious energy unique to this ever-hopeful place at the bottom of the world, shakes me out of my aeroplane grog. 'It started with one man on a corner ringing a bell, then another, and then another. Everyone knew instantly what was happening. People came out of their houses banging pots. Baa! Baa! Baa! We knew that this was the end, this was our day. We took over the whole city. For one day the city was ours.'

That was the day of '*La Crisis*', as it is now known, when hundreds of thousands stormed on Congress shouting '*Que se vayan todos!*' and brought down the government of De la Rua. Then came looting, the repression and total financial collapse. Ever since, the country has been in the care of a janitor president, former Buenos Aires province governor Eduardo Duhalde, ex-Menem ally. The power vacuum waits to be filled.

I walked through Plaza San Martín, the beautiful square of my childhood. Homeless people were sleeping on benches under the octopus branches of ficus trees where I used to roll. A seventy-something bag-lady was plucking her eyebrows, a ritual that perhaps made her feel still the *señora de casa* she was a year ago before she was stripped of her pension and life savings.

Entire families rummaged through bins, looking for cardboard to sell on for recycling. *Cartoneros* they call them. In the Menem years you'd find engineers and university professors driving taxis; now they go through bins. I walked down Florida. 'THIEVES', 'PIRATES' in dripped white paint covered Citibank's magnificent Victorian architecture, as the swarms of hagglers outside called in a deafening chorus of broken English.

'I've had it up to here with your ledder factory, ledder factory!' snapped a newspaper seller to the leather haggler.

At the Plaza de Mayo, I sat on a bench, contemplating the dreams, the nightmares that began here in this square. The thousands of *cabezitas negras* who came to welcome Perón only to be disowned for their revolutionary intentions and so delivered to military death squads. And here their mothers walked round and round, defying the stone-faced military police, to demand answers for their 'disappeared' children. 'Thank You, Mothers' says the graffiti, for keeping the memory alive while the country floundered.

I got on a bus up to my old neighbourhood. A man with a grubby silk scarf tied round his neck and a trilby perched on his head stood at the front, pitching novels in a tango tune. 'This one is no usual romance, a love story between a man, a woman and... a cat. Yes, incredible as it may seem, but a delicate and tender read, I can assure you, an exquisite little tale of furry love nuzzling between anger and frustration...'

The audience stared pitifully at his ambulant professionalism.

I got off and walked towards Plaza Cortázar, the square of my neighbourhood, down Armenia Street, and noticed that the Lebanese cantinas and immigrant community centres had been replaced by designer boutiques selling funky chrome and cow-hide furniture. In Scandinavian minimalist restaurants and Almodóvar surrealist bars, *cartonero* children held their hands out to flinching plastic-breasted babes and dodged security guards just like in Bogotá's pink zone. None of this existed three years ago. Palermo Viejo, rebranded Palermo Soho, the land of the new-new rich.

Before the devaluation, private banks had helped their richest customers whisk an estimated twenty billion dollars out of the country, making them four times richer. Partly because of this flight of capital, the government had to 'freeze' the small accounts of the lower classes, pennies saved over generations.

On the way home I bought the papers. Will Argentina default on its IMF debt? Will the *piqueteros,* the community leaders whose roadblocks had forced the government to release unemployment benefits, loot the supermarkets to commemorate a year since the end of government? Ex-president Menem, based in Chile is apparently expressing his approval of the *piqueteros* from the sidelines in the hope that they might pave the way for his return. In a little cartoon, a journalist asks Menem, 'Is it true you are trying to encourage the *piqueteros* to come back and loot the supermarkets?' 'Of course not!' replies Menem, 'All I want is for the IMF and the multinationals to come back and finish looting the country.'

'What is there left to rob?' said a man on the bench sitting next to me. 'They have taken everything, all of them together.' In front of us a *cartonero* family rummaged in the bins. 'Is this what we murdered a generation for? For *this*?'

■

'No, it is worse than back then,' Taba corrected me. 'Much, much worse.'

Taba is the father of a friend of mine, a militant from the old days, a survivor. I was told I could find him in the offices of the Central de Trabajadores de Argentina (CTA), the new trades union group when their leaders allied themselves with Menem.

'How can you keep going?' I asked. 'How can you keep believing, after all the deaths, the devastation and broken dreams?'

'I don't know...' Taba said, frowning as he sipped his *mate*. 'I suppose being here is a way of reminding myself of what I have been, to stay true to the things I always believed in. To understand this country, why it has all gone so wrong, is to understand myself.'

He poured some more water in his *mate* and stroked the cat that sat on top of the computer monitor.

'In those years... we were very young. The average age of militancy was eighteen. You have to understand, it wasn't just a small group of us, it was an entire generation. Being indifferent wasn't an option. We thought we could change the world. It was a very powerful feeling.

'We were fighting an ideological battle of which we were hardly aware. It was a battle for economic power. We didn't stand a chance and we didn't see it. We began to lose with the massacre at Ezeiza when Perón returned. I remember a friend of mine saying, "This isn't a little Caribbean island. Do you think the Vatican, the military or the Americans are going to let us get away with this?" None of us listened. We were so reckless.'

'So what's different now?'

'We know that we cannot fight dogma with dogma. Ideology that has military backing will always win. The truth is not a constant; the moment you think it is in your hands it has already changed. *We* thought we had the truth also, eh? We hated also. We thought that anyone who thought differently deserved to die. If we had won the battle it would also have been a problem. Now our aims are concrete. I have learnt that one's goals should always be tangible. Ideology is too vague, too dangerous.'

Some kids interrupted us, wanting Taba to approve the slogan for the CTA's first National Congress in two weeks' time. It read: 'For the future of our children: Bread, Work, Sovereignty, Democracy.'

'No,' he told them. 'The first bit should just be: "For our children".'

He paused, caught by a thought. 'You want to know why I go on? In the end it's the same struggle as before… for the right to work, for an organized, transparent society. Why should I not have hope? They haven't won. They have not killed us all. The oligarchy, the multinationals, they need a *pueblo muerto* to dominate. As long as we are alive as thinking beings and still fighting, they cannot win.'

■

I know that in the *piqueteros* is the key to my action. In them I will find my new vocation. This new generation of *cabecitas negras,* the dark-haired masses Evita patronized, have started from scratch. In my way, I too have gone back to the drawing board, with my palette of new convictions.

In the midst of destruction, with 90 per cent unemployment in some areas of greater Buenos Aires, the *piqueteros* began by taking over abandoned land and built houses, installed electricity and water and then negotiated with the government to make the settlements legal. With the *planes de familia* (unemployment benefit) they've wrested from the government, they run soup kitchens and put the unemployed to work in their communities, either practising their skills or teaching in workshops. They pool resources to keep families alive. The CTA needs the *piqueteros.* They are its power base, just like the Landless Movement is for Lula in Brazil.

I got up at dawn and took three buses to La Matanza, the biggest district of Greater Buenos Aires, the land of Evita's *negritos* that she turned into the country's Perónist stronghold. Everywhere were painted slogans – 'With us, things were better – Vote Menem 2003' – the disgraced face of corrupt neo-liberalism still trying to lure its confused victims. I saw more graffiti: 'We want to consume what *we* produce,' and I knew the *piqueteros* were close. My dad had always said that it wasn't foreign investment that was the problem, but that the investment was never the kind that added value to the local economy, only the kind that took profits out.

In one of the soup kitchens, *Referente* Carlos, one of the district leaders, told me the *piqueteros* were not the same *cabecitas negras* that Evita manipulated. 'The days when they bought our votes with a bit of bread and wine are over. We will not prostitute ourselves for any agenda any more, whether political or corporate, whose consumer culture wants to make us passive individuals, not citizens who feel part of a society. We are re-educating people to think about the community. Our strength is in our organization. Our power is in the autonomy we build here.'

Carlos took me to a sports hall down the street, where big honcho Luis D'Elia, a huge sloth of a man, was hosting a meeting of *piquetero* reps from all the districts of Greater Buenos Aires. They were here to discuss the movement's relationship with the CTA, which they would present in a document before the big congress. 'We do not want to be used by the CTA to make up numbers and then be discarded,' shouted D'Elia, to a roar of approval. 'We must be respected and treated as equals.' But also we had to discuss the nature of the social movement, and whether each *piquetero* group (there were many) should be integrated separately into the CTA or whether they should be united under the biggest *piquetero* movement, which was this one, the Federation of Land and Housing (FTV), headed by D'Elia. We split up into groups to discuss the issues and were to return with our conclusions. The emphasis on democracy was repeated at every instance, as though they were terrified of losing sight of it again.

'It is not that the other *piquetero* movements aren't valid, only that we have to work under one umbrella, represented in each city, otherwise we will be divided like the last time,' said an old man. 'I remember when the *Cordobazo* happened in 1968, Buenos Aires didn't rise up in solidarity because the capital thought it was better than the provinces. That must not happen again.'

The *referente* asked someone else to read the proposals set out by D'Elia but nobody volunteered. He convinced a reluctant teenager and we waited patiently as he struggled through the words. The nature of this new social and political movement seemed strange to the elders, so a younger *referente* began to explain that the *piqueteros* were different from what had gone before.

'The idea is not that power be "taken" in an instant moment; our power is in becoming a constant source of pressure on whoever is in power, to ensure that our rights are always respected. It is direct democracy.'

'We have always put our blind faith in charismatic leaders – Perón, Menem…' began a young girl. 'You cannot put your life in another's hands. By doing that you are asking to be abused.'

'Yes, Perón centralized power,' agreed one of the elders. 'We must keep our power in the neighbourhoods so that we do not get lost and forgotten.'

We were called back to the hall to give our group's opinions on the document. Everyone had their say. Their democracy took hours.

■

 There was something different about Buenos Aires, a feeling of wartime solidarity. Middle-class women, who despised Evita's *negritos,* now banged their pots to the chant: '*Cazeroleras, Piqueteras, la lucha es una sola.*' (Cazeroleras, Piqueteras, we are united in our fight.) People were fleeing the crisis, but it was also a calling. Mum's friend Patricia came back from years abroad and started a street magazine sold by the homeless based on the *Big Issue.* Now the magazine is everywhere. I found it ironic that Levi's had placed an ad. 'The best investment of your life: another person.' It's the talk of the town as an example of a multinational that's not so bad.

'It's good of them to support you,' I admitted.

'Well, I gave them the ad for free,' Patricia said. 'They say they don't have the money. But I keep the advert because it gives the magazine credibility.'

Levi's 'investing in people' only went as far as perception management, not far enough to pay the magazine on time for the ad. Of course, it's the share prices, I remember as I think of the man on the plane. The thought of Levi's inspired me to call the bubbly girls who had done Levi's PR when I did my first report here. Their company had thrived during the Menem years when multinationals sought local marketeers. 'What a coincidence!' Sandra exclaimed. 'Guess who's sitting next to me?' I heard a scuffle as she passed the phone to someone. 'Hello, Amaranta, it's Bill.'

I searched for something to say. 'I tried to convince them not to...' Bill burst out, filling my silence. 'The risk has become too big for Levi's to keep its operation here. I came down personally to try to soften the blow.' Even dreams of blue jean glory had been shattered. Everyone had lost. The countless local textiles factories that had folded before the crisis, unable to compete with the likes of Levi's, factories built on two immigrant generations' work, had all been for nothing.

■

At midnight, thirty buses left La Matanza heading for Mar del Plata to the CTA's new congress. Argentina's new beginning. My baptism.

The journey would take six hours, so we'd arrive just in time for breakfast and the start of the congress and we would stay at a campsite, even though nobody had any tents. It was after eleven when we arrived, eleven hours freezing in a windowless bus. The *piqueteros* stared longingly at the beach and shimmering ocean; the congress had supposedly already started. As we walked through the stadium doors with our banners and drums, ten thousand delegates inside erupted into a version of Argentina's favourite football song:

Ole, Ole, Ole
Ole, Ole, Ola
Ole, Ole, Ole
Cada dia te quiero mas
[Each day I love you more]
Oooooh Piqueteros
Es un sentimiento, que no se puede parar!
[It's a feeling that cannot die]

 How could I have ever thought that they would start without the *piqueteros*, the heart and soul of Argentina's new social movement? We were the largest single group in the auditorium, taking up an entire bank. The stadium's frenzy was fit for a world cup final, not for a meeting of three thousand unemployed people.

The hundred or so foreign delegates, who had come from as far as Canada and France, looked on from behind the podium. 'We are making history!' shouted Victor de Gennaro, leader of the CTA, as the celebrations finally died down. Over his head Taba's banner read: 'For our children: Bread, Work, Sovereignty, Democracy.'

A short video played, commemorating the cost of the last thirty years: the thirty thousand 'disappeared', a thousand Falklands victims, forty-three protesters since December and children dying of hunger now, as a result of structural adjustment.

'*Compañeros y compañeras,* politics is not a snapshot, it is a process!' de Gennaro began. 'We will decide our destiny on the streets and in the neighbourhoods, constructing democracy and distributing power. We will change this country, *compañeros y compañeras,* and to change society we must first change ourselves. Let the congress begin!'

Then it was down to serious work. Every clause of the new constitution had to be debated and voted on by the congress tomorrow. The CTA's resident intellectual, Claudio Lozano, proposed a broad, open and democratic movement, then delegates from all over the country were invited to speak.

'I am all for unity, but why should our movement include small and medium businesses, when they are and will always be against the interests of labour?' said a man from Córdoba. 'The only unity we need is the unity with *piqueteros* from all over the country. I don't want to share the movement with capitalists; they are the ones who have betrayed us.'

The session continued, one delegate after another hurling insults at the CTA, and it began to look like consensus would be impossible. Too many factions, too many positions. Impatient, Lozano attempted to hurry up the process. 'Please, please... will each delegate reduce their time—' he began, but the crowd don't let him finish.

'It's not your turn!' they shout. 'You've had your turn, let everyone else speak!' They get up on their chairs and start stamping. 'You think what you say is more important than anyone else?' one said. 'People have come from all over the country and you won't let them speak. You call that democracy?' said another. Lozano was forced to concede the platform.

The congress went on until ten at night. In the campsite, everyone was exhausted and nobody had a bed. The rain began to pour down. *Piqueteros* everywhere ran for shelter: under the food hall, into the buses. On the damp floor of the bus I watch Vicky, the girl I'd sat next to on the way, unpack the mountains of make-up and tight-fitting outfits from her bag, her weapons of feminine dignity against the reality of her new poverty. She was no natural militant. Circumstances had made her so. Her conservative parents worried about her new radical status, she told me, but being a *piquetero* has kept her busy since the hospital laid her off, and at least allowed her to practise her nursing skills.

■

The next morning we made our way down to the stadium again. I noticed different *piquetero* groups outside in heated discussion, including the Movement of Land and Freedom (MTL), which had contested the FTV's proposal for *piquetero* exclusivity.

In the auditorium everyone was singing again, with even more fervour than the day before. There was more at stake today. *Referente* Carlos was in a shirtless frenzy, flinging his top around and leading the chants.

Now you see, now you see
There's only one FTV!

It was more a gloat than a song, directed at the other side where the MTL was. The two sides chanted insults at each other as if they were at a football match. In the middle they sang 'To the plaza, to the plaza', reiterating the demand for action on the 19th, the anniversary of the crisis – for another government downfall, this time definitive. Little by little, the different songs began to merge into one, until finally the whole stadium was singing in unison:

CTA, de los trabajadores
El que no le guste, que se jode, se jode!
CTA belongs to the workers
Whoever doesn't like it, stuff 'em, stuff 'em!

The voting began. Nearly every motion was voted for unanimously. Only the one on exclusivity was close. Our *piqueteros* start hissing and booing: 'Now you see, there's only one FTV...'

Carlos shouted, 'Throw them out!'

'Please!' De Gennaro begged. 'Respect the feelings of the opposition. We will not have any bullying in our movement. Let's have the vote again. Please put your hands up, those in favour of the motion.' The hands went up again, and this time the support for the motion was clear. Our side threw its cards in the air and began to celebrate. This was the last motion. The stadium ran amok. Their song filtered through the showering paper.

No queremos mas al ALCA
No queremos mas traición
Tenemos un nuevo movimiento
Para nuestra liberación!

We don't want the Latin American free trade agreement
We don't want more betrayal
We have a new movement
For our liberation!

■

The next day I went to the Levi's office, to spy on the spyer. Could they tell I was no longer on their side? 'Terrible, terrible,' said the general manager about the 'crisis', huffing and puffing. Despite having to sell the operation, the year had not ended too badly for Levi's. Within the new-new-rich niche market the brand was very well positioned. 'Alternative' was the way they described this new market (as opposed to benefactors of misery), more Palermo Soho boutique than shopping mall, where Menem's crass old-new rich hung out. Levi's had not lost money and they had not had to get rid of too many jobs and... suddenly I felt dizzy. I ran to the toilet just in time.

The PR girls had also not lost too much business on account of the new-new-rich market. What's more, Sandra told me, as she intermittently yapped on her mobile like a New York exec-chick, her company had branched into doing 'informal research' (inspired by my Levi's job) to help multinationals take advantage of crisis mentality. And yes, terrible, terrible, she huffed and puffed, 'We all have to work together to overcome.' Meanwhile, she got local journalists to investigate how Argentine women were maintaining their aesthetic dignity under the crisis, and sold the report to Unilever. She even managed to publish unconfidential bits of the research in *Clarín*, Argentina's main newspaper, as an article sponsored by Unilever's Sedal shampoo.

Sandra let me have a look at the Sedal report. It concluded that 'crisis women', though depressed, were more dynamic and multifaceted, so that Sedal's old beauty message, 'Are You Ready?', was now redundant. Instead the report recommended that the ego-boosting 'Because You Deserve It!' could now apply to the Argentine woman, since the crisis had taken its toll on emotional relationships and ego-boosting *piropos* were scarcer. I saw *piquetera* Vicky's face in the bullet points, her struggle to maintain feminine dignity making her the prototype Unilever target. Must squeeze her brand loyalty to its last drop. 'As long as she spends that dollar a day…' I hear the Pepsi man say…

Branding the crisis was the new business, and it was big business. I began to see empathy advertising on billboards everywhere. FEDEX, for example, had become the saviour of devaluation Argentina with a picture of Argentine goods being loaded onto planes under the slogan: 'Export is the way forward'. A glass of clear water on a billboard was how the Spanish-owned water company showed its solidarity with the Argentines' disgust at corruption. Much Music, the channel built by my friend Ralph who sold it to the Cisneros, had a boy on a mountain bike pointing yonder, in the image of the Argentine liberator San Martín, with the message: 'Argentina needs new role models.' All had guzzled Menem's corrupt new liberalism, though.

Sandra put me in touch with a girl called Papaya she had hired to do the kind of work I did. 'I work for big companies, Camel, British American Tobacco, Nestlé, Unilever and I earn $10,000 a month. If you want my ideas, there's a price,' snapped the little bulldog of a girl. We met in the red velvet lounge of a San Telmo gay hotel called Painted Lips, inspired by the novelist Manuel Puig. 'These companies hunted me down because I am an urban psychic. I know everything that happens here. I know what is going to happen before it does. I know the streets here, the guts of this city. If I go into a bad neighbourhood, they know not to touch me; they know who I am. I know the lowest of the low. I am bubble-up, not trickle-down.'

She hired young informers. But, like me, she didn't tell them who their information was going to.

She dragged me off to one of her events, where she brought low-life boxers from the ghetto to a nightclub to box to drum and bass. In the middle of the fight she flung herself into the ring and tried to make the boxers fight over her. One of them knocked her in the head, and she bounced around the ring looking totally deranged before collapsing on the floor.

■

The 19th, the anniversary, finally came. The buses from La Matanza were to drop about fifty thousand of us on the motorway ten miles from the city centre, and we would walk on Plaza de Mayo. 'Where is everyone?' shouted Angelica, between stuffing biscuits and cigarettes into her mouth. Only her, a toothless old man and myself had turned up on time. *Piquetero* laziness always sent Angelica into a rage. She ordered her daughters to go and knock on people's doors, and people slowly dribbled out yawning, including Vicky.

'Nobody wants to come today,' laughed the toothless man.

'Are they scared?' I asked.

'Scared? Nooo. It's payday today. People want to get their plan money.'

Angelica ordered us to get on the bus. 'But, Angelica,' said the toothless man, 'how can we get on the bus when there are so many people blocking the way?' Angelica didn't find this funny.

Finally, with the yawning hordes rounded up, we set off for the centre. The convoy stopped on the motorway that leads into Plaza de Mayo. We were a million, drumming and chanting under the burning sun. I walked with Vicky and told her of Bill's trauma about Levi's leaving Argentina. 'Tell him he doesn't need to feel sorry, that it's very nice that he came down and shared his grief with us, but that he can just pack up, taking all those traitors who worked for him, and leave us alone.

'They want to replace identity with consumerism,' she added, as if learnt from a workshop. We had arrived at the same conclusion through a different route. 'So we do not have expectations, only greed. They want to patent our cultural values and emotions, take away our strength and leave us doubting who we are. They want to appropriate the things that make us know who wc are, what we stand for and what we want.'

Levi's just sells jeans, Papaya is only making a living, the PR girls are trying to get by and sell someone's shampoo. All hate Menem, the traitor. And yet Menem's betrayal lives on in their actions. But what else should they do? These are the opportunities open to them, a way to get by, just like everyone wants. It's dog eat dog, opportunities are scarce, who wouldn't grab one when it came along? It is not the devil's work, just an assumed activity, the normality within the institutions that dominate global society.

How different would it be if the dominant institutions of this new global order encouraged solidarity, fraternity, compassion, respect and cooperation instead of greed, power, self-interest and profit? Then the interaction between people would reflect those things. Things like common ownership, democracy in the workplace, shared profits wouldn't sound crazy. Those who dismiss them as utopian and communist ideas are those who have found their patch in the status quo. But the thousands here on this avenue, millions all over the world, the majority world, believe another way is possible. As Lula says, it is up to us to change the values of society, in our everyday actions to break with the normality, shed our stakes in it. If you take out the bricks, the wall will crumble.

By the time we reached the centre we were dying of thirst. I wanted to go and get a drink. Shops were boarded up in expectation of frenzied looting, but it was clear by now that nothing of the sort was going to happen. Even though the great and the good of militant tourism had flown in specially for something to happen, Plaza de Mayo resembled a Cotswold country fête. People wondered around basking in the memory of last year's momentary empowerment, but now they were tired. Nobody was in the mood for bringing down another government. Something more long term was brewing.

■

So I leave Argentina, South America, thirty years on, still fighting for their destiny.

While the new generation try to pick up the pieces of three decades of IMF policies implemented by corrupt governments, brands are still tapping into the weakness, and end up making more money out of the confusion and damage. In Perú, the stories I listened to sceptically on the beach turned out to be true. Just after I left in September 2000, President Alberto Fujimori and his *eminence grise* Vladimir Montesinos fled the country after a leaked video showed Montesinos bribe an opposition congressman to defect to Fuji's government. Fuji's third election victory weeks before had depended on twelve or so defections like this. At first, Fuji promised to sack the hated Montesinos and call new elections in which he would not stand, but the video turned out to be only one of 2,500 others which showed Montesinos giving cash to media moguls, judges, army officers, politicians.

Scared that the 'Vladivideos' might feature one of its own officials, the US government helped persuade Panamá to give Montesinos asylum. The Peruvian courts, meanwhile, continue the investigation of an alleged million-dollar donation from Pablo Escobar for Fujimori's 1990 presidential campaign. After Fuji's and Vladimir's departure, the Peruvian currency mysteriously surged against the dollar. Civilian traffickers regained control over the drugs trade, bringing dollars back into the banks. While the Clinton administration had boasted of the success of the Peruvian drugs crackdown, sidelined exporters flogged cheap *pastabase* to the children of Lima.

The courts want Fujimori back to face charges, but he has taken up the Japanese nationality he had always denied having access to, and is thus protected from extradition.

In Venezuela, my old employers, businessmen tried to topple Hugo Chavez in a US-backed coup. In an extraordinary finale, the whole of Petare descended on the presidential palace demanding their president be reinstated, during which time they managed to convince the palace guards to turn on the hijackers. Cisneros television stations, which went blank during the coup, are now promoting a general strike against reinstated

 Chavez, and the middle-class pot-banging scenes reminiscent of the ones that ousted Chile's elected socialist president, Salvador Allende, thirty years ago. Despite the economic sabotage, however, Chavez has the poor majority's overwhelming support.

In Colombia, Alvaro Uribe, the hard-line governor of Antioquia, became president on the promise to deliver 'Democratic Security' and destroy the FARC. Backed by George Bush and Tony Blair, he is extending the system of informant networks and peasant soldiers he experimented with in Antioquia to a national level, a system reminiscent of that which Bush Snr backed in Central America. As multinationals move in, peace communities have no place in his full-scale military solution, exercised in the form of strange-named 'operations' by army brigades, often in conjunction with paramilitaries. Any opposition is dealt with as the enemy.

In Medellín, Raúl tells me, Operation 'Orion' officially took the guerrillas out of a neighbouring *barrio* called Comuna 13, but the community is begging the army not to leave, hoping they may at least exert some restraining influence over the paramilitaries. The people of Cacarica in Urabá, displaced to the sports stadium, got their land back, but since Uribe took power the 13th Brigade and paramilitaries patrol while by night timber companies fell their forest illegally. One of the biggest areas of military operations is the oil region of Arauca, which British and US multinationals are increasingly anxious to exploit. In November 2002's Operation 'Heroic', the military rounded up two thousand people into the sports stadium, where hooded informants pointed out suspects. But now concrete evidence is emerging of past links between some of those in the regime and the drugs cartels as well as paramilitaries. Maybe they too will have to flee the country, disgraced as the latest in the recent trend of corrupt US and British supported 'democratic dictators'.

And so to Chile, the 'success story', the region's fastest-growing economy, where the poor accept poverty and watch the rich grow richer, for they have grown up believing that their own will is dangerous. Only the children of Pinochet's losers continue the search for their lost identity buried beneath the debris of Americanization. They remind Chile of the dreams it must rescucitate.

■

After a night of cheap tequila I spent this morning with my head down the toilet cursing the country. But it was good. I'm paying my *derecho de piso,* my rite of passage, spewing out the impurities.

Because that was what the 19th – the *Argentinazo* – was. Not a 'crisis', as the world's media portrayed it, but Argentina's final rejection of the poison unleashed by Menem's neo-liberal economic plan. Not a crisis, but the people's own operation, a liberation of the Argentine soul.

The spontaneous burst of Argentine-ness that spread from street to street was more than an economic reaction; it was a unanimous assertion of identity, a reclaiming of destiny. The rest of the world looked on horrified at the barbaric scenes of savages clawing at supermarket shelves. The looting was politically engineered, but the unseen story was a sublime expression of collective will.

The expectations are different today. As the *piqueteros* said: 'We cannot stop them exploiting us, but we can stop prostituting ourselves.'

For all the hardship, Buenos Aires is bursting with culture and life. Local actors and artists now occupy the grand Corrientes theatres where international stars lit the lights in Menem's years. They represent the city's desire for creative self-expression, its desire to understand its own weakness and confusion. Glum tube travellers light up when kids, one with a drum-set attached to a luggage trolley, another carrying a bandoneon and another with electric bass guitar, get on and play Piazzolla compositions.

In this music they can see themselves reflected, they can see the shoots of their awakening and the rejection of the false progress the new 'investors' imposed on the nation. However much wealth is invested, a country will never flourish if it does not know who it is, what it exists for, where it is going and why. Progress is rooted in one's own essence, driven by one's own will.

■

Perhaps Bill is right, I have taken it all to heart, blown it all out of proportion. I cannot say that everything would have been different for Latin America had others allowed it, helped it even, to choose its own destiny, instead of taking advantage of its weaknesses to further their own wealth.

An old friend at Levi's argues that, of all the multinationals, Levi's is the most ethical. Its foundation invests money in Aids programmes and community-related programmes. But all that is nothing but a drop in the ocean, plasters on a haemorrhage. The sum of the mundane, not our exceptional gestures, expresses and shapes our world. Market forces cannot be our star of Bethlehem, when from behind them the iron fist of military force and corruption is working to get laws through and create the convenient conditions.

I have asked myself what my function is a product of, what lies went into creating it and what lies it continues to create. I was born into a country's dream and I became part of the lie. We are all responsible for the historical process of which we are a part. Now I know, at least, which side I am on, here in Buenos Aires, there in Britain or anywhere. It is the side asking questions, not questions to serve strategies of might and greed, but questions to understand and heal. I am on the side of letting the young develop the ability to question before the branding machine converts their questions into false symbols of progress. It is the side of action, because you can only whine so much. So give me the irrational, utopian, dreaming, commie, unreliable world of the losers any day. This is my final report.

epilogue

I arrive in London in need of a job. Britain and the US are on the warpath again, in yet another attempt to control another people's destiny in the name of progress. At this very moment Tony Blair is helping Colin Powell convince Chile, one of the unfortunate members of the security council, that a regime change in Iraq would be an act of humanity. Perhaps if it wasn't recovering from a similar 'act of humanity', Chile might believe him.

The news from Latin America gets better each day. Menem lost the election and for the first time in thirty years, with Brazil's Lula and Argentina's Kirschner leading the way, Latin American presidents are reaching out to their neighbours and forming negotiating blocks to stand stronger and more united on issues of global trade. All over the continent new social movements are building cultures of autonomy to make sure their own political and financial elite never betray them again.*

Meanwhile, I watch Tony Blair trying to convince sceptics of the need for war, in that impatient urgent tone of his, as if people were morons for not understanding. He is the presentable face of the Bush administration. I can see their graphs, accompanied by bullet-point analysis, placing countries along their axes: Good–Evil, Christianity–Islam. As persuasion and manipulation fails, the Bush-Blair coalition borrow Pinochet's motto: by reason or by force. They are building themselves in the image of old tryants. Islamic fundamentalists are the new anti-brand.

I get calls from marketing experts who believe the bombing of Iraq will open up new opportunities in the Arab world. They want my guerrilla marketing expertise on getting inside the minds of dark youth of another region. I detect desperation in their mid-Atlantic confidence. I know the tide is turning. Like little *piqueteros*, kids block Crouch End Broadway and urge cars to beep for peace and justice. Brands, having ironed former youth 'tribes' into one monolithic consumer identity, try to tap their anti-war feeling. But the kids are getting wise to the game.

■

* *In November 2004, Uruguay's Tabaré Vasquez became the latest addition to a wave of Latin American presidents voted in to end neo-liberal policies by a new generation set on vindicating past injustices. Vasquez broke seventy years of two-party rule with the same party, the Frente Grande, that he founded thirty years back to oppose Uruguay's dictatorship and was consequently banned. In the same month, under the centre-left government of Ricardo Lagos, General Pinochet was arrested by the Chilean courts to be tried in Chile. Earlier in the year, Venezuela's Hugo Chavez finally silenced the opposition by holding and winning a referendum. In Argentina, President Kirchner's first move on defeating President Menem's attempted return was to lift the amnesty that prevented dictatorship officials from being brought to trial. The second was to take a firm stand against the IMF. While both Menem and Fujimori remain abroad, avoiding charges brought against them, Montesinos as least was captured and brought to trial. He received thirty-seven years for the first four convictions. He has almost seventy more charges to be heard. Menem remains in Chile, avoiding corruption charges being brought against him. Popular movements against privatizations in Paraguay and Perú forced their governments to declare states of emergency. In Bolivia, Aymaran Indian Evo Morales's Movement to Socialism won second place among eleven candidates, despite US threats to cut off aid to Bolivia if Morales won. A year later the US-backed mining magnate who won, Gonzalo Sanchez de Lozada, was forced to resign after his repression of protests against the proposed sale of the country's gas reserves left seventy people dead.*

At a conference on Colombia at the London School of Economics I meet Jaime. He tells me how, two days after his last meeting with Carlos Castaño, the paramilitary leader had to let him go, barking: 'It's not the first time I've had to concede.' US congressmen, the European Union and eighty-two other countries lobbied for his release. Protests took place daily in Bogotá and a group of bishops even visited Castaño to appeal.

'You were lucky,' I said.

'No, it wasn't luck. I have international solidarity to thank.'

On his return, the neighbourhood threw a big party and people came from all over Medellín to celebrate his safe return, including some of the policemen he had been working with. They claimed that a senior police officer, who had opposed their project, had tipped off the paramilitaries. One month later, the offices of Jaime's institute were blown up and Jaime finally understood that he really should leave the country and went into exile. The whereabouts of Carlos Castaño, wanted for multiple massacres and assassinations, is uncertain. He is rumoured to have staged his own death to avoid extradition, a condition the US Congress set for its support of the proposal for an amnesty for the paramilitaries. Reports have it that he is in Israel.

In the conference a young Uribe government adviser wows future Colombian business leaders with dramatic graphs that attribute Colombia's entire violent history to peasant greed and cocaine funds. He also proved that the average FARC combatant earned more than the average Swiss citizen. *Malicia indigena* scientifically proven. They remind me of the data I once moulded into a preset ideology. Mine was to back commercial invasion; his is to justify US-backed military action.

Not once does the starch-shirted yuppie mention Castaño's own known dabbling in cocaine money, the army's collaboration with the paramilitaries or members of the regimes personal links to them. Jaime sits calmly in silence. Those who possess true knowledge need not resort to insult.

■

With sluggish pessimism I flick through the *Guardian*, looking for an alternative vocation. Something catches my eye.

DO YOU WANT TO CHANGE THE WORLD?
REVOLUTIONARY YOUTH CHARITY NEEDS GUERRILLA
MARKETING WUNDERKIND WITH CHARISMA, CONFIDENCE
AND KILLER COMMUNICATION SKILLS TO HELP LAUNCH
OUR KIKASS STREET TEAMS PROJECT. HAVE YOU GOT WHAT
IT TAKES TO DO A JOB THIS EXTRAORDINARY?

I whiz to the website of this revolutionary youth charity called kikass.com where I learn of its ambition to spread sex and drugs awareness to the inner city through guerrilla marketing techniques.

My job as Street Team leader would be to recruit the coolest trend-setting ghetto geezers of Newham, Tower Hamlets and Hackney as volunteers in a Street Team network. 'The Heineken of charities – refreshing the parts that other organizations can't reach.'

Through the chirpy Americanized ad-lingo, however, I can't see what the charity actually *does.* 'Hook them, engage them, involve them!' it says. 'Coach them to spread the word about the Kikass projects... Make joining the Kikass Team something they'd really wanna do for fun, because it's cool. Sell it to them on the peg that it could boost their career too!'

'We LOVE this idea...' they say, '...and so do Levi's!'

I pause. It transpires that Levi's is the sponsor. Who is kicking whose ass here exactly?

'BUT ENOUGH ABOUT US!' the ad goes on, as if not to let the reader brew on this minor corporate element. 'We want to hear about you...'

There follow two pages of questions, the kind I used to ask my kids, each one requiring thoughtful and lengthy responses. Some of the questions are direct marketing questions.

Do you think young people could be persuaded to buy Levi's rather than another brand through sponsorship of Street Teams?

If you had the chance, what would you tell the General Manager of Levi's UK?

'If you don't think the job's for you,' they say, 'we'd still like to hear from you anyway.' i.e., your answers will be useful to Levi's. From my perspective I wonder, is simple espionage too obvious for a more sceptical British youth? Does Levi's need now to *be* the concern to engage the selfless loyalty that only social movements or ideologies have the power to generate? A new function for charity outreach: while you are tackling social problems of the inner city, why not get your victims to do a bit of youth trend-spotting on behalf of our brand partners? While you are busy being concerned, why not encourage a bit of greed and brand slavery? While you are encouraging underprivileged youth, why not exploit their vulnerabilities? Tell them: No!, don't throw away your talents on drugs, give them to Levi's. We can make better use of them!

No wonder, in Kikass's list of 'social problems', the silent corporate takeover of our lives is not included. How the mixing of interests and hidden agendas conspires to confuse and distract children from their path of development into independent thinkers. Soon children will be blaming their parents for not understanding them as well as Levi's do.

I apply for the job, to see what they are up to. Kikass replies saying I sound just the person they are looking for. I meet up with them in an appropriately trendy Hoxton bar. What's with the corporate sponsorship? I ask.

'Conventional charities don't understand,' says Neil, the charity mastermind, 'that branding is the language of youth. They only understand through brands.'

I ask him how, as Street Team leader, I would merge the social work with the market-research service for Levi's; he says the latter would be done on an informal basis. Of course. I ask him what kind of practical assistance they would offer the kids of London, and he says classes in networking. Philanthropically teaching that in everyone and everything is something to be had, I think. They say I would be useful, with my experience, for their International Development section. Perhaps Levi's are bidding for one of the contracts in Iraq's reconstruction, preparing their market through social work with other do-gooders, like Halliburton.

I know there is no point in debate. In this world of consumer fundamentalism you are either with them or against them. Those whom it suits will believe it is normal for corporations to have their hand in the formative years of youth, be it education or social work, as the key place to establish the framework of assumed truths that limits the development of independent thinking, and to manage perceptions.

I leave these visionary charity-branding gurus to their strategy building. I do my own research, on Parliament Hill Fields, where the teens sit and chat in groups. They are not hardened by the me, me, me culture, or reeking of self-satisfaction as I feared. Just like their Latin American peers, they are open and friendly, vulnerable and anxious. They have hope that inspires action. They want to be listened to, not sold to.

'The way they went to war… despite the whole nation being against it, shows we don't matter,' one girl says. 'We only matter when they want to sell us things. I have nightmares about a girl just like me having her home, her city, her friends blown to bits, while I can go to school, I can sit here freely and enjoy myself. It's not fair… it makes me feel sick.'

'They say it's in the name of democracy,' says a white freckly boy. 'But what kind of democracy are we spreading when our own elected leaders take no notice of the people? No, it is not them and us… we are all in this together.'

No longer will I stash these answers in a report for corporate use, while the kids remain helpless in their solitude. It would be great to build a platform, connecting young people in Britain to their global peers. They will share ideas, create new visions and act for a fairer world order based on solidarity. An idea germinates…

My search is the search of millions: for freedom from an ideology that converts every aspect of humanity into an opportunity to acquire, to exploit; for the right to principles over dogma, to identity over brand illusion, to creative self-expression over consumer tyranny. Pier Paolo Pasolini said, 'The new fascism is the consumer society, because it profoundly transforms young people. It has touched them. It has changed their feelings, their ways of thought and their way of life.' You cannot take out of your head what they have put in, they told me in Chile, but you can fight it and it can be broken. All fascisms can be broken.

Acknowledgements

A special thank you to: Jane Lawson and John Saddler for putting me on the right track; my agent David Milner for helping me find what I wanted to say, reach deeper and write the best book possible; John Pilger for your guidance and encouragement; Kevin Simpson for your generosity and contagious enthusiasm that sold the book; Di Riley for taking the leap; my editor Hannah MacDonald for understanding and nurturing its spirit; Mari Roberts for taking such care; Ken Barlow, Sarah Bennie, Ed Griffiths, Hannah Telfer and the whole team at Ebury for your support and hard work.

A very special thank you to: my father and mother for your faith, support and criticism; my love, José Luis, *por tu cariño* and for your indefatigable ability to put up with *mis locuras*; to all those in Latin America who have embraced me, made me laugh and cry and shown me new sensations and truths.